Endorsements

Applying rigorous critical thinking and psychological research, Dr. Kuiper offers a timely and authoritative expose of the sexual ideologies undermining our civilization. In contrast, he presents a powerful apologetic for historic sexual traditions and biblical values. A must-read for concerned students, professors, pastors, and other thought leaders.
—Rev. David Branson, Ph.D., author, *More Love: How to Experience More of the God Who Loves You*

Michael has brilliantly documented the various currents driving the cultural chaos and insanity of our day. His analysis points the reader back to the foundational design which reflects the Designer and has served mankind so well. This inspiring book reminds the reader of what is timeless, true, and worth championing, even against a cancel culture unwilling to hear. Michael has presented an invaluable gift to those longing to understand this cultural moment.
—Steve Martens, MDiv, former missionary

While Vice-President for Student Development at a small private college, I and my student development staff interacted with students who either had questions about or were struggling with gender issues. Kuiper's book, written at a level suitable for the upper-division college student, graduate, or post-graduate reader, gives answers to my staff and those students as to the meaning and application of the terms "God's design" and "God's order."
   In his, *Idols for Destruction*, Herbert Schlossberg identifies the attitude that says, "modern thought is the best thought." The result is arrogance toward any traditional views held by previous generations. In *Sex and Society*, Kuiper exposes the

consequences of such an attitude in a society wanting a new sexual order. Using an abundance of evidence from well-known researchers, both past and present, he unmasks the law of diminishing returns in a society that is rejecting the historically and biblically accepted view of gender. Drawing from theological, biological, and philosophical constructs, he presents a case for embracing a sexual order grounded in a sacred order.

This is a thought-provoking book that is not a quick read. But it is a well-documented and well-presented book that forces both the progressives and the traditionalists among us to understand the implications of their positions while, at the same time, vigorously recommending that the road to a "flourishing culture" is marked with divine reference points.

If you are looking for a book that answers the questions, "How did our society's sexual values and behavior get to where we are?" and "How, as Christ-followers, can we support and defend a position on sexual and gender morality that is being attacked?" I recommend *Sex and Society: God's Design, Tradition, and the Pursuit of Happiness*.

—Dr. Rich Brown is a retired college professor, Dean, and Vice President; author, *Extended Stays: A Closer Look at Longer Pastorates*

I appreciate Michael's courage to write a book on such a relevant and controversial topic. And even more than that, to do it in such a wonderfully articulate, scientifically accurate, and biblically sound way.

—Shawn Vander Mark, Senior Pastor, Trinity Alliance Church

Well written and extremely well researched, but it is not easy, in that it confronts some of the most outrageous lies propagated by universities and media regarding sexuality. As a clinician and theologian, I am grateful to Dr. Kuiper for writing this courageous work to help enlighten, first the church, and hopefully, the larger community of the wrong path post modernism and libertarian attitudes and actions have taken us. My hope is that the reader will remain truly open-minded as she or he reads...it will certainly challenge thinking for the better."

—Dr. Stan DeKoven, President, Visions International University and author, *Marriage and Family Life: A Christian Perspective and Journey to Wholeness*

An intelligent and scholarly work, firmly anchored in history and research. This project takes us on a deep dive into many of the theoretical underpinnings of modern-day concepts that influence our society. I appreciate the way Michael Kuiper has dared to address what others have been too timid to tackle. The reader is challenged to a deeper level of contemplation throughout the book, as differing views about traditional roles and religious concepts are examined. In the final chapter, the author provides a beautifully detailed multicultural lens to give us a fresh set of eyes to look beyond what we may have thought religion to be and to see what we may have totally missed in the midst of our struggles.

—Joan W. Ellason, Ph.D., LPC

Impressive scholarship and sound reasoning. A truly must-read for every seminary student and every graduate student in psychology in Christian universities in America!

—Steve Weathersbee, LMFT, seminary grad, and former missionary

SEX
SOCIETY

God's Design, Tradition, &
the Pursuit of Happiness

J. MICHAEL KUIPER, D.MIN., PH.D.

VIDE

Bible versions used:

New International Version (NIV). Holy Bible, New International Version®, NIV® Copyright ©1973, 1978, 1984, 2011 by Biblica, Inc.® Used by permission. All rights reserved worldwide.

New American Standard Bible (NASB). New American Standard Bible®. Copyright © 1960, 1971, 1977, 1995, 2020 by The Lockman Foundation. All rights reserved.

Vide Press
6200 Second Street
Washington D.C. 20011
www.VidePress.com

PB ISBN: 978-1-954618-47-3
e-Book ISBN: 978-1-954618-48-0

Printed in the United States of America

Table of Contents

Introduction..ix

Chapter 1:   Crumbling Traditions.....................................1

Chapter 2:   The Garden Plan: Together in Union..........21

Chapter 3:   Beyond Eden: A Divided World 39

Chapter 4:   Descent into the Sensual 51

Chapter 5:   Hope Beyond the Sexual Self.....................73

Chapter 6:   Belonging Together and the Primacy of
Woman..99

Chapter 7:   Belonging Together and the Primacy
of Man...115

Chapter 8:   Traditions of Connection or
Competition 151

Chapter 9:   In Celebration of Old Ways.....................175

Chapter 10:   Secular Prophets and the Road to Sexual
Suicide 185

Chapter 11:   The Search for Wholeness: Personal and
Public Theories 209

Chapter 12:   Ideas Carry Consequences; Division
Spreads...241

Chapter 13:   Engaging Culture with Promise and
Hope...261

Index..281

Introduction

The mystery of sexuality reveals itself only when the mystery of humanity and what it is intended to be is revealed and only when love – in this fullest sense of the word – is perceived to be the very theme of life itself. —Helmut Thielicke[1]

Could love really be "the very theme of life itself"? John tells us that God is love (1 John 4:8). Genesis declares that God created humankind to be like himself; and that we reflect this nature as a duality of male and female (1:27). Clearly, then, we are fashioned to love each other and are like God as we do so. The Bible also teaches that together male and female were given great purpose and possibility: to be fruitful, to fill the earth and domesticate it (Genesis 1:28). Tragically, sin soon infected the minds of Adam and Eve and confusion and conflict have colored the human story ever since. Today is no exception.

Monica Cline did not last long as a sex educator. After her uncle died of AIDS in the 1990s, she wanted to help teenagers avoid the horrors of sexually transmitted disease. So she volunteered for training with Planned Parenthood in Austin, Texas. Monica learned that "risk avoidance," advocated by the Comprehensive Sexuality Education (CSE) movement, was the best way to help kids avoid pregnancy and STDs. She learned to teach students how to have safe sex using condoms and lubricants. This she did until the day she got a question that caught her up short. Monica had been describing which bodily fluids were more likely to carry HIV and other STDs when a girl asked, "How do I provide oral sex without gagging?" Stunned, Monica hesitated, unsure of how

---

[1] *The Ethics of Sex* (Grand Rapids: Baker Book House,1964), 51-52.

to respond. Finally, she stuttered, "It sounds like you don't enjoy it... maybe... have you ever considered not doing it?" At this point, the kids just turned in their seats and looked at her. It soon became apparent they were relieved to consider such a thing.

Monica explains, "Planned Parenthood had taught me that if I were to say something like that, they would be upset like I was judging them." When she asked the class if they had ever considered that they "don't have to do any of this stuff—vaginal, anal, or oral sex—they replied, 'no one ever told us that!'"[2]

Monica also learned that parents could be a problem, i.e., a "barrier to service." Therefore, this campaign thought it necessary not to tell parents when she would visit classrooms or inform them of the content. Now, Monica carries a different agenda: to spread the news that CSE sexualizes children, has swollen to global proportions and must be stopped.[3] Not content to push abortion and birth control, this crusade now *requires* teachers to inform first-graders that they themselves decide whether to identify as boys or girls.[4]

"Lisa" shares a different kind of story. She writes, "Last year, my brother Josh, a thirty-seven-year-old married father with five kids under the age of nine, announced he was becoming a woman." After sharing how she just could not call him "Melissa," he severed the relationship. Now heartbroken, Lisa misses her brother. She also chaffs at being labeled "transphobic." She simply cannot accept an ideology that denies reality: the proposition that one's inner truth trumps all realities. This "True Self" must be celebrated, an authentic identity

---

[2] "Comprehensive Sex Education 101" July 16, 2019. https://www.youtube.com/watch?v=xsSxdDre4oM (accessed May 12, 2020)

[3] See Gabriele Kuby, *The Global Sexual Revolution: Destruction of Freedom in the Name of Freedom* (Lifesite, 2015).

[4] Ibid.; See also, www.stopCSE.org; https://familywatch.org/resources/family-policy-resource-center/#PRC-sex-ed

that only harsh, archaic societal structures would deny. To doubt such a discovery is mean-spirited and makes Lisa an "unsafe" person. However, she is neither of these. She writes, "I love my brother. But love does not mean supporting him as he slowly destroys himself... Love means speaking the truth."[5]

Norfolk Police Chief Constable Simon Bailey is also troubled by changes in sexual behavior in recent years. He is Great Britain's national officer in charge of child protection. A new group of young men who have grown up with pornography has become so desensitized that they are now "getting their kicks" from child porn. Every month, his police arrest 500 people possessing this material, but the "scale and level of depravity" just keep growing. "We've got to start coming to terms with the fact that there are some appalling things taking place online... We have to start looking at that, and we have to start genuinely asking the question, how much more are we going to tolerate."[6]

Children are having sex, and adults teach them how. Fathers decide they are mothers. Instead of protecting the innocent, young men exploit them. One wonders: what would our grandparents say? Since the so-called sexual revolution took flight back in the 1960s, did anyone predict how a culture so open and preoccupied with sex would impact children?

Changing sexual modalities

Today, it would be difficult to overstate how profoundly attitudes toward sex and its meaning have changed. Nevertheless, old-fashioned stories still surface. For example, Kevin James stars in a movie called "Mall Cop." Too fat, too short, and not handsome, this hapless hero, having been turned down by the police academy, had settled for a job as a security guard in a

---

[5] Ibid.

[6] "Rise of paedophilia among young men desensitized by Pornhub," *Metro*, April 13, 2020.

large shopping mall. Bumbling but dedicated, he faithfully makes his rounds until one day, a lovely redhead sets up her kiosk. Stricken to the point of stuttering, he knows she is way out of his class. Fortunately, she is kind enough to talk to him and wise enough to rebuff the other potential suitor—a handsome, but arrogant guy. Then the entire mall is taken over by terrorists, and she is one of the hostages. As you might guess, our man finds courage and, in his fumbling way, risks life and limb to rescue everyone and save the day. Seeing his good heart and bravery, she agrees to marry him. Happy ending, yes? But is it realistic?

Since the "women's liberation" of the '60s and '70s, many females appear not to want to be rescued. Many young men hesitate to embrace a heroic role. Further, many males fail to discover *any* significant role for themselves. Warren Farrell and John Gray identify a severe "boy crisis." They cite data, for example, that 70 percent of valedictorians are girls while boys achieve most all of the Ds and Fs. They rightly decry the horrible way the media depicts men "... a perpetual bombardment of *Father Knows Less.*"[7] But their solution, aside from urging dads to become more involved, is to mimic feminist attitudes. They scorn traditional sex roles as "social bribes." They believe we should relieve our boys of the idea they should stand out, be tough, and go for some protector or hero role.

> The degree to which our sons become as free to be who they wish to be as our daughters are is the degree to which we will have taken a huge step—from women's liberation to gender liberation... a gender liberation movement freeing both sexes from the rigid roles of the past toward more flexible roles for our future.[8]

---

[7] *The Boy Crisis: Why Our Boys Are Struggling and What to Do About It* (Dallas, Tx: Ben Bella Books, 2018), 193.

[8] Ibid., 397.

In other words, "From killer/protector to nurturer/connector."[9] Cute, but it will not happen. Males and females are not the same. Farrell and Gray ignore crucial developmental, psychological, and biological differences. However, the question indeed lingers: Are the old ways of women and men outdated?

Mark Cherry, in his comprehensive analysis, *Sex, Family, and the Culture Wars,* concedes that a "liberal social-constructivist theory" of the family has gained broad ascendance in the Western world. This view denies any essential difference between the sexes and assumes that intra-family social roles ought to be interchangeable. Cherry presents a disturbing argument that such beliefs—increasingly enforced by the state—fly in the face of sociobiological realities, deny any place for God, undermine morality, and are rapidly forcing us to the brink of nihilism.[10]

Cultural progress?

The position that people should just be who they are regardless of what their parents, their society, or their genitals tell them reflects the attitude of many feminists and sexual libertarians. Blinded by the myth of inexorable cultural progress, these believers assume human advance parallels technological advance. Regressive traditions that would bind sex to biology, marriage, or progeny must not be allowed to impede the quest for personal expansion. But are we progressing? Are we witnessing self-actualization or self-destruction? In his prescient monograph, *The Abolition of Man,* C.S. Lewis, in 1943, had already discerned a growing trend toward

---

[9] https://citaty.net/citaty/1723780-warren-farrell-in-the-past-socializing-men-to-become-the-best-ki/

[10] New Brunswick: Transaction Publishers, 2016.

subjectivism in education.[11] Feelings supplanting truth. A kind of soft, emotion-driven attitude toward life was being taught by those he called "men without chests." Today, this drift away from empirical realities in favor of subjective experience has grown to universal proportions. Today, we find a tragic counterpart to Lewis' image of chestless men: the 16year-old girl, now a breastless woman, after a "top surgery" obtained without her parents' permission.[12]

How is it that a society fails to protect the innocence of its children? Or pretends that sex differences do not exist? Or remains indifferent to the fact that thousands of pornographic videos cheat millions from real relationships? We might also inquire as to whether the turnaround in sexual attitudes in the last half-century has brought more peace or joy to our world? What about love? No society, of course, has ever provided an ideal platform from which to satisfy these needs.

Nevertheless, despite drowning in information and technological brilliance, our own culture in the 21st-century garners no stars for fostering love or joy. This book presents evidence that a freefall from tradition has produced a freefall in happiness. In particular, we discern a correlation between the jettisoning of attitudes and customs allied with our Judeo-Christian roots and a decline in mental and spiritual health. Despite an insatiable quest for freedom and self-fulfillment, we have become a troubled and confused society.

Naming as culprits the relentless campaigns of radical feminism and sexual libertarianism, Chapter One underscores the personal costs wrought by these anti-establishment movements. Thanks to these forces, traditional attitudes about sex and the sexes have all but disappeared. Despite promises of freedom and equality, these movements have done no favors

---

[11] "The Abolition of Man," in *The Complete Works of C.S. Lewis* (N.Y.: HarperCollins, 2002). Originally published, 1944, 1947.

[12] In Oregon, the age of consent for minors is 15. https://www.oregon.gov/oha/PH/HEALTHYPEOPLEFAMILIES/YOUTH/Documents/minor-rights.pdf

for boys or girls, men or women. Drifting from the moorings of faith and tradition, our people have become lonelier, sadder, and sicker. The next chapters explain how, according to the biblical narrative, the human race fell to a terrible mistake: while the God of the universe provided a design for the greatest self-actualization possible, the humans turned away. Away from God and away from each other. Representing the relational nature of God, the man and woman *together* were called to fill the earth and domesticate it. They were to reflect *together* his very nature of compassion, joy, and creative love. This was the original formula for human flourishing.

Repudiating the Creator's design, the humans fell into a dark hole of sin and self. Civilization has ever since stumbled along, wrestling with division and disorder. Emotional symptoms of such disorders have always included anxiety, loneliness, strife, and depression. Such personal pain cries out for relief. Chapters Four and Five describe the futile descent into sensuality and identify common disorders of sexuality, none of which are new today. These represent private efforts to resolve deep divisions within a soul cut off from its Maker. Chapter Six reminds us of the central role females hold as life-givers and nest builders and argues for a more traditional understanding of sexuality that better fits the data of personality development.

Chapter Seven proposes that the male of the species also possesses an essential role in the family and society. Complementary forms of love are described. As creatures fashioned in the likeness of a triune deity, we find our freedom within an ordered hierarchy and "reciprocity of being." Specific passages of Scripture elucidate the doctrine of male initiative as the two become one flesh.

Chapter Eight highlights the differences between a generative, future-oriented sexuality and the individualistic mentality of social progressives. Chapter Nine offers practical insights as to why traditional attitudes better prepare the young to face adult sexuality. In Chapter Ten, we discover several "secular prophets" who sounded early warnings that the social fabric of the West was beginning to fray. These include George Gilder's forecast that a wholesale capitulation to sexual license and the feminist agenda would lead us to a kind of "sexual suicide." We should have listened to these thinkers. Can we hear them now?

Diabolical and destructive ideologies do not show up like crop circles overnight. Rather more like rats chewing through wooden planks, subtle and insidious forces have long been eating away at the floorboards of our society. Chapters Eleven and Twelve examine key philosophical underpinnings behind the assault on traditional values. The final chapter invites each of us who has fallen short to follow the one man who got it right. As believers in Jesus, can we engage with a secular world with gracious understanding and wisdom to stand for truth as we know it? Most importantly, can we share the love of God and his Son, the one who shines in the darkness, the hope of the world?

CHAPTER 1

Crumbling Traditions

Where there is no revelation, the people cast off restraint.
—Proverbs 29:18

Although we had just met, we were all Christians and the dinner conversation flowed along cordially. Until the word "Trump" popped up and the gloves came off. I do not remember who won. Perhaps you, too, have experienced firsthand how divided we are as a people. Left versus right. Black lives matter versus all lives matter. In recent decades, a different polemic has infiltrated public discourse. This debate circles around sex. What does it mean to be a man or a woman? This debate touches every area of living—from simple codes of conduct to complex philosophies of life. Can a boy open the door for a girl? Does the girl try out for the cheerleading squad or go for the quarterback spot? If two people love each other, do they marry or live together? Who takes care of the babies?

After World War II, the protests of the civil rights movement challenged us to become a more just society. The debate about the Vietnam War further badgered the powers that be. However, mistrust of authority structures did not stop there. Opposition to government grew to open defiance against moral and societal traditions as well. Freedom to do your own thing became the new watchword as Timothy Leary invited the hippies to "tune in, turn on and drop out." This new freedom included freedom from sexual restraint. As Crosby, Stills, and Nash so helpfully sang, "If you can't be with the one you love, love the one you're with." Unfortunately, a quick tour of San Francisco's Haight-Ashbury district ten years later would reveal a heartbreaking sea of homeless, drug-addicted, and lonely individuals. Free love had become no love at all. Love had become sex, and persons had become bodies.

Believing the moral codes of the past to be just another expression of "the Man's" agenda to control the masses, the sexual revolutionaries, with a hearty boost from rock 'n roll, preached satisfaction now. Easy access to birth control fed the conviction that taking the time to know your partner was a waste of time. While the hippie generation outgrew its disdain for money, attitudes about easy sex became well embedded in the cultural mindset.

A question of "I" or "we"

In less socially turbulent times, people assumed that the sexes were designed for each other's benefit. They dated, got to know one another, fell in love, and dreamed of family. They believed they needed each other and felt complete together. Sex itself was precious and protected—a significant thing designed to seal the union of persons. Since the '60s, the "I" has mostly overtaken the "we." Picturing their lives in individualistic terms, the young today tend not to think they need the other sex. As males and females become less significant to each other, sex itself loses meaning—now a cheap thing, to be bought for the price of dinner and drinks.

Judeo-Christian tradition teaches that God, revealed as love personified, created men and women in his own image. Christians understand God as one being, yet three persons. Differentiated, yet functioning in complete union. To exist in God's image thus carries the impetus of love as a communal and uniting force. From the perspective of theological anthropology, individual self-expression and self-actualization occur in the context of intimacy and the well-being of the other.

Enacting our god-like nature, love of self and love of others flow together.

In stark opposition to such an ethos, individualistic ideologies saturate our culture. Marriage is denounced, postponed, or abandoned in favor of fun or career. With too-easy sex has come too-easy divorce. Thanks to the Internet, pictures replace persons.[13] As a further sign of rank self-centeredness, we do little to protect our children from Internet porn.[14] An anti-male bias infiltrates the worlds of education, television, and film media, further driving the sexes apart. Purporting to address wrongs done to sexual minorities, homosexual and transgender activists work to normalize sexualities that fail to support natural procreation or bring the sexes together. Such a troubled climate produces troubled children. Just this morning, a distraught neighbor reported that her twelve-year-old daughter declared she was a lesbian. Twenty years ago, such an announcement was rare. Today, it would be unusual to meet someone who does not have a friend or family member flummoxed by some such child or grandchild.

When Judeo-Christian attitudes formed the bedrock of the Western world, we generally assumed we lived our life in some way before a creator. We understood ourselves to be engineered by a loving God and fashioned in his image. We assumed we were responsible to God and thus responsive to others. We did not expect to define ourselves without reference to other people. We understood that every self is, in fact, a gendered self[15] and carries a responsibility to the opposite

---

[13] Patrick F. Fagan, Ph.D., psychologist and former Deputy Assistant Health and Human Services Secretary, details this 16 billion dollar industry's destructive impact on youth and families. https://www.webroot.com/us/en/resources/tips-articles/internet-pornography-by-the-numbers

[14] One wonders, *Where have all the grown-ups gone?* Such as Dr. James Dobson when he chaired the Meese Commission on Pornography.

[15] Nicolosi, Joseph, *Shame and Attachment Loss: The Practical Work of Reparative Therapy* (Downers Grove, Il.: Intervarsity Press, 2009).

sex. Men were to be strong and responsible, and women were to be prized.

A question of decline

Of course, one does not have to be a historian to realize that "the good ole days" held their own portion of evil. Furthermore, anxious hand-wringing—*what is this world coming to?*—is unbecoming to thoughtful discourse. Nevertheless, as Anthony Esolen points out, some societal shifts ought to be questioned. He offers two examples:

> "Perhaps the amalgamation of family farms into vast tracts of agribusiness is not an *entirely* good thing," or, "Perhaps the nearly universal exodus of women from homes and neighborhoods into offices does not bode well for the homes and neighborhoods, and that is something we should consider." [16]

More significantly, he writes, *"Sometimes entire civilizations do decay and die, and the people who point that out are correct."*[17] (italics his)

Rather than idealizing any past period or culture, the thrust of this study is to posit that certain behaviors and thought-forms are indeed destructive while others, having withstood the test of time, foster more salutary outcomes for children and families. Societal change, of course, is inevitable and often brings blessings. Nevertheless, the severe tampering with customs and assumptions about sexuality carries disturbing consequences. Most cultures—those having achieved stability—follow traditions that guide and protect individuals at the very area of greatest personal vulnerability,

---

[16] *Out of Ashes: Rebuilding American Culture* (Washington, DC: Regnery Publishing, 2017), 3.
[17] Ibid.

viz., their sexuality. When affirming that humans are God's creatures, people naturally lean toward modesty, self-control, and the desire to know and love one another. There is no question of their investment in the launching and protection of the young. Traditions that honor faith, delay of gratification, loyalty, and commitment help a community to survive and flourish. As our society has wandered from its theistic roots, these virtues have not thrived. Nor can we say that individuals have flourished.[18]

An offended generation

The destruction of traditional customs has not been motivated, of course, by any wish to make people miserable. Instead, each step clothes itself in a kind of self-righteous indignation. As if rules and traditions equal oppression. A recent article in the local newspaper announced the victory of an eleven-year-old girl who refused to wear a dress for a school ceremony. Not satisfied that the administration backed down, the parents now demand an apology, as if to say, "Your customs hurt us and we are mad."

In contrast to such a spirit of offense, traditions that foster religious faith tend to cultivate trust. Trust in the wisdom of older generations. Trust that there is design in nature, order, and purpose in the world. With diminishing faith in God, an anxious atmosphere of suspicion grows, breeding both fear and contempt. Seeing a world of victims, secular humanists spread a message of struggle. Activists on college campuses preach that masculinity is toxic, and sex roles operate only to dominate women. A compare and contrast style of identity

---

[18] The suicide rate since 1999 has risen by 30%. Sally C. Curtin, MA, and Margaret Warner, Ph.D., Division of Vital Statistics; and Holly Hedegaard, MD, MSPH, Office of Analysis and Epidemiology *Suicide Rates for Females and Males by Race and Ethnicity: United States, 1999 and 2014* https://www.cdc.gov/nchs/data/hestat/suicide/rates_1999_2014.htm (accessed December, 2019).

politics demands equality in every possible way. Natural gender differences are resented or denied altogether. The superior tone of equity activists is more than intimidating. As Harvard president Larry Summers discovered, you are not allowed to suggest that perhaps women fail to achieve equal representation in physics and math might be due to prefer-ence rather than sexism. After the public outcry and his subse-quent resignation, we can only wonder how many academics, like the silent crowd watching the naked Emperor, keep their thoughts to themselves. Will no one say, "Ah, excuse me... but only *women* can have babies"?[19]

For decades, educational policies have been shaped by the assumption that girls are shortchanged and boys are pred-atory. Despite the fact that the data do not support these assumptions, the impact in enforcing "equity" has been profound.[20] As boys grow up, they not only realize that girls learn faster and mature earlier, they also discover girls are groomed to compete with them. Deprived of distinctive masculine roles, many fall behind or simply pull away. As a boy absorbs the message that his masculinity is suspect, he may embrace a "bad boy" persona or group together in the pursuit of mischief, including a preoccupation with sexual conquest.

Exploitative behavior by immature males deepens cycles of conflict. High school and college girls, emulating impulsive male patterns, agree to quick sex. As teenage boys conclude they have no particular contribution to the woman, instead of taking care of her, they take advantage of her. The girls soon find themselves used and objectified. Angry young women

---

[19] Stephen E. Rhoads, *You Can't Imagine Facts Away: A Response to Bridgett Schulte and Gary Barker.* https://ifstudies.org/blog/you-cant-imagine-facts-away-a-response-to-brigid-schulte-and-gary-barker (accessed December, 2019).
[20] Christina Hoff Sommers, *The War Against Boys: How Misguided Policies are Harming Our Young Men* (New York: Simon and Schuster, 2013).

conclude they cannot trust men. For many, marriage and children are the last things on their minds.

When schools make sure women are pictured in equal numbers as police officers, engineers, or construction workers, but *never as mothers* with babies, girls may conclude they have no particular purpose in relation to boys. In studying forty social studies textbooks, Paul Vitz could not find a single reference to marriage as the foundation of the family. Nor was there any indication that being a mother or housewife represented a vital job.[21] This kind of tacit devaluation of motherhood is most disturbing. When a society negates the primacy of mothering, how can it not devalue its children?

Striving against oppressive social structures, identity groups resist the thought of a natural order to the universe. Or a wise God who orders life and relationships. Tradition and authority are the problem. For some, the family itself, with its assumption of patriarchy, is the enemy. Progressives pretend the sexes are the same. The assumption that boys and girls are designed to build a future together has vanished. Dreams of family have disappeared along with home economics classes. With growing secularization, students are less likely to assume they belong to God. They certainly do not learn they belong to each other.

But is it so bad? Is the sky falling? Let us take a brief survey. So, we ask the question: Boys, girls, persons—"How is it going?"

Are the boys okay?

Perhaps the most significant observation is also the most subtle. No riots in the street, no cries for justice or angry

---

[21] "Indeed, the words marriage, wedding, husband, wife do nor occur once in these books. Nowhere is it suggested that being a mother or homemaker was a worthy and important role for a woman." *Censorship: Evidence of Bias in our Children's Textbooks*, 2.

letters complaining of loss of position or purpose. Instead, the attitude of many boys today seems to be one of pure indifference. High School teacher Joshua Pauling recalls observing his students as they listened to the student council election results. Neither sex was surprised and seemed to accept uncritically the discrepancy that out of forty-three positions, only eight had been filled by boys. Of the school's thirty clubs, girls run twenty-five of them.[22]

Psychologist and family physician, Leonard Sax writes:

What's troubling about so many of the boys I see in my practice, or the boys I hear about from parents and teachers, is that they don't have much passion for any real-world activity... The boys I'm most concerned about don't disdain school because they have other real-world activities they care about more. They disdain school because they disdain everything. Nothing really excites them. Even more disturbing is the fact that so many of these boys seem to regard their laid-back, couldn't care less attitude as being somehow quintessentially male.[23]

Pauling believes these trends are a direct consequence of "second-wave feminism," a movement of the '60s and '70s which pushes past equality to sameness. Pauling warns that promoting the idea of no difference between the sexes misleads girls and completely neglects boys.[24]

I see it in my classroom, where many of the boys are happy to sit back and watch, as if to say, "You want

---

[22] "Where are the men? A public school teacher confronts gender illusions and sexual reality." In *Salvo*, Spring, 2020.
[23] *Boys Adrift: The Five Factors Driving the Growing Epidemic of Unmotivated Boys and Underachieving Young Men* (New York: Basic Books, 2007), 7.
[24] Pauling, 13.

girls to be leaders? All right fine; I'll just goof off and then go home and watch Netflix (or worse)." What I see emerging are disordered forms of masculinity— the hyper-masculine male on the one hand, and the effeminate male on the other. The twin problems of aggressiveness and passivity both result from disordered masculinity, and both can stem from a sense of weakness and impotence that can erupt in unhealthy outbursts as a way of compensating for a stifled masculinity.[25]

Another perceptive observer, Christina Hoff Sommers, has long been concerned about how boys have fallen behind. She writes:

For most American women, especially young women, the problem is not the futility and monotony of domestic life; it is choosing among the many paths open to them. Finding male partners as ambitious and well educated as they are is another challenge. Life for women may be difficult, but the system is no longer rigged against them. The new problem with no name is the economic and social freefall of millions of young men.[26]

In my counseling practice, I encounter men in their twenties who have not yet obtained a driver's license. Skilled at video games, perhaps, but motivated? Disciplined? Too many boys inhabiting men's bodies still live with parents who are

---

[25] Ibid.
[26] Sommers, 28.

reluctant to give them the boot. [27] The data are alarming.[28] Among the troubling statistics are these: Less than 65 percent of American men have jobs today, compared with 80 percent in 1950; most college students are women—undereducated men will have that much more difficulty finding jobs or supporting a family; men lost twice as many jobs during the last recession as did women; one in three children is living in a home without a father; although the US has only 5 percent of the world's population, we house 25 percent of the world's prisoners, the vast majority of whom are male;[29] Women make up more than half of all health care and middle management jobs; young urban women make more money than young urban men; boys achieve 70 percent of all Ds and Fs in the public schools. Male SAT scores in 2011 were the lowest in forty years; some 30 percent of all internet traffic contains pornographic web sites, and men consume significantly more pornography than do women. Recent research makes it clear

---

[27] See "As Video Games Get Better, Young Men Work Less and Play More," Brian Wallheimer, *Chicago Booth Review*, December 20, 2017. Comparing the periods 2004–07 and 2012–15, the researchers find that young men increased the number of hours dedicated to leisure by about the same number of labor hours they lost, or 132 hours over this time span. They used three-quarters of these hours for gaming and other computer leisure activities, significantly more than did women or older men."

[28] Michael Snyder, "32 Facts that show how young men are being systemati-cally emasculated in America today." *The Economic Collapse Blog*, June, 2013. Young men are not the only males languishing. A Brookings Institute study reveals that mortality rates for men have been rising – preventable deaths called, "deaths of despair." "The entire trend is driven by premature mortality among less-than-college-educated whites, mainly in the middle-aged years. That's a pretty big marker that something's really wrong." https://www.yahoo.com/finance/news/deaths-of-despair-why-this-group-of-americans-has-higher-mor-tality-rates-130633528.html

[29] Ibid. This statistic includes some 21% of all black men who have been to prison compared with 9% of black men after World War II who had been to prison.

that porn not only has a detrimental effect on relationships but damages the male brain as well.[30]

Looking past statistics, have we not noticed a pervasive media assault on the male? Long gone are the wise role models found in "Father Knows Best," "My Three Sons," or "Marcus Welby, MD." In contrast, have not the likes of Ed Bundy and Homer Simpson, as well as thousands of beer commercials, taught us that men are little more than pleasure-seeking, self-centered dopes?

Diane Passno writes that the spokeswomen of feminism,

…portray all men as potential predators, rapists or abusers, or just plain mentally deficient… The advertising world has completely bought into this feminist mindset… I challenge you, the reader, to keep a pen handy while you watch television. Record how often the woman in the commercial is all-knowing, even when it comes to purchasing an automobile, and the male is a good-looking, dumb guy, just pleased as can be to have her lead him by the nose! So often television programs and advertising depict men as buffoons.[31]

The other day I watched a Kia commercial in which a precocious little girl explained financing options while a little boy, in mock reference to other sales techniques, danced foolishly in the background. Growing up with the constant drumbeat of "girls are smart, boys are useless," is it a wonder that boys today hold back? Or do not know where or how

---

[30] William Struthers, *Wired for Intimacy: How Pornography Hijacks the Male Brain* (Downers Grove, Il.: Intervarsity Press, 2010). See also, "Your brain on porn: How internet porn affects the brain" https://www.youtube.com/watch?v=7oFVOJf0TzY&feature=youtu.be

[31] Diane Passno, *Feminism: Mystique or Mistake?* (Wheaton Ill.: Tyndale House, 2000), 32.

they fit in. Are we surprised to find that gender confusion is spreading?

In a multifaceted, high-tech world, we understand that roles for men and women would have changed. Perhaps feminism has simply facilitated a necessary correction. On the other hand, in the legitimate desire to right wrongs and give women the equal freedom to pursue their dreams, did anyone realize there would be such a corresponding cost to the other sex?[32]

And the girls?

At any rate, the girls are flourishing! But are they? Are they happy as they cast about searching for some man they can trust? Or respect? Are they happy as they suppress innate longings for children? After decades of freeing women from the confinement of home and the strictures of sexual taboos, we ask: "Are the girls thriving? How much better off are they?"

Although one may argue that social media and other factors are to blame, the statistics for girls are also alarming.

---

[32] Nathanson and Young argue that "ideological feminism" has created a culture of misandry. Their book, *Spreading Misandry*, analyzed what they considered to be pervasive messages of hatred toward men in greeting cards in "pop cultural artifacts and productions from the 1990s." *Legalizing Misandry* (2005), the second in the series, gave similar attention to laws in North America. In 2002, pundit Charlotte Hays wrote "that the anti-male philosophy of radical feminism as filtered into the culture at large is incontestable; indeed, this attitude has become so pervasive that we hardly notice it any longer." (Wikipedia-Misandry) Wendy McElroy wrote in 2001 that some feminists seem to have moved from a "hot anger" toward men to a "cold hatred." She argued it was a misandrist position to consider men, as a class, to be irreformable or rapists. McElroy stated, "a new ideology has come to the forefront...radical or gender, feminism," one that has joined hands with [the] political correctness movement that condemns the panorama of western civilization as sexist and racist: the product of 'dead white males. " (Wikipedia-Misandry)

Religious Studies professors Paul Nathanson and Katherine Young made similar comparisons in their 2001, three-book series, *Beyond the Fall of Man*, which treats misandry as a form of prejudice and discrimination that has become institutionalized in North American Society.

A British study reports that the number of girls ages seven to twenty-one who describe themselves as "very happy" has dropped from 2009 to 2017 by 41 percent.[33] According to a Pew Research study, the rate of depression in teen girls grew significantly from 2007 to 2017. While both sexes experienced an increase, the rise was sharper for girls; one in five teenage girls reported at least one major depressive episode in the last year, an increase from 12 to 20 percent.[34]

Campus psychiatrist Miriam Grossman is troubled by these trends. For one thing, she does not relish the frequent need to treat girls suffering from STDs. She also finds it painful to listen to the parade of girls who come into her office heartbroken after casual sex. Most people fail to realize how despondent a young woman can become after being caught up in the "hook-up" culture prevalent in so many colleges. Depression and suicidality are three times more likely to be experienced by sexually active girls than virgins.[35]

In another vein, Grossman decries the lack of honest communication by feminist groups and sexual counselors regarding the medical and psychological consequences of abortion. In their guide for the career counseling of college students, "experts" from the American Psychological

[33] "UK Survey finds sharp decline in happiness among young women and girls." https://www.theguardian.com/lifeandstyle/2018/sep/19/uk-survey-finds-sharp-decline-in-happiness-of-young-women-and-girls?CMP=Share_iOSApp_Other (accessed July 10, 2020).

[34] A.W. Geiger and Leslie Davis "A growing number of American teenagers—particularly girls—are facing depression" *Fact Tank: News in the Numbers*, July, 2019 Pew Research Center https://www.pewresearch.org/fact-tank/2019/07/12/a-growing-number-of-american-teenagers-particularly-girls-are-facing-depression/ See also, Haidt, J., & Twenge, J. (2019). *Is There an Increase in Adolescent Mood Disorders, Self-Harm, and Suicide Since 2010 in The USA and UK? A Review.* Unpublished manuscript, New York University. https://docs.google.com/document/d/1diMvsMeRphUH7E6D1d_J7R6WbDdgnzFHDHPx9HXzR5o/edit

[35] Miriam Grossman, *Unprotected: A Campus Psychiatrist Reveals How Political Correctness in Her Profession Endangers Every Student* (New York: Sentinel, 2007).

Association completely pass over both established psychological principles and medical reality. Among other omis-
sions, they ignore the wisdom of the revered psychologist
Erik Erikson regarding the critical task of early adulthood
concerning generativity; the guide neglects to inform girls
that these are the years to be considering parenthood. Nor do
they mention that pregnancy in the later years can be increasingly problematic. "Between one third and one-half of all
high achieving women in America do not have children…
The vast majority of these women did not choose to be childless."[36] Instead, the APA's guide focuses the young women's
attention on discrimination, occupational and gender role
stereotypes, workplace harassment, the glass ceiling, and the
like. "The only reference to children in this chapter, devoted
specifically to the guidance of women, is to say that they can
be a barrier to career success."[37]

Nicole King summarizes the overall outcome for women
fifty years after Betty Friedan's seminal treatise that launched
feminism on the world stage.[38] While women have entered
academia and the workplace in record numbers, they are far
from happy. They experience:

> … historically low fertility rates, no-fault divorce, and
> abortion on demand. The emotional consequences for
> women have not been rosy. Stevenson and Wolfers
> report [39] that, in spite of the fact that all objective
> measures of women's happiness have risen, both

---

[36] Sylvia Ann Hewlett, *Creating A Life: The Professional Women in the Quest for Children* (New York: Miramax, 2002), (cited in Grossman, 138).

[37] Grossman, 129. "More than 50% of Women are childless at 30." https://www.youtube.com/watch?v=BoqjKqt__tI

[38] Betty Friedan, *The Feminine Mystique* (New York: Norton,1963).

[39] *The Paradox of Declining Female Happiness*, 2009. The National Bureau of Research, Http://www.nber.org/papers/w14969

women's subjective well-being and their well-being relative to men have fallen since the 1970s.[40]

In a sharp rebuke to feminist ideology, King argues that Friedan's drive to set women free from the bondage of home and family has, in the long run, turned out to be a social experiment gone awry. Friedan preached that women should develop a career outside the home; to do so also implied an embracing of their sexuality apart from the strictures of marriage. King notes that in sex education today, as schools promote contraceptives to twelve-year-olds, the separation between sex and fertility has been learned all too well. In 2011, 41 percent of all births were out of wedlock. "The implication is clear: sex and marriage no longer go together, and so, babies and marriage no longer go together, even though research overwhelmingly shows marriage to be the best environment for raising children."[41]

In 1963, Friedan declared that the real work of America was business, not homemaking. King writes:

> Women have taken her advice, leaving home and children to the care of others in ever-increasing numbers... But those careers, it turns out, are not as meaningful as they had hoped, and most women still cannot squelch that maternal instinct that drives them to *want* to bear and care for children more than anything else in the world.[42]

A recent survey of a thousand mothers by Forbes revealed that

---

[40] Nicole King, "Feminism through the life cycle: Women bought into a mystique that left them even more alone and conflicted in their pursuit of fulfillment," *Mercatornet,* July 5, 2013.

[41] Ibid.

[42] Ibid.

while only 10 percent of stay-at-home mothers wished they still worked, about half of working mothers wished they could stay at home.[43] Study upon study has indicated that most women want to have children, and most women who want to have children want to stay home with them or at the very most work part-time.[44]

With the dream of "housewife" thoroughly denigrated, many girls assume they ought to set their hearts on a career first and, if possible, to have a family as well. Having both at the same time is difficult. Although *The Feminine Mystique* addressed some real problems in 1963, the proposal to elevate career over homemaking has produced dismal results. Nicole King concludes that a woman today

> ...finds herself in constant conflict with her own nature... In trying to straddle the worlds of career and homemaker, today's woman finds herself stressed, tired, and, according to most studies, wanting to return home to be with the children. In her later years, she is more likely to be alone and separated from her children and husband.[45]

In her brave book, *Sex Scandal: The Drive to Abolish Male and Female Gender*, Ashley McGuire summarizes multiple studies supporting the conclusion that egalitarianism has done no favors to women. For example, while the spread of STDs affects both men and women, deleterious long-term consequences, such as cancer, are far more likely to be experienced in women. There are subtle symptoms of dysphoria, as well.

---

[43] https://www.forbes.com/sites/meghancasserly/2012/09/12/forbes-woman-and-thebump-com-parenthood-and-economy-2012-survey-results/#6063d7213212

[44] King, ibid.

[45] Ibid.

It's not just STDs taking a toll on the female body. Women are experiencing an epidemic of body insecurity. Our culture's insistence on wiping out sex difference in the name of sexual equality has done nothing to slow the tide of plastic surgery, something that tends to *enhance* sexual difference, which is on the rise, especially among teenage girls.[46]

More liberated, but less happy, women struggle with twice as much anxiety and face significantly more depression than men. It would also appear that the transgender craze sweeping across the West affects females in greater numbers, in particular, young ones. In her disturbing study of rapid-onset gender dysphoria (ROGD), Abigail Shrier writes, "Among preteen girls aged 10 to 14, rates of self-harm are up 189% since 2010, nearly triple what they were only six years before."[47] In the recent past, pubescent angst about one's body was managed on a more face-to-face level with family and friends; today, teens seek refuge in electronics. As they search for friendship or information on Tumbler, YouTube, or Snapchat, they become subject to a heretofore unthinkable question: "Maybe my problem is that I am trans"—a diagnosis that ultimately carries chilling consequences, the destruction of genital tissue. Although most girls who come to think of themselves as trans or non-binary do not seek sex reassignment surgery, any confidence in their emerging femininity remains nonexistent. They "flee womanhood like a house on fire."[48]

Although the issues are complex, certain conclusions become apparent. As boys find themselves vilified or unnecessary, they flounder. Lacking positive sex roles and powerful

---

[46] Washington, DC: Regnery Publishing, 2017,150.
[47] *Irreversible Damage: The Transgender Craze Seducing Our Daughters* (Washington, DC: Regnery Publishing, 2020), 3.
[48] Ibid.

masculine models, many fail to develop the qualities or the inclination to rise to the challenge of family life. On the other hand, as girls are groomed for nothing but achievement, their natural disposition to home and children must be suppressed. Under the ever-present banner of independence, they learn not to look to men for anything. Inevitably, each sex grows up believing there is nothing special the other sex brings, except, perhaps a romp in the hay.

An astute observer of teenagers, high school teacher Pauling sums it up this way: Thanks to equity indoctrination, the young have lost the mystery of the "other."

> Second wave feminism's campaign of sameness (and the concomitant sexual revolution's deconstruction of sexuality) has been all too successful in creating the emasculated male who sits back and wallows in permanent adolescence, and the masculinized female who is a go-getter and dons the business suit.[49]

A question of health

Many of the troublesome consequences of the sexual revolution and feminist agenda have been subtle. Depression and anxiety are unseen, private agonies. In contrast, the Centers for Disease Control brings us face to face with alarming public data. While the effect of the Coronavirus has yet to be evaluated, pre-covid statistics are noteworthy. In 2016, for example, there were 1.59 million new cases of chlamydia, 468,514 cases of gonorrhea representing 4.7 percent, and 18.5 percent increases over the previous year.[50] CBS News reports: "Young people and gay and bisexual men continue to be disproportionately affected by STDs. The data show that

---

[49] Pauling, 13.

[50] https://www.cdc.gov/std/stats16/infographic.htm

Americans aged 15 to 24 accounted for nearly two-thirds of chlamydia diagnoses and half of gonorrhea diagnoses."[51]

Dr. Jonathan Mermin, the Director of CDC's National Center for HIV/AIDS, Viral Hepatitis, STD, and TB Prevention warns that, "We have reached a decisive moment for the nation… STD rates are rising, and many of the country's systems for preventing STDs have eroded."[52] Other symptoms of disturbance are evident as well.[53] For example, in 2019, 61 percent of Americans reported being lonely.[54]

In summary, the evidence suggests we are not a happy people. Many worry about the decline of the family. Others wonder if this is not such a bad thing. They celebrate the possibility of different kinds of families as well as different ways people can relate to each other sexually. Indeed, for these folks in their demand for tolerance, traditions are the enemy—repressing the human spirit and blocking cultural development. But is it true that moral and spiritual traditions are the problem? Is it wise to throw out conventional wisdom under the banner of enlightenment and progress? As C.S. Lewis noted, progress cannot be progress if one is going the wrong direction. Is it not time to reevaluate? Is it not time—at least in some ways—to think about turning around?

The next two chapters invite us to pause for a bit to consider ancient biblical wisdom regarding the nature of persons and the function of sexuality. Borrowing from Dietrich Bonhoeffer's insightful investigation, *Creation and Fall: A Theological Interpretation of Genesis 1 – 3*, we examine

---

[51] https://www.cbsnews.com/news/stds-at-an-unprecedented-high-in-the-u-s/

[52] Ibid. These stats continue to alarm. https://nationalistreview.net/2018/08/28/study-liberal-sex-culture-caused-rapid-10-percent-spike-in-stds/

[53] Suicide rates for the young of both sexes are at an all-time high. https://www.latimes.com/science/la-sci-suicide-rates-rising-teens-young-adults-20190618-story.html

[54] According to a survey by health insurer Cigna, more than three in five Americans are lonely. The study found that Gen Z had the highest loneliness scores while baby boomers had the lowest.

what it means to be created in the image of God "as male and female."[55] From a Judeo-Christian standpoint, we ask, what was God's intention and design? What went wrong? And what is the plan for recovery?

---

[55] New York: Macmillan Publishing Co., 1959.

CHAPTER 2

The Garden Plan:
Together in Union

*"And they were both naked, the man and his wife,
and were not ashamed."* —Genesis 2:25

Before delving into the theistic roots of our Western world, we might pop a few questions. "What is the big deal about sex? Or gender or sexual orientation? Why did you do a double-take when you noticed that tall man wearing a mustache, lipstick, and a skirt? And why care if our teenagers text each other's naked bodies? Or watch pornography?" Perhaps we who resist cultural changes are just old-fashioned, moralistic, and judgmental. Another answer, however, has to do with genuine concern, a desire that humans do well on this planet, that they find meaning, satisfaction, and purpose. We want the young to feel that they belong, that they fit—with themselves, with one another, their community. When things fit together, we experience harmony. There is order, and the world feels right.

Disorder does not feel right. When things do not fit, we do not feel right. The momentary pleasure of a one-night stand does not fit with good feelings in the morning. The joining of genitals without the joining of persons is a bad fit. *"I thought he loved me, but he just used me. I thought I knew him. He doesn't know me at all."*

So why is sex a big deal? One reason is that it can hurt. Sexuality implies vulnerability. To be naked is to be without protection. The consequences of "unprotected" sex are both costly and wide-ranging. Beyond the risk of an STD or inconvenient pregnancy, one might find their nude photos flashed on social media. Not only is sex a delicate thing, but it is *significant*. It produces a *child*. Sex brings two people together. The old-fashioned word is "consummate." Sex cements the bond. Biblically, the two become "one flesh." When that consummation is publicly acknowledged, the broader community supports that union. There follows a harmony among physical, psychological, and social systems. In a way, you could say that sex built from knowledge and love pulls all these systems together.

The following notes provide a framework by which to understand the Maker's intention for the sexes. Bonhoeffer offers the phrase, "at the origin."[56] We catch a glimpse of that original design in the book of Genesis. A God of perfect love creates a perfect world. The paradise of the Garden of Eden.

Life "At the Origin"

The first chapters of the Bible reveal in elegant simplicity the story of God's original plan. We note that before God's intervention, the earth was "formless and void" (Genesis 1:2). Then God speaks, creating light and order. After each day of creation, he pronounces his handiwork "good." After creating the humans and in summary of everything that was created, God calls it "very good."

It would appear that the void of the earth represented *possibility*. God is here pictured as one who envisions, one who imagines what could be. He fashions creatures who resemble himself, and he shares his power by giving them dominion over the other creatures. He provides for them everything they need.

---

[56] *Ethics* (New York: Macmillan, 1955).

In Genesis One, "Elohim" is the word used for God, a word that may carry a more generic translation as "deity." In the second creation account in Chapter Two, we find a more intimate tone and the more personal "Yahweh" is used, generally translated as "the Lord God." Here we see the care in which the Lord fashions the man from the soil and then breathes his own breath into him. We see the foresight of the Creator who has a special love for his creature, the one like himself. We see how he plants a garden and causes beautiful trees to grow and to produce "good fruit" (2:9). We also get a glimpse of the discerning judgment of God, who observes that it is "not good" that the man lives alone. God then acts on his evaluation. His remedy is to form a "helpmate" or "suitable companion" for him. God is pictured as intimately involved in the process as if he wants to please the man. "He formed a woman out of the rib and brought her to him" (2:22). This operation turned out to be highly successful. Adam is elated, declaring, "At last, here is one of my own kind..." (2:23).

In reading the accounts of creation, one discerns God's delight in anticipation. One can imagine that God is having fun. Verse 19 hints at curiosity in the Lord when he brings the animals to Adam "to see what he would name them." God is happy to share with Adam the creative ability to make choices. One imagines too that God anticipates enrichment of his own being as he participates in the choices and creativity of his humans. We discern glimpses of this attitude where we find God enjoying humanity and "delighting in his way" (Psalm 37:23). In the astounding statement that Jesus endured the cross *for the joy set before him* (Hebrews 12:2), we find a God who eagerly anticipates a restored relationship with his creatures.

The original gifts of being

Brennan Manning quotes the Latin phrase, *Bonum diffusum sui,* "good diffuses itself".[57] In other words, creation is the overflow of God's love. He gives Adam and Eve a place of their own, a "garden of delight." The word picture of a garden suggests a place with boundaries, a home, a field of operations for play and work. A place for living things to grow and to produce fruit. Ultimately, this field would extend to the whole earth. God gives them life, an everlasting life untroubled by any danger to that existence. They are given position—a high status, an identity as beloved and belonging to the eternal God of the universe. They are declared to be the very "image and likeness of God." The Hebrew word for image is *se'lem,* a common word in the ancient Near East for "idol." Richter writes:

> When a polytheist from the ancient world sets out to make an earthly representative of their deity (understood as the incarnation of that which could not be fully incarnated, a lifeless object that must be animated by the deity), that polytheist fashioned a *se'lem.* When the language of Genesis 1:26-27 is combined with the images of Genesis 2:7, we see that Yahweh is presenting himself to us as a divine craftsman, who is making an idol of/for himself, which he himself must animate. And that idol is us. Within the worldview of the ancient Near East the message here is clear: we are the nearest representation of Yahweh that exists.[58]

Along with this elevated position, the first humans receive a purpose—to be fruitful, to fill the earth and subdue it

---

[57] *The Ragamuffin Bible* (Grand Rapids: Zondervan, 2013).

[58] Sandra L. Richter, *The Epic of Eden: A Christian Entry into the Old Testament* (Downers Grove, Ill.: Inter-varsity Press, 2008), 107.

(Genesis 1:28). God gives them, as male and female together, this vocation, a mandate full of rich possibilities and meaning. In summary, Genesis tells the story of a loving God who shares his nature, including his capacity to create and to love. He does so by offering to his creatures "like himself" possibility, provision, place, and purpose.

Bounded possibility

God is pleased with his creatures who can think and act. He has given them the capacity and freedom to thrive, to grow, and eventually to have dominion over the whole earth. Yet, these powers are limited, bequeathed by another. As Ray S. Anderson puts it, they are "derived powers."[59] Humans are creatures, not self-existent creators. Their abilities are gifts to be used for specific purposes. All created things have boundaries and must fit within a grander scheme of things. Every creature is designed to function within its nature. By instinct, animals do that for which they were designed. Bound by nature, dogs do not mate with cats. God did not give them the freedom to be or to do anything else. They are not, after all, made in the image of God.

Adam, too, in order to properly live out his nature, is given a boundary. However, this is not the boundary of rigidly prescribed physical space, as is the case with a plant or a tree. Nor is it the determination of instinct. One cannot bind a free spirit with such methods without withdrawing the gift of freedom, without diminishing the *imago Dei*. Nevertheless, the Creator requires his creation to function within its proper order. To step outside that order would be to miss the actualization of its own being. To step outside the creature's order would be to create disorder. And to introduce evil.

---

[59] Ray S. Anderson, *Theology of Personhood*, class syllabus, Fuller Theological Seminary, 1978.

God places two trees in the middle of the Garden. These seem to represent possibility, the tree of life and the tree of the knowledge of good and evil. In the second creation narrative, God has not yet formed Eve, and it is to Adam that he commands: "You are free to eat from any tree in the garden; but you must not eat from the tree of the knowledge of good and evil, for when you eat from it you will certainly die" (2:16-17). Anderson writes:

> Prior to a knowledge of good and evil, the original man and woman had knowledge of the command of God, which was both limiting and liberating. They were free to eat of any fruit of the garden, but not of the tree of the knowledge of good and evil. The question as to which fruit could be eaten in such a way as to authenticate and complete the personal life of each could only be answered in this way: any fruit that God has set before you as a possibility. In this case, self-enactment was completed by choosing and eating, not by questioning and reflecting.[60]

In no uncertain terms, God tells Adam he may not eat of the tree of knowledge of what is good and what is bad. Herein lies the boundary to human possibility. The Lord's intention for his creatures is that they live in freedom from the need to judge life in that way. This capacity does not belong to them. It is not in the design of their nature. To defy this boundary brings death. Standing before the human creature whose nature is to think and to choose, in other words, is both possibility and prohibition. Just as instinct binds the animal to its own created order, so then, does the word of God bind the free spirit to its own created order.

---

[60] Anderson, *On Being Human: Essays in Theological Anthropology* (Grand Rapids: Eerdmans, 1982), 59.

God had designed a field of rich possibility—a playground, if you will, for delightful human existence where the creatures can expand in joyful co-regency with the Creator, sharing the Maker's enjoyment in the world. Adam's possibility, the very actualization of his nature, was to be found in his relation to God as the source of all possibility. To live, then, meant that Adam lives in God, in his subordinate and dependent status as a creature who is like God but is not God, who is made in God's image but whose glory is not that he is his own source but that he is the crown achievement and pride of the One who is the ultimate source. The paradox for the creatures is that their freedom to be themselves is ontologically bound to their nature as belonging to another. Being made in the likeness of this "Other" who is freedom personified, they may choose not to be so bound. Such a choice, however, has no ontological legality since it would ruin their very nature.

Nevertheless, such a choice remains a possibility—an evil possibility. God cannot determine that such an illegitimate choice not be made. The free spirit cannot *be forced* to obey without denying its own natural being as "like God." God can only warn.

The prohibition not to eat of just one particular tree, then, was a necessary address to Adam's core being as a free soul. Unable to force obedience, God addresses him as he would address another being like himself: He speaks to him. Not that this speech is that of equals. Indeed, God speaks with authority and commands Adam not to eat. Yet, the nature of this command is in the form of Word, not determining power. Because the man is like God, he has a choice. As he chooses to obey, he enhances his being, stays intimately connected to the source of that being and lives.

Happy innocence

We ask, then, what could be the nature of the prohibition? Surely, this is a protective boundary. We must assume that the prohibition was for the human's own good, designed to maintain and enhance the created order. Second, we assume that to disobey would open the door to possibility that is not good. To know good and evil, God says, is not good and will diminish Adam's being. The warning is dire, indeed. "In the day that you shall eat of it, you shall die." Why, we ask, did God not intend for man to know good and evil? In what way would such knowledge corrupt or diminish the human's natural being? To answer, we may imagine what such being was like before disobedience. What might life have been like before such knowledge? To speculate is of course a stretch because, born in sin, we have never known such a life.

Nevertheless, the Bible gives us hints, seeds of insight that resonate in the soul and stir longings difficult to articulate. Such a hint is found in Genesis 2:25: "The man and the woman were both naked and they were not ashamed." Picture the toddler playing in the sprinkler in the backyard. Unaware that adults are watching her, she laughs as she splashes and dances on the grass. Alive only in the moment, she knows nothing of whether the rent was paid or what will be for supper later that day.

Not only were Adam and Eve naked in the garden, they were unashamed. This description was a way of saying, "... the first couple was physically, emotionally, and spiritually one."[61] In this unity, any self-conscious judgment, guilt or fear were unknown.

God had provided everything, including each other. The loss of companionship would not be a problem. Boredom

---

[61] Paul House, *Theology of the Old Testament* (Downers Grove, Ill.: Intervarsity Press), 467.

would be unknown. The earth itself would be a field for discovery and self-expansion. In knowing God, the creatures knew they were loved. If anything were to happen that was "not good," Yahweh himself would make that judgment. To stay within the perfect life of Eden and remain within the boundaries of their created order, the humans must simply obey the ban from knowing good and evil. In knowing the generosity of the Creator, why would anyone in their right mind defy him?

The temptation to unboundedness

But now Eve is tempted. The serpent questions the prohibition, inviting doubt as to why God would keep knowledge from them. There is no necessity for her to give in. There is never a reason for sin. She simply saw that the fruit was good to eat and pleasing to look at. She imagined what it would be like to be like God himself and decided that that would be a better thing than what she was. In short, she used the gift of her freedom against the One who issued that freedom. Failing to intervene, Adam also succumbed.

There appear, in disobedience, to be four interlocking forces at work. The first of these is deception. The serpent deceives Eve, questions the good intent of God, denigrating his character. The serpent implies that God was afraid they would become too wise for him, that they would know too much (Genesis 3:5). Being impressed with the physical beauty of the tree and imagining how wonderful it would be to have unlimited wisdom, she ate. The second dynamic of sin is what we might call "solipsism"—a kind of hyper-individualism, an attitude of complete self -containment. Not only was Eve deceived, she acted alone, without consultation. She thought of herself alone and decided by herself alone. After disobedience, love of God and love for each other vanishes from the minds of Adam and Eve, replaced by self-concern.

Luther termed this core aspect of sin, *curvitas im se*, "a curving in on the self."

The third dynamic is simply pride. This is the wish to be great, to expand your sense of importance or power. Already made in the likeness and image of God, such a self-inflationary conceit wants to be even more like God—*just* like God. As the history of kings and princes shows, mankind has not been above vaunting himself to *be* God. Finally, we discern "lust," a detour away from God's purposes to the short-term goal of immediate gratification. The temptation is packaged with the promise of immediate appeal. "Take it now. Have it now," whispers the tempter.

Now the Lord has a problem. Having already created the perfect world, he now must decide how to respond to their failure to manage their freedom in ways that conform to their nature as belonging to himself. He can no longer trust them to remain within their created order. By defying their limits, they have introduced evil into the world.

God begins his plan of redemption

The Lord's intention was then as it is now: To take back that which was lost, to restore and repair that which was broken. He begins by attacking the problem of deception. When we are deceived and believe that which is false, a corresponding reality is that we lose that which is true. I recall taking LSD as a rebellious teenager. One night, my friend and I were so impressed with ourselves as we talked on and on about the secrets of the universe, we decided to grab a tape recorder so we could capture for all time our drug-induced profundities. As you might guess, we were quite disappointed the next day to play back our conversation—a hodge-podge of nonsense. A step toward redemption from a life of drugs was for me the awareness of the deception woven into that lifestyle.

To counter deception, God invites self-reflection. He begins with a simple question, "Where are you?" Indeed, the third chapter of Genesis records God asking three more questions before making any statement. He asks, "Who told you you were naked? Did you eat of the fruit? What have you done?" He does not respond with raw power as an angry father might immediately spank a child. He addresses the creatures with words. The intent, it would seem, is to correct the deception by stimulating thought, by creating awareness of wrong-doing. They must understand they have stepped outside their created order. They must recognize the disorder.

The Boundaries grow sharper

Knowing the humans cannot now be trusted, God must limit the damage. He curses the serpent and condemns him to crawl in humiliation. Eve will experience pain in childbirth and a conflicted relationship with her husband. Adam will have to fight with the land to survive. Is God angry? Disappointed? Surely, he is. Are these judgments the direct result of his rage? Do they reflect the motive of retaliation? I don't think so. A parent will certainly discipline a naughty child and may feel deep anger, but if the parent is wise, that anger is not what drives the response. Good discipline is directed by thoughtful consideration of the good of the child and motivated by the goals of restoration and redemption. This is axiomatic. We cannot assume less for the loving Lord of the universe.

We note that the decrees do indeed seem to have a redemptive purpose. This is so inasmuch as severe curtailment is precisely the effect of each curse. In refusing the original limit, the creatures revealed they could misuse their freedom. When someone cannot be trusted, his power must be curtailed. So, the loving thing to do is to limit the power of the man and the woman. To reduce the realm of possibility requires an increase in the degree of physical determinism as their freedom is diminished. Any pain involved in these curses also limits the pain they can inflict upon each other.

God addresses each person at the very nexus of his or her unique glory. The woman is the bearer of life—all of the future is bound up in her womb. At this very point of pride, God brings pain. Further, she shall not be able to elevate herself to independence, and her attachment to the man will be colored with conflict.[62] Adam, in his turn, receives a curse that challenges his pride and power of initiative. He can no longer speak his wishes or simply act on his intentions but now must worry about survival, must wrestle with the ground to provide food. At the very point of his glory as worker and cultivator and husband of the earth, the man is severely restricted and must suffer.

Clearly God's redemptive discipline is at work. Pain invites the awareness of something wrong—out of order. Such awareness invites repentance. Since the creatures did not listen to mere words, did not adhere to the spoken boundary—then the boundaries must be sharper. Physical limitation now enters along with verbal imperative. To continue to live and not die, the humans must conform to their nature as belonging to and submitting to the One who gave them existence. This is their proper and natural order. We might surmise that in the future, they will take the word of God more seriously and be less deceived. In the future, they will experience more sharply

---

[62] "Your Desire Will be for Your Husband and He Shall Rule Over You" (Genesis 3:16). For interpretations of the Hebrew for *desire* and *rule,* see Andreas J. Köstenberger and Margaret E. Köstenberger, *God's Design for Man and Woman: A Biblical Theological Survey* (Wheaton, Ill.: Crossway, 2014). They write, "The loving harmony that prevailed before the fall will be replaced by a pattern of struggle in which the woman will seek to exert control over her husband (interpreting "desire" as "desire for control," cf. Gen. 4:7), who will respond by asserting his authority. See also Raymond C. Ortlund, Jr., "Male-Female Equality and Male Headship: Genesis 1 – 3" in John Piper and Wayne Gruden (eds.) *Recovering Biblical Manhood and Womanhood: A Response to Evangelical Feminism* (Wheaton, Ill.: Crossway, 2006), 107-110.

their need for God and for each other, and be less likely to succumb to solipsistic decisions. Humbled, they will be less likely to be tempted to self-aggrandizement. Immediate gratification will be impossible so they will learn discipline.

The limit may be a hard wall. In the counseling office, we observe that those addicted to drink or drugs often "hit bottom" before becoming ready to turn their life around. When there is an abusive husband who is bent on blaming everyone else for his problems, we notice that only after a period of loneliness—because the wife has left or because of a restraining order—does he repent or show remorse. I recall a newspaper article about a man who searched for the cop who had arrested him several years before. When he found the officer, he embraced him with a bear hug for saving his life.

Sin entails the deception that one can be more than one is. A mistake of nature, sin diminishes self and other selves as well. Sin is characterized by the law of diminishing returns. Jesus put it succinctly: whoever sins becomes the slave of sin. The prideful person who basks in achievement, sooner or later experiences set-backs and the fiction of being above others gives way to reality. The individual who has little self-awareness, however, strives to keep the myth of specialness alive, uses primitive ego-defense mechanisms such as denial and projection and raw blaming to avoid adjusting his own image of himself. The sin of pride, as are other sins, is costly. It costs psychic energy to distort reality, to rationalize and explain away failures. It costs friendships and loss of love to blame others. Without some self-awareness, this kind of pattern goes on. One pictures a trapped animal as it bares its teeth to the world, not knowing why it is cornered or why it has so many enemies. Without reflection and awareness, repentance is unlikely. Without pain, such awareness is unlikely. Like a disease without symptoms, sin without pain would slowly steal a life away allowing a soul to wither and die.

In the curses God seems to be saying: Since you deceive yourself when I give you everything and only limit you by warning you not to experience evil, then your limitations must be, for your sake, made clearer. You can change and repent and find life and wholeness only as you repudiate the ontological mistake of attempting to be more than you were designed to be. But to do this requires an act of your own will. A necessary and central component of will is the perception of consequences. In the first world where there was no evil and no pain you misused your will and wanted to be greater than you were meant to be; in so doing, you deceived yourself and chose to know evil. You must know that with the evil of falsehood and deception there is suffering and death. So you will not be totally lost in self-deception, you must also know pain.[63]

Expelled from the perfect world, the humans now function in a world split apart, forever torn between good and bad. God, however, did not abandon his special creatures.

Salvation history

The rest of the Old Testament chronicles God's pursuit and protection. As a sign that sin is costly and in a foreshadowing of the system of animal sacrifice, God kills. Animals must die to fashion leather coverings—better protection than leaves (Gen. 3:21). He sets in place a system of offerings and sacrifice whereby the humans could acknowledge their dependent status and make atonement for their sin. When Cain misuses this system, God corrects him by not receiving the offering. When Cain responds with anger and resentment—possibly depression—God speaks to him as if to counsel him. God

---

[63] Many have turned away from faith because of the difficult questions arising from the basic problem of evil: If God is good and if he is all powerful, how do we explain suffering? Theologians and philosophers wrestle with answers called "theodicies." A sample of recent thinkers: C.S. Lewis, *The Problem of Pain,* 1940 and Peter Kreeft, *Making Sense Out of Suffering,* 1986.

begins, as he did with Cain's parents, with questions. "Why are you angry?" he asks. "And why has your countenance fallen?" (Gen. 4:6). Then God attempts to encourage Cain and to explain to him the way of well-being. "If you do well, will not your countenance be lifted up? And if you do not do well, then sin is crouching at your door; and its desire is for you, but you must master it" (Gen. 4:7).

God tells Cain how he can feel better. He explains the correlation between right, submissive behavior, and joy. Disobedience, on the other hand, gives sin increasing power over the soul. This wise counsel was not received. Cain murders his brother. Again, God confronts Cain with a question. This time one can hear the distress in the voice of God as he demands of the man, "What have you done? The voice of your brother's blood is crying to me from the ground!" (Gen. 4:10). Again, a curse follows. Cain, the farmer, will no longer be able to pull fruit from the ground, but is condemned to wander the earth. When Cain protests that the punishment is too great and that he will be hidden from God's face and that anyone could kill him, God acts to guarantee his life. Even with a murderer God is gracious.

The next chapters tell us of both the geographic spread of humankind and the growth of wickedness. The pattern of sin as refusal of boundaries again is illustrated in the folly of the Tower of Babel. The intention of the builders involved both a rejection of God's mandate to fill the earth and raw hubris:

> And they said, "Come, let us build for ourselves a city and a tower whose top will reach into heaven, and let us make ourselves a name; lest we be scattered abroad over the face of the whole earth" (Gen. 11:4).

The response of the Lord is noteworthy. It is reminiscent of the heavenly alarm expressed in Genesis 3 where God laments that indeed, "The man has become like one of us, knowing good and evil..." (v. 22). Concerned that the creatures eat from the tree of life and live forever, God drove them from the garden. After observing the tower, God again expresses alarm—as if the threat of raw, harnessed, and cooperative power is in fact *a very real one*.

> Behold, they are one people, and they all have the same language. And this is what they began to do, and now nothing which they purpose to do will be impossible to them. ... So the Lord scattered them from there over all the earth, and they stopped building the city (Gen. 11:6, 8).

In the following chapters, God chooses Abram (Abraham) to follow him to a land where he will develop a special people, a great nation to be blessed by God and through whom the entire world would be blessed. Abram's response is to obey. The stories of Abraham, Isaac, Jacob, and Joseph depict the beginnings of a people of faith, who would walk with the Lord, doubt him, wrestle with him, and are rescued by him. It was to these people that the covenant of the Law was given. What was the Law but a gracious expression of how the humans could thrive in the fallen world, now split between good and evil. The Law articulated and reaffirmed in the context of the destroyed world what the boundaries are for being human. To know the limits is to know possibility, freedom, and growth. The first commandments reaffirm the demand that God alone be God (cf. Exodus 20). God must be first, the object of obedience, the only object of worship. The natural order for humans as subordinate creatures is reestablished. Their power is a derived power. Their prerogatives are gifts. The demand for proper submission to God is articulated in the first four commandments of the Decalogue followed by the demand for proper treatment of others. As elaborated in the New Testament, the love for God always must find expression in the love for others.

Underneath the demand for obedience to the law is the call to trust. As the writer of Hebrews saw, Abraham himself was not able to be the Father of so many because of special abilities or even a particular commitment to obey the commandments. Rather, it was because of his faith. Faith that God is good and can be trusted. Repeatedly, the people of Israel lost sight of God's goodness, went their own way, got into trouble. Repeatedly, God responded—with patience, with mercy, with anger, with miracles and at times with threats. But God never turned his back. God never gave up his pursuit of his lost creatures. After sending kings, prophets, and priests, finally, he sends his son.

The Son of Man

God's relentless drive to redeem lost humans finds ultimate expression in Bethlehem. In the Messiah, we discover not only a savior, but we encounter the "second Adam" or as Karl Barth calls him, the "real man."[64] In Christ, we find a sinless lamb of God who himself became the ultimate sacrifice for sin. In the man Jesus, we also find an outline of what God originally intended in fashioning Adam and Eve. While our first parents disobeyed the order of protection and fell into disorder, we find in the man Jesus one who *obeys*. "My meat and my drink is to do the will of the father…" (John 4:34). This subordination works as it was designed to work in Eden, viz., to the enhancement and empowerment of the humans. Rather than being diminished by submission, Jesus is trusted. He is given ultimate authority. As a man, Jesus does not step

---

[64] *Church Dogmatics*, Vol. 3, "Doctrine of Creation, Part Two," G.W. Bromiley and T.F. Torrance, Eds. (London: T &T. Clark, 1960).

beyond his order, but in his obedience is entrusted with the right to judge the world and with life itself (John 5:27).

In the beginning, God warned that the misuse of the power to make choices would catapult the creatures from design to disorder and they would die. Failing to heed the word of God, they fell into pride and self-deception. Repudiating pride, Jesus comes to us as one "humble in heart" (Matthew 11:29). In contrast to the falsehood of sin, Jesus *lives* from the truth of God's word: "Man does not live by bread alone but by every word that comes out of the mouth of God" (Matthew 4:4).

In contrast to the self-absorption and individualism of sin, Jesus was, in Barth's phraseology, a "man for others."[65] Taking the role of a servant, Jesus repudiates this sin of self-centeredness. In addition, Jesus does not give in to the demand for immediate satisfaction. Even at the point of starvation, he resists the devil's offer of bread. Finally, although sinless, he identifies with sinful man and takes up the death that belongs to sinners. In the resurrection from that death, he offers once again life to all of us who have fallen into disorder.

---

[65] Ibid.

CHAPTER 3

Beyond Eden: A Divided World

*"Then the eyes of both of them were opened,
and they knew they were naked..." —Genesis 3:7*

"I can't do this. Can't do it anymore... I don't want to do it anymore." We sat in silence as she dabbed her eyes with the Kleenex. "Where do we go from here?" I thought to myself. "She has three children. Where does she go from here?"

Connie had been working with me for several months. She had originally called the office for help to deal with stress and depression. By the middle of her first session, it became obvious that the major source of her emotional pain was her husband's behavior. I understood that problems tend to be multifaceted and that there are generally two sides to any story. At first, I resisted the assumption that Sam was just a jerk. Perhaps he was just a person suffering from chemical dependency or an underlying personality disorder that motivated his violent and cheating behavior. Thinking that it indeed takes "two to tango," I assumed that Connie must have some degree of codependent or controlling tendencies that contributed to Sam's failure to be faithful or to hang on to a job or to face his cocaine addiction. However, after months of his refusal to get help or do much else beyond slapping Connie around and doing as he pleased, it became obvious that this was not so much a "system" problem as it was an issue of Sam's terrible behavior.

How is it that some people behave so badly? What is going on when a mother of a seven-year-old decides she has had enough and disappears? Or when a man in midlife announces to his family that he is moving out to live with his boyfriend? What are they looking for? What is any sinner looking for? Of course, each situation needs to be carefully understood and responded to with compassion. After all, as the book of James reminds us, "…we all stumble in many ways" (James 3:2).

Having ingested the fruit of disobedience, Adam and Eve must now live in a world infected with evil. No longer one with God or each other, they must live with disunion. In this chapter we look at some of the difficulties of navigating life and love under a canopy of division. Are there common denominators underlying human disorder?

An inverted order

Before disobedience, the humans lived and breathed in the presence of God. In paradise, "clothed in greater splendor than any earthly potentate,"[66] they radiated his glory as they walked and talked with God. With free access to the Tree of Life, they possessed immortality. Knowing they belonged to God, they knew they belonged to each other. Selfishness was unknown. But that was before the unthinkable. That was before sin. From glory to shame, from wholeness to division. What have we become? How could our first parents—how could *we*—be so stupid? Having fallen from the original design, we now must see ourselves under a psychology of brokenness. Bonhoeffer writes:

The fall of man in God's creation is both inconceivable and unalterably inexcusable, and therefore the

---

[66] Josiah B. Trenham, *Marriage and Virginity According* to St. John Chrysostom (Platina, Ca.: St. Herman of Alaska brotherhood, 2013), 91.

word "disobedience" does not exhaust the facts of the case. It is revolt, it is the creature's departure from the attitude which is the only possible attitude for him, it is the creatures becoming Creator. ... The Fall affects the whole of the created world which is henceforth plundered of its creatureliness as it crashes blindly into infinite space, like a meteor which has torn away from its nucleus.[67]

Created "like God" (Genesis 1:26) to live from his care and presence, man succumbed to the temptation to be "just like God." In defying the limit, he now "lives out of his own resources... Now he lives out of himself, now he creates his own life, he is his own creator."[68] He now misunderstands himself as he misunderstood the prohibition. This limit was not to take away his freedom, but to guarantee it. This limit was a gift not only to protect him from operating out of a false center as the judge of good and evil, but as a guide pointing him always back to his true and proper nature, which is freedom for God.

A bifurcated world

The simple refusal to partake of the tree of knowing good and evil insured the creatures' status and destiny—which was to enjoy God and one another forever. In innocence and unself-conscious freedom they could, in a way, "dance like no one is watching." To live without judgment, in union with God, self and all of creation. To eat of the Tree, however, would split their world into good and bad or in the Hebrew, *tov,* meaning that which is pleasurable and therefore good and *ra,* that which is painful and therefore bad.[69] Sin splits apart,

---

[67] *Creation and Fall,* 76.

[68] Ibid., 74.

[69] Ibid., 77.

bifurcates experience. In sin, the human creatures arrogated to themselves that which they were not designed to do: the judging of good and bad. All of life is now infected with this duality and every choice and every experience must now be evaluated, assessed as to its relative value as good or bad.

The experience of self is the area where the wreckage is most immediate. The fallen ones could no longer be at one with themselves. Having defied God's order, they now experience disorder deep within. This happens as soon as they eat the fruit. At once they become aware of themselves in a new and different way: as exposed. The hitherto seamless experience of their body as part of and belonging to themselves now becomes a split experience; they now know their naked bodies as alien, different in a way that is wrong somehow. They taste for the first time a split between subject and object. They become self-conscious in a negative way, aware of wrong, of inadequacy, of missing the mark. They feel shame. They become aware for the first time of vulnerability. They feel danger. They attempt to protect themselves with fig leaves. Later, when aware of God's presence, the shame intensifies and they hide.

The freedom just to be one's self is now corrupted. Psychic energy originally designed to be focused in the activities of creative loving and subduing the earth, is now diverted. Energy must now be expended to cover up and hide, to defend and justify. As the self is no longer experienced as a unity, the actions of choosing, willing, creating, loving and enjoying are now saddled with the specter of conflict. Part of the self must now separate from itself, watching and evaluating. Pure being and pure action have disappeared as a kind of cognitive dissonance infects every waking moment. An observing conscience now accusing or defending every thought and action. Chronic conflict replaces eternal innocence.

The knowing of good and bad no longer remains in the tree but now has come to reside inside the self, often in the form of a stream of negative self-talk. The self is now thrown back on itself, judging and comparing. In big and little ways:

The Harvard student: "All these smart people. I'm the only one who doesn't belong here."

The nurse: "Oh darn. What does that lady in 312 want now?! Ugh. Look at me, I'm supposed to care, but I don't. What's wrong with me?"

The driver: "That idiot deliberately cut in front of me."

The mom: "Her child speaks in complete sentences! Mine can hardly say, 'dada.'"

Comparison and judgment. "I'm not OK. You're not OK." The peaceful mind now echoes with noisy, negative internal dialogue. In the Genesis story, this internal split quickly grows to a division between persons.

The gift of sex: limit and potential

After the Fall, the two humans see each other through clouded eyes. Adam no longer jumps for joy at the sight of Eve, who appears happy to go her own way. Judging life from their own center, they have lost sight of the Creator's original design. As the limit not to know good and evil contained promise, so too, the creation of male and female to be one flesh entailed both boundary and possibility. Before sin, such a duality was not contradictory. After the Fall, possibility fights with boundary as male and female fight with each other. In sin, we forget that we are mere creatures and that our freedom is actualized only as we live within the natural order of creation. This order includes sexual order.

At the origin, only God discerns good and evil. He determines it is "not good" for the man to be alone. And God acts on man's behalf. But first he enables the man to come to realize something is missing. He brings other creatures to Adam and eventually, "no suitable helper was found" (Genesis 2:20). Anderson writes:

> In naming them, the man was searching for that encounter with his own being which would free him to experience himself as addressed and recognized by another, as a *Thou* for which he could become a corresponding *I*.[70]

God next fashions the perfect counterpart for Adam who joyfully recognizes, "This is bone of my bones and flesh of my flesh." Now the man is complete, free from a lonely autonomy, free from an existence for self, living out of himself alone. Free to be for another.

> The true source of the human experience of freedom to be for another and to know oneself is in the divine determination to exist as co-humanity; or, as the basic text in Genesis 1:26-27 tells us, to exist in the image of God, male and female. This existence for and with the other is the source of the openness of being which issues in speech, hearing, and love.[71]

The prohibition affirmed that God is the one to evaluate anything "not good" and to act toward his creatures for their good. The keeping of that limit guaranteed their joy and life potential. In the creation of Eve, another "limit" is introduced, alive, organic, and throbbing with potential.

---

[70] *On Being Human*, 81.
[71] Ibid.

In the creation of woman from Adam's rib, Adam's own being as creature is intensified in a way he never imagined. The limit within which he lives has now taken on bodily form… Man's limit has drawn near to him and has become all the more sharply defined. But it is just this bodily revelation of the limit in the love for the other person which gives Adam an ever deeper knowledge of the grace of the Creator.[72]

The man and woman together represent the nature of God as a loving union and together represent to each other both limit and potential. They are not designed to be self-existent. Before Eve, Adam had no counterpart to complete him. To be a self that images God as relational love, the human must have a counterpart who is also a counterforce.[73] To be a self, there must be a not-self—another being who stands in distinction ready to respond, to challenge, to bless, and to help. Imaging God, the human does not act without reference to another. But this "other" must correspond as a limit for it is only within limits that creatures must live. The limit is a grace. The limit enhances possibility, enabling fullness of life as it focuses the purposes of that life. The limit as a person with her own choices represents synergistic possibility. She is no empty Echo to proud Narcissus. As helper, she is her own person as she guides Adam to the actualization of his manhood, which requires guiding and caring for her in her feminine calling. In this fellowship they enact together their destiny in the life of God.

To transgress the limit is to misuse the gift of freedom for God and for the other. To transgress the limit is to invert the created order and live as self alone, an unnatural self. One

---

[72] *Creation and Fall*, 74.

[73] As the movie, *2050x* warns us, mindless, submissive "sexbots," which are becoming more life-like and popular every year, lead only to dehumanizing dead ends.

cannot do so without also being against the other. "The violation of the tree of knowledge has to be at the same time a violation of the other person."[74]

Alienation between the Sexes

Prior to the Fall, that which is different only brought delight. Now, where others dwell, so dwells danger. Now ever watchful, the monitoring of other selves becomes a terrible necessity. Now knowing each other as sinners, they quite logically realize they cannot trust the other. Fear now contaminates love. In placing blame, they assert that the good lies within and the bad belongs to another. In their shame and fear they not only hide from God but from each other as well. According to Karl Barth, they became alienated at the very point of their differentiation, their femininity and masculinity.[75] In this separation, we find an inevitable loss of wholeness for it was within their union that they were truly human. It was together that they reflected God's image and as they blessed and loved the other, they were most truly themselves, most truly alive and free. Before sin, Adam and Eve could walk with God and with each other in unself-conscious harmony. Different, yet functioning as one. Before sin, they did not fear the different nature and function of their Creator but understood that God, as an essentially different being, was the source of their own being. So, too, before sin, Adam was excited about Eve. He was drawn to her naked embodied self as he saw in her a reflection of himself ("bone of my bones") as well as one who offered, in her essential difference, a completion of himself. I'm sure they soon discovered that their different genitals fit perfectly, bringing together the joy of attraction and the ecstasy of physical pleasure. Knowing no split between self and body, the

---

[74] *Creation and Fall*, 74.
[75] Karl Barth, *Church Dogmatics, vol. III*, 292.

different gendered selves would "fit" as well. They would be "one flesh." But in the futile attempt to advance the self away from the ultimate Other, the unique thing about Adam and Eve, their sexuality, is now a thing to cover and to protect. In contrast to the design of their sexual organs as enticement to ecstatic union, these same body parts now represent disunion and must be hidden.

A terrible dilemma ensues. *I want you; I don't trust you. I need you but you might hurt me.* Nevertheless, each partner continues to hold the potential to bless and complement the other. And for all of us on this side of Eden, this remains the hope. As a spouse feels loved and affirmed, he or she grows in spontaneity and self-expansion. The more one feels known and accepted, intimacy feels less risky and more risks are taken. When believing his wife won't scorn him, a husband might risk acting silly or telling a corny joke. Happy and emotionally stable couples thrive together in a sea of what John Gottman calls "positive sentiment."[76] Such couples respond to each other with fondness, affection, and understanding. They tend to agree with each other and see each other's point of view.

On the other hand, each spouse invariably carries the power to criticize as well. After the fall, as Bonhoeffer saw, now living between good and evil, every good holds in its underbelly a flavor and potentiality of evil. The potential to promote self-doubt, defensiveness, and disharmony is never far away. Intimacy, after the fall, always seems to carry with it a yes and a no. The satisfaction that only a soulmate can offer is like trying to dance on a floor that shakes and moves. Love and fear. Satisfaction and frustration. The potential for pain is never far away. For many, intimate relationships are chronically fraught with conflict. Such bifurcation of experience woven within this most primal level of existence cries out for relief.

---

[76] *The Relationship Cure: A five-step Program for Recovering Relationships* (New York: Random House, 2002).

In summary, the fundamental problem according to the Genesis narrative, is that humans were designed to "be with." God designed them to do and to dream, to laugh and to love in intimacy with himself and with others. They were to flow with life, experiencing the safety and the permission to "just be." There was no disjunction between being themselves and being with God. The single prohibition protected their innocence, guarding the relationship from which that innocence and freedom arose, binding the self to the Source of selves. To defy that protective limit constituted an unnatural act, an action outside of human nature and therefore incompatible with human life which could only flow from the origin of that life. No longer experiencing themselves alive in union, the creatures turn inward. No longer "being with" they now experience life as "being alone." Or *being against.*

Happiness is fleeting. We miss the bliss of Eden. An inchoate dis-ease lingers as judgment has replaced intimacy. The longing for communion is shadowed by apprehension. We are fearful and restless. Relief might come in many forms. Maybe the solution is another person, a different person. The longing for an ideal love—one who could complete us, as if to make us whole. Some people live their lives in search for an ideal romantic partner. On some level of consciousness, they retain the belief that the right match will bring lasting relief from the anxiety of division.

The midweek lovemaking was over in a flash. Max, anyway, seemed to have a good time. Now as he snored away, Marcy found herself staring at the ceiling. Restless, she climbed out of bed and went to the next room where she turned on the computer. Before long, she found herself absorbed in story after romantic story in the various entertainment websites. "Why couldn't Max be more attentive? All he thinks about is himself." Her mind wandered back to her high school sweetheart. She recalled the experience of sexual excitement, the exhilarating feeling of being desired. He wasn't such a bad guy. They were just too young. With an inno-cent curiosity, she typed his name in the search engine.

Most people come to realize that inasmuch as they them-selves are sinners, so too, will a potential mate possess that affliction. Individuals who get this sooner are more likely to negotiate realistic compromises and therefore work toward relatively satisfying unions. Oddly enough, in recent decades, the search for an ideal love has diminished. Some observers believe the hope for lasting love has all but disappeared from among our young.[77] For many, sex without personal compli-cation has taken its place. Sex for its own sake. Disillusioned with romance, lust has replaced love.

As a corollary to this emphasis on sensuality over person-ality, guilt has gone out of fashion. As Marcy cruises the Internet, she is shocked to discover how this is so. She finds herself easily stumbling onto websites in which every sort of "hooking up" and sexual experience is promoted. She wonders, "Is there no shame? What is to become of our society?" Quietly, she shuts off the computer and returns to bed.

Unfortunately, for many, neither the mind nor the computer gets turned off. The search for that missing some-thing or someone goes on unabated. We don't know that we miss God—that we have fallen out of sync with our Maker. So we keep searching. We feel fear and want serenity. We do know we feel alone and want connection. We feel power-less and want power. But expelled from the Garden and tone deaf to the promise of reconciliation with the Gardener, we grasp for what is at hand. Having lost the spiritual, we find ourselves lost in the sensual.

---

[77] For example, Nancy Pearcy, *Love Thy Body: Answering the Hard Questions about Life and Sexuality* (Grand Rapids: Baker Books, 2018).

CHAPTER 4

Descent into the Sensual

Whatever my eyes desired I did not keep from them I did not withhold my heart from any pleasure. —Ecclesiastes 2:10

They had just come up from Las Vegas. As the two sisters found their seats, I was struck by the concern etched across the elder one's face, the one who had made the appointment. She began the session by announcing that she had brought her twenty-something sister back from "a horrible" situation. As I considered the pretty woman in old jeans, I wondered if she had been beaten or raped. Not exactly, as it turned out. What her sister had rescued her from was her position as a "cam girl," one who strips on the internet for money. The younger woman did not seem so concerned as her sister, although she might have been numbing her feelings. When it dawned on me what precisely she had been doing, I was the one who needed to manage his emotions. As I arranged my face to exhibit a bored curiosity, my head was screaming: "What is wrong with you that you would show your private parts to the whole world!" She told me her brother got her into it and the money was good. As if, "big deal." They did not reschedule, so I never got the whole story. That was fifteen years ago. Since then, "camming" has become big business and the girls who take their clothes off in chat rooms number in the thousands.

After the fall from God's order, the early humans slipped into disorder. Designed for harmony, they now know conflict. Designed to be together, they know themselves alone. Instead of protecting the woman, the man exploits her. And the man who watches? The one who pretends? When he shuts his computer off, the chat girl is gone, and only silence follows him to bed.

The need for transformative experience

Defying God's order, the humans ingested the fruit of contradiction. Pure being dissolved into disturbed consciousness, every thought and action now infected with *tov* and *ra*. Having lost innocence, every choice is now subject to judgment. Is it good or bad? Am I good or bad? Having turned from God, they find themselves distant from his presence, his provision, and his protection. They have lost much and the burden is heavy. Not only must they grapple with judgment and guilt, they must work to put food on the table, and worry about enemies. Most of all, they must live under a shadow of death.

Such is the postlapsarian condition of the world into which we are born. Transient satisfactions are swallowed up by difficulties. We long for palliation, for freedom from conflict and fear. We long to feel good, to forget. As detailed in Chapter Six, transformative processes from states of hunger, cold, or other stressors are an integral aspect of everyday experience and foundational for healthy personality development. As adults, we continue to search out various methods to relieve us from anxiety or depression. Of course, God has not left us without good things to enjoy and pursue. As Kreeft reminds us, signs of heaven everywhere haunt the earth.[78] Yet, these joys are laced with impermanence. "Every good and perfect gift" is to be a sign, not an end. The pleasures of love or sex are to be understood as referential, penultimate values. Nevertheless, as an infant loves the breast and not the mother, we can become attached to pleasurable things as primary objects of hope and transformation from anxiety.

---

[78] *Heaven: The Heart's Deepest Longing* (San Francisco: Ignatius Press, 1980).

Sex as a tranquilizer

In his Pulitzer Prize winning book, *The Denial of Death,* Ernest Becker enumerates uneasy attempts to resolve the terrible dualism of spirit and flesh, of life bound to a body. A body bound to die. We are soul longing for life; yet we are body—not unlike our pet, equally defenseless against microbes or bullets. Or time. To face the contradiction head on is terrifying. So we develop what Soren Kierkegaard called "character armor." Strategies to anesthetize against dread. We tranquilize ourselves with great or trivial pursuits. Or with pleasure. We do this with romance. We do this with sex. In the Twenty-first Century, the noisy and ubiquitous assertion that sex is the key to satisfaction is heard by big and little ears everywhere. While some people retain the myth that romantic love brings happiness, others pursue orgasm for its own sake.

Following the writings of psychoanalyst Otto Rank, Becker argues that the deification of romantic love and sex reflects a loss of faith. He writes:

> Sexuality, which Freud thought was at the heart of the Oedipus complex, is now understood for what it really is: another twisting and turning, a groping for the meaning of one's life. If you don't have a God in heaven, an invisible dimension that justifies the visible one, then you take what is near at hand and work out your problems on that.[79]

One's genitals are not only close at hand, so to speak, they also carry the potential for transformation from dysphoric states to ones of pleasure. They bring an immediacy of experience—a "nowness" to absorb guilt and anxiety—that creaturely dread that haunts the psyche. This is a knowing just

---

[79] Ernest Becker, *The Denial of Death* (New York: The Free Press, 1975), 162.

below the surface that we were designed for living but the end of our living is dying. Sensuality focuses the mind, strengthens for a time the power of repression.

> We are witness to the new cult of sensuality that seems to be repeating the sexual naturalism of the ancient Roman world. It is a living for the day alone, with a defiance of tomorrow; an immersion in the body and its immediate experiences and sensations, in the intensity of touch, swelling flesh, taste and smell. Its aim is to deny one's lack of control over events, his powerlessness, his vagueness as a person in a mechanical world spinning into decay and death.[80]

Sensuality invites us to forget that without a creator, we creatures are doomed. A secularized education joins the fiction and celebrates sex while denying its purpose. Students at major universities sponsor an annual "sex week." Northwestern's 2020 version highlights the possibility of manifesting your desires by visualizing them at the point of orgasm. The training, "Masturbation for Manifestation," is apparently a form of sex magic along the lines of the book, *The Secret*. To round out the schedule, the performer, "Cunty MeMe," who uses the pronouns "they" and "them" offers a workshop to "explore sex outside of the five senses and how individuals can develop intimacy with themselves."[81] Yale, after banning sex week for several years, has brought it back with a vengeance. Nathan Harden writes that the school has "…positioned itself as a leader in a radical new form of sex

---

[80] Ibid., 84.

[81] Brittainy Slaughter, "Northwestern hosts 'Masturbation for Manifestation' virtual event as part of online sex week" *The College Fix*, May 12, 2020. https://www.thecollegefix.com/northwestern-hosts-masturbation-for-manifestation-virtual-event-as-part-of-online-sex-week/

education, complete with sex toy pageants, porn star lectures, sadomasochism seminars, and fellatio demonstrations."[82]

As God has disappeared from common discourse in the academy, young people must cast about for meaning, for ways to negotiate the contradiction that is their lives. Without revelation, such a search stumbles along without boundaries. Students assume traditional taboos against promiscuous or anonymous sex are passé. Or antithetical to freedom. Unfortunately, such a stance leaves them essentially stranded, without a hope that would transform the raw, existential anxiety of a soul caught between eternity and a dying body.

As one denies God, the longing for transcendence hardly disappears. Sexuality awakens passion. Intensity merges with feelings of significance. But can *eros* really be an effective tool to overcome the burden of living between *tov* and *ra*? Following Rank, Becker argues that the transformation away from the creaturely fear of death through the intense physicality or merger with another body inevitably fails to absolve individuals of guilt or relieve existential anxiety. An impossible contradiction arises. "Sex is of the body, and the body is of death."[83]

The body telegraphs our limitations. Its daily aches and pains remind us of vulnerability and how fragile life is. To live in a body is to be bound to a body—not unlike our dog and cat. Animals procreate. They have sex. They bear young and die. We, too, male and female, have sex and procreate. We, too, grow old and die. This is not right! Were we not born to live? We are not animals! "He has set eternity in their hearts..." (Ecclesiastes 3:11).

---

[82] "When Sex Isn't Sexy: My Bizarre Education at Yale University," *The Daily Beast*, July 13, 2017.
[83] Becker, 162.

Taboos of protection

Traditional societies have always had ways to soften the contradiction and to keep us from the worship of sensual experience as a pathway to wholeness. As if to remind us that we are not mere fornicating animals,

> ... sexual taboos have been at the heart of human society since the very beginning. They affirm the triumph of human personality over animal sameness. With the complex codes of sexual self-denial man was able to impose the cultural map for personal immortality over the animal body. He brought sexual taboos into being because he needed to triumph over the body, and he sacrificed the pleasures of the body to the highest pleasure of all: self perpetuation as a spiritual being through all eternity.[84]

Indeed, societies that survive for any length of time invariably embrace sexual taboos and punish deviance. As we see from the book of Leviticus, however, defiance against sexual self-control is as ancient as history itself. The Israelites thus were enjoined to engage in none of the practices of their neighbors in Egypt and in Canaan. Chapter 18 catalogs a host of sexual perversions including child sacrifice, adultery, prostitution, homosexuality, incest, and bestiality. Such activities represent false attempts at transcendence as if emergence in sensuality can offer relief from the anxiety of existence. Such activities deny the Creator as the only source of wholeness while repudiating the original aim of the sexual act in consummating the union of two people designed to love and complement each other.

---

[84] Ibid., 163.

Increasingly, taboos themselves have become taboo. A deadly synergism between a secularism that replaces sex for God and crumbling traditional restraints cannot help but beget extreme forms of sexuality. Hunger driving the hunt. For some, the search for satisfaction leads to truly disturbing scenarios. Pedophilia, for example, despite the specter of prison, continues unabated. One in three-to-four girls, and one in five-to-seven boys are sexually abused before they turn eighteen. These statistics are well known among industry professionals, who are often quick to add, "and this is a notoriously underreported crime."[85] Incest is a common subset of pornography. Bestiality or zoophilia is an even more grotesque defilement. Many websites testify to a kind of growing participation and acceptance of such perversions. Sex as an answer to life's conundrums will always leave us frustrated and disappointed. And prone to stretch the limits.

"Perversions:" A human problem?

Becker suggests that sexual deviance, unlike other deviations from tradition, touches core issues in the human condition. Deep needs rumbling in the human soul. Could he be correct in relating a rise of sexual preoccupation and sensuality to a loss of faith? And love. Already in 1987, Allan Bloom had noticed that college kids had stopped holding hands.[86] And rarely spoke of love. Sexual interest was already migrating from the assumption of relationship to that of individualistic motives. As these trends have continued, we find a burgeoning of extreme forms of sexual self-expression.

---

[85] https://www.theatlantic.com/national/archive/2013/01/america-has-an-incest-problem/272459/
[86] *The Closing of the American Mind: How Higher Education Has Failed Democracy and Impoverished the Souls of Today's Students,* (New York: Simon & Schuster Paperbacks, 2012).

Watching YouTube videos of Gay Pride parades in New York and San Francisco, I am struck by the energy and intensity of both the participants and the onlookers. One sign reads, "Loud and Proud Since 1969!" The reference is to the Stonewall riots when the homosexual community rose up against repeated police raids on gay bars. Many marchers wave large rainbow flags. These stand for unity, equality, and pride. On a slow-moving float, several muscular men in colorful G strings thrust their pelvises as they dance and gyrate to upbeat music.

I wonder about why these men exaggerate their genitalia, or why the drag queens flaunt their "femininity" in such colorful but garish ways. How did sexuality become so central in their lives—a loud and constant assertion that "this is who we are"? One can appreciate the angry energy in 1969 to battle oppression and discriminatory laws. Yet, today, same-sex marriage is legal and the LGBTQ community has gained wide public acceptance. Nevertheless, the intensity remains. The demand to be recognized lingers long after recognition. The self-sustaining energy around homosexual and transgender issues seems as well to parallel the unremitting agitation of feminists long after achieving parity with men in the workplace. What is this restlessness that remains? Of course, any group may develop a self-sustaining bias and energy. Those who join a cooking club or motorcycle club, as they bond together, certainly enjoy meeting and inevitably, they reinforce each other's likes and prejudices. But they don't find their *identity* in these behaviors.

Considering original design, preoccupation with sex does make some sense. Sexuality promises loving communion. The sex organs are the vehicle for intimacy; they represent the continuation of life itself, as well as offer a pathway to physical ecstasy. In this sense, sex pulls the soul and body together. Sex hints of transcendence, represents the possibility of overcoming dualism, the contradiction between mind and body. But can it?

As Becker saw, "…the body is a bind. It overshadows our freedom."[87] But, the sexual rebels cry, *we will not be bound!* So, pushing the limits, we push the body, defy it even as we worship it. "Don't cast me in your old rules" say the dancing men in pink tutus. When the seventeen-year-old declares that she is non-binary, she gives the finger to fixed forms. In a secular society, she will find her own way, molding her body to her will, repudiating the contradiction that is her life.

The extremes of sexuality draw our attention. Indeed, the search for sexual transformation finds its culmination around the edges of sexual expression. Here, the fundamental issues become clear and they are not sexual. Following Rank and psychoanalyst, Medard Boss, Becker argues that the sexual perversions are not marginal issues in human discourse. In fact, they reflect

> the core problem of human action. They reveal what is at stake in that action better than any other behavior because they narrow it down to essentials. In this sense the perversions are truly the sub atomic theory of the human sciences, the nucleus where the basic particles and energies are concentrated.[88]

In other words, "more normal" sexual problems may reflect no deeper issue than a toothache, fixable at the clinic. The treatment of erectile dysfunction, for example, may require medication or involve simple behavioral strategies. The extremes of sexual behavior, on the other hand, go to the heart of the human condition:

---

[87] Becker, 164.
[88] Ibid., 222.

The self finds itself in a strange body casing and cannot understand this dualism. Man is aghast at the arbitrary nature of genitality, the accidentality of his separate sexual emergence. He can't accept the impermanence of the body casing or its incompleteness—now male, now female. The body makes no sense to us in its physical thingness, which ties us to a particular kind of fate, a one-sided sexual role.[89]

The extremes of sexual behavior uncover realities that most people have been able to repress. In other words, deviant sexuality represents desperate attempts to manage this knowledge. Pascal is quoted as saying, "Men are so necessarily mad, that not to be mad would amount to another form of madness." The sexual deviant has failed in this normal "madness," is overwhelmed by dread, comes face to face with his existential contradiction. The "pervert" rips away the veil of repression; the traditions that provide others with security, meaning, and direction are impossible. "Your normal life doesn't work for me! I don't fit your culture or your nice little rules. My body doesn't fit." So the sexual rebel will not bow to some myth of normalcy. He or she must defy taboos with their demand for conformity. And their implied threat of exposure. In defiance of the body, he beats the body. Or "beats off" three times a day. In a race against decay, he wrests from it what meaning he can. The middle-aged nymph, proud to be a MILF, exposes herself on the internet, thinking her sexuality is "empowering." In the moment of a late-night hookup, she does not know she is lost and lonely. Paradoxically, those drawn to abnormal sexuality in some ways come closer to the truth. They fail, of course. All *causa sui* attempts at transcendence fail. But in tragedy, they expose the lie that sexual solutions resolve the bifurcation brought by sin. They are correct: life

---

[89] Ibid., 224.

should be more than a happy heterosexuality—a white picket fence, two cars in the garage, and two kids in the yard.

Absent the call of faith, a deeper disturbance and despair lurks behind the compulsions, obsessions, and magic rituals woven into the lives of sexual outsiders. Often, those drawn to abnormal sexuality come with disturbed childhood histories. Some have been molested or otherwise neglected or abused. After thirty years of counseling with sexually confused individuals, a friend puts it this way: "They do not know what love is. The docking station to receive love never got formed. All addictions have this in common: artificial intimacy demands massive amounts of stimulation." Desperate for love and the safety of belonging, the dread of life in a body that decays and dies is not so easily dismissed. As Becker puts it, "…the species' role becomes a frightening chore, a possibly annihilating experience. If the body is so vulnerable, then one fears dying by participating fully in its acts."[90]

All forms of intimacy carry a certain risk. Individuals with little emotional or spiritual capital, however, have more to lose. While others enact convenient narratives of normalcy and mental health, the sexual deviant knows better. Feels acutely the wrongness of his animal body. He may protest the body "by abandoning his sexual role entirely."[91] The arbitrariness of being found in one sex and not the other, the determinism and boundedness of it, is too real, too much.

Nevertheless, there is no escape. The self is hopelessly ensconced within that casing, always near with its groaning and needing and desiring. Satisfaction eludes the sexual deviant who becomes like the obsessive-compulsive woman who spends hours arranging her cupboard "just so." In this ritualized activity, she shields herself from the chaos of the larger world and comforts herself with the feeling of control.

---

[90] Ibid., 230.
[91] Ibid., 232.

So, too, the male fetishist constricts his sexual world. A real woman as a real person is a terrible prospect. But a shoe or panties—these are more manageable.

Ritual operations numb existential dread and offer pathways on the road to transcendence. The psychoanalysts of the last century (who were as yet free to distinguish normal from abnormal) observed the religious quality of drama queens and fetish rituals. "The fetish object represents the magical means for transforming animality into something transcendent and thereby assuring a liberation of the personality from the standardized, bland and earthbound flesh."[92]

I recently watched a YouTube video depicting the numerous, precise steps a young man took as he transformed his face into that of a beautiful woman. The attention to detail was impressive. Such careful rituals take on a religious quality as "…ways of overcoming anxiety, the terror of the body, in a reassuring, magical way."[93] For a while, this boy has assuaged nagging self-doubt. He has exercised control. He is empowered. "See? I defy the arbitrary determination that I should be this and not that! I shall not be bound!"

The tragedy of such defiance is only known later. When the breasts are gone and the twenty-three-year-old condemns and sues the doctors who affirmed her wish as a sixteen-year-old to begin puberty blockers.[94] Or when the polyamorous woman discovers her favorite guy has not only left her for another, but left her with gonorrhea. In short, sex as an end in itself is a dead-end. In the final analysis, any answer to the questions of human existence that involves a preoccupation with our physical existence, denies the fact that we are spiritual beings. As belonging to God, we were created to live as his creatures under his laws. We defy that reality to our own peril.

---

[92] Ibid., 235-236.

[93] Ibid., 236.

[94] NHS gender clinic 'should have challenged me more' over transition https://www.bbc.com/news/health-51676020 accessed July 10.2020.

Boundaries and freedom

After the fall into sin, the need for limits and boundaries has continued to exist as the *sine qua non* for any community to do well. Dr. James Dobson told the story about a one-room schoolhouse set in the middle of a large field located in the countryside. During recess, the children would play outside but they stayed clustered closely around the building. At some point, it was decided to build a fence around the property. The contrast amazed the teacher who observed that the children now spilled out all throughout the entire yard. Freedom always requires a fence. Nature's laws, what C.S. Lewis, borrowing from the Chinese, called the *tao*, provide boundaries to guide our development. As we discovered in the last chapters, boundaries both limit possibility and invite possibility.

Paul warned in Romans 1 that as we deny the Creator, we ultimately degrade the creature. As we defy natural order in pursuit of limitless freedom, we lose freedom. As we defy natural order, we diminish the possibilities of our own nature. This nature is relational, communal. Thus, to grow and thrive as an individual, we must not remain alone, functioning as if we are the center of the universe. It is only in concert with others that we find ourselves, that we find meaning and purpose in life.

In contrast, an individualistic mentality denies the other as significant to the self. Such a denial represents an inversion of the Creator's definition of a person as inherently relational. Reflecting God's nature, the self can only find self-actualization and freedom in one kind of possibility. This is a possibility that includes the other who may in fact represent a solid limit to our freedom. More will be said on this in Chapter Seven. For now, let us posit that real freedom takes us beyond the prison of the self, beyond endless rumination about one's needs and feelings. Real freedom draws us away from unending sensual searching and self-feeding.

Confrontation: kindness and truth

Recalling the story of King David and Bathsheba, one wonders if David had developed a sexual addiction (2 Samuel 11). At the pinnacle of his power, he had been taking it easy avoiding the leadership of his army, when from his roof, he spied the beautiful wife of Uriah bathing. Led by lust, he summoned her and had sex with her. After she became pregnant, he tried to conceal his paternity. He brought her soldier husband back home so he would lie with her. Out of respect for his comrades still on the field, Uriah refused. In response, David instructed his general to put Uriah in front of the battle, effectively ensuring his death. Understanding the situation, the prophet Nathan was not pleased. Directed by God, Nathan told David a story about a wealthy man with many sheep and cattle who stole the only little ewe lamb of his poor neighbor. David was furious and demanded the man be executed. At that moment, the prophet said, "You are the man" (12:7).

When confronted with the truth of our sin, two possibilities arise. To live in cognitive dissonance is stressful. Therefore, one response is to deny the data. To turn away from acknowledging our condition. This action may involve justification and the projection of responsibility onto others. The other possibility echoes David's own response: "I have sinned against the Lord." Psalms 32 and 51 each record his heartfelt confession, repentance, and belief in God's forgiveness and cleansing. Acknowledging our sin, we are invited to believe in the perfect one who himself takes that sin.

Christ did not see a contradiction between love and telling the truth. In love, Jesus had ways of stopping people in their tracks—inviting them to acknowledge their pain and their missteps. In the ancient Middle East, the sexual double standard was profound and a woman's sexual behavior was understood to directly reflect the honor of the family. Perhaps that is why the New Testament offers three key stories illustrating

Jesus' approach to women who were seen to be sexual misfits. New Testament and Near East scholar Kenneth E. Bailey notes that "evil cannot be redeemed until it is exposed."[95] Jesus shrouds such exposure in grace and surprise. And "costly love." In each case, Jesus puts himself at risk or some disadvantage. We find as well, in each confrontation, the underlying theme of atonement—that traditionalists and rebels both stand in need of saving.

Jesus and the transformational encounter

In the story of the woman at the well (John 4), we discern both an iconoclastic confrontation of hurtful traditions as well as a gentle and deep understanding of human motivation. It was around noon and the disciples had gone shopping. A Samaritan woman comes alone to draw water. The fact that she was alone at the well when other women came early in the morning tells us that she had been shunned. Bailey writes, "Only a 'bad woman' would be so blatant. She is either a social outcast or knows that travelers can be found at the well at noon and wants to contact them."[96] Jesus blows past several customs. He asks the woman for a drink. Bailey sees this request as both strategic and exemplary of the self-emptying of Jesus. Middle Eastern wells do not come with buckets. Jesus could have requested the disciples to leave the bucket, but he had a plan.

> By deliberately sitting on the well without a bucket, Jesus placed himself strategically to be in need of whomever appeared with the necessary equipment. The woman approached. On seeing her, Jesus was expected to courteously withdraw to a distance of

---

[95] *Jesus Through Middle Eastern Eyes: Cultural Studies in the Gospels* (Downers Grove, Il.: IVP Academic, 2008), 226.
[96] Ibid., 202.

at least 20 feet, indicating that it was both safe and culturally appropriate for her to approach the well. Only then could she move to the well, unroll her small leather bucket, lower it into the water, fill her jar and be on her way. Jesus did not move as she approached. She decided to draw near anyway. Then comes the surprise.[97]

Jesus asks for a drink. The immediate result is typical: she is thrown off balance. "You are a Jew and I am a Samaritan. How can you ask me for a drink?" Bailey discerns four surprises in this request.

1. He speaks with a woman, a violation of a social boundary that is all the more notable in an isolated area. Even today, strange men do not make eye contact with a woman in public.
2. Jesus ignored the centuries-long hostility between Jews and Samaritans.
3. Jesus totally humbles himself. He is at her mercy. He is thirsty and has no means to get a drink. (We note that Jesus required his disciples to echo such humility when sending them on their first missions trip. "Take nothing for your journey..." Mark 6:8-9.)
4. Jesus affirms her self-worth. "In this story the woman was no doubt amazed that a male Jew was talking to her, a female Samaritan. The idea that he really wanted to drink out of her (defiled) leather bucket was a second shock."[98]

How is it he asks her for a drink? He does so because he understands exactly who she is and exactly what she needs.

---

97 Ibid.
98 Ibid., 205.

"If you knew the gift of God and who it is who asks you for drink, you would have asked him and he would have given you living water." Jesus does not shame or judge her but he does *see* her: "You have had five husbands and the man you have now is not your husband." Squirming, she quickly changes the subject. In the theological conversation that follows, her awareness deepens, both of her underlying need for "living water" and with whom she is speaking. Clearly blown away, she drops her water jug and races to tell the villagers of the encounter. "Come see a man who told me everything I ever did! Could this man be the Messiah?"

The man who heals division

Sin, as we saw, brings a deep bifurcation of experience. Shame or honor. Law or license. Punishment or mercy. Ultimately, life or death. In John (7:37-8:11), we witness an event that brings together these dualities in dramatic fashion. What places these elements before us in a very public way is sexual behavior. It is one thing to be accused of adultery, but can you imagine being "caught in the very act"?

During the Festival of Tabernacles, Jesus had made it increasingly clear that he was the Messiah. This proclamation divided the people and seriously threatened the authority of the Pharisees. They tried to arrest him but were thwarted because of his popularity. So, overnight, they set a trap. "If they could humiliate Jesus in public by posing a question of interpretation of the law that Jesus could not answer without destroying himself, his popularity would fade and their problem with him would be solved."[99]

Waiting until Jesus had drawn a crowd, these religious leaders, presumably having arrested her the night before, brought the humiliated and terrified woman and "made her

---

[99] Ibid., 231–232.

stand in the center" (8:3).[100] Knowing the Roman soldiers were listening, they quoted the Mosaic law requiring stoning for such an offense. A perfect set up! If Jesus argues for patience or explains that the Roman occupation necessitates adjustments to such enforcement, his opponents could accuse him of discounting the law of God and of cowardice. On the other hand, if he were to say, "Stone her," he would not only lose the crowd's sympathy but would be arrested on the spot for it was against Roman law for Jews to execute people.

At first, Jesus ignores their question. He bends down and writes in the dust as they pester him for an answer. The tension builds. Finally, he stands up and announces that the one without sin ought to throw the first stone. They are stunned into silence. As they walk away, Jesus again writes on the ground. When alone with the woman, he asks her if there is anyone to accuse her. After her acknowledgment that there was no one left to condemn her, Jesus replies that he too does not condemn her and to go and sin no more.

In the story, we find a dramatic foreshadowing of the atonement itself, a confrontation between sin and righteousness in which Jesus himself resolves the contradiction. Both the lawbreaker and lawkeeper are guilty. He is the only one who is just. And justifier. He is the one who stands in front of both sinners, the unrighteous and the self-righteous.

We see that this action of rescue is costly. Despite knowing the temple guards the day before had tried to arrest him, Jesus returns the next morning and submits himself to the rage and cunning of the legalist leaders. He thus offers himself in costly love.

A few minutes earlier the terrified woman had expected brutal violence and a painful death. Suddenly the

---

[100] If they really cared about the law, they would have included the man as instructed in Leviticus 20.

Pharisees are angry at Jesus rather than at her. At great cost he has shifted their hostility from her to himself, and he doesn't even know her name! The famous Servant Song of Isaiah affirms, "with his stripes we are healed" (Is. 53:5 KJV). She knows that Jesus' opponents will be back with a bigger stick and that Jesus is in process of getting hurt because of what he is doing for her. She is the recipient of a *costly demonstration* of unexpected love that saves her life.[101]

Bailey notes that Jesus' compassion extends to the scribes and Pharisees. He is aware that he has humiliated them but does not rub it in. In silence, he once again bends to the ground, not watching as they withdraw. The theological import is profound. Beyond his courage and compassion, Jesus walks a "razor's edge between trivializing the woman's sin and condemning her as a person." In doing so, he "upholds the sexual ethics of the biblical tradition but removes its penalty."[102] In effect, he says that both sides are wrong. Yes, adultery is sin. But to act as if tradition and law matter more than people is also sin.

The religious leader and the sex worker (Luke 7:36 – 50)

In the story of the Pharisee and the prostitute, we again find a clash between law and license, traditional sexual mores and sexual immorality. The scuttlebutt on Jesus had been that he was hanging out with drunken partygoers, tax collectors and sinners. Luke follows with this story:

Then one of the Pharisees invited him to eat with him. He entered the Pharisee's house and reclined

---

[101] Ibid., 236.
[102] Ibid., 238.

at the table. And a woman in the town who was a sinner found out that Jesus was reclining at the table in the Pharisee's house. She brought an alabaster flask of fragrant oil and stood behind him at his feet, weeping, and began to wash his feet with her tears. She wiped his feet with the hair of her head, kissing them and anointing them with the fragrant oil. When the Pharisee who had invited him saw this, he said to himself, "this man, if he were a prophet, would know who and what kind of woman this is and who is touching him—she is a sinner!"

Again, we find three actors: the religious ruler, the sinner and Jesus. As before, we see a Messiah who sees the heart of both the law keeper and the law breaker. Once again, the stage is set for encounter.

Jesus replied to him, "Simon, I have something to say to you." "Teacher," he said, "say it." "A creditor had two debtors. One owed 500 denarii, and the other 50. Since they could not pay it back, he graciously forgave them both. So, which of them will love him more?" Simon answered, "I suppose the one he forgave more." "You have judged correctly," he told him.

Turning to the woman, he said to Simon, "do you see this woman? I entered your house; you gave me no water for my feet, but she, with her tears, has washed my feet and wiped them with her hair. You gave me no kiss, but she hasn't stopped kissing my feet since I came in. You didn't anoint my head with oil, but she has anointed my feet with fragrant oil. Therefore, I tell you, her many sins have been forgiven; that's why she loved much. But the one who is forgiven little, loves little." (40-48)

Several observations stand out in this dramatic story:

- The language describing the scene suggests a formal occasion "where the traditional roles of guest and host are expected to be acted with precision by all concerned."[103] Hosts were expected to engage in several customs of hospitality. Simon's failure to provide water for his feet or to kiss him on either cheek was a "marked sign of contempt" and implied that he considered Jesus an inferior.[104]
- Simon's motivation was not to understand Jesus' teaching, but to test and scrutinize him. He is driven by judgment of both Jesus and the woman, not love.
- The woman had clearly heard the message of Jesus and violated custom by touching him, risking public humiliation to show her gratitude. Jesus allows this and himself violates custom by not shooing her away.
- Again, the tension is allowed to build, revealing Simon's heart.

Bailey offers the contrast that "sinners," the law breakers, often know they have fallen short, while the legalists seem to lack such self-awareness. Jesus sees the woman's heart and defies expectations by honoring her as restored and forgiven. On the other hand, he openly confronts Simon on his shameful hospitality. In doing so, he severely defies customs as such a confrontation is *never done* even to this day in the Middle East.

As with other parables and stories of encounters with Jesus, the ending is left open. We are not told how Simon responded, whether with faith or offense. Bailey writes:

---

[103] Kenneth E. Bailey, "The Parable of the Two Debtors," *Poet and Peasant and Through Peasant Eyes: A Literary- Cultural Approach to the Parables in Luke* (combined edition) (Grand Rapids: Eerdmans Publishing, 1983), 4.

[104] Tristram, cited in Bailey, 5.

For Simon, either Jesus is a rude young man who insults his host, fails to show gratitude for a meal prepared in his honor, and presumes to act in God's place, or he is in fact God's unique agent who mediates forgiveness and appropriately expects humble and costly devotion to his person.[105]

In a way, the two extreme forms of being in the world—the self-righteous rule keeper and the rebellious rule breaker—are not so different. Each style issues from the position of self as center. Each style represents futile attempts to make whole a soul that is divided. Jesus understands that both orientations fail and that he himself is the solution to the human condition (What the law could not do, God did, sending his son…). But he addresses each individual differently as he sees their heart, whether it be proud and hardened or broken and repentant. In an encounter with those who might be rigid traditionalists or legalists, Jesus might discern the sin of pride. With lawbreakers, who may or may not feel guilty, Jesus might expose their destructive lifestyle as he did with the woman at the well. Some, like Simon, need to be broken before they can become whole. Others, already broken, need to be lifted up. The message to all is the same: that Jesus alone is the Savior, the one who makes all things new.

We understand that sex was designed to consummate the union of two lovers and bring the fruit of new life. A "sexual disorder," on the other hand, can be distinguished by its fruits. These include division and diminished life or even death. The next chapter samples the ways we humans can stumble sexually. Perhaps, as did Jesus, we can see beyond the surface to the inner world of those whose behavior might be problematic. And, following Jesus, assert that nothing is beyond the redemptive work of God.

---

[105] "The Parable of Two Debtors," 21.

CHAPTER 5

Hope Beyond the Sexual Self

We all stumble in various ways. —James 3:2

Chip was getting the boot—again. His wife had had enough after discovering his second affair in this year alone. With tears in his eyes, Chip explained that he really does love his wife and does not know why he cheats. "But I do. I cheat and I lie. The story of my life." In the following sessions, it became clear that this story began early—a story of ambivalence: two contradictory feelings, one of which is darker, hidden, and forbidden. In exploring an individual's childhood, it helps to look not so much for excuses, but insight, factors to help us understand. In Chip's case, it was not hard to discern the ingredients that fostered a deceitful, double minded lifestyle: public school teacher and church-goer vs. private philanderer. Again, no excuses, but here are some facts. Chip's dad was often not home and when he was, he drank. When he drank, he would switch from kind and funny to cruel and abusive. Chip both longed for his dad and feared him. Chip's mother, on the other hand, was stable as a rock—a cold, hard rock. Rigidly religious, she sought to manage his every move. The most telling event, however, occurred when he was nine or ten. His mother's nineteen-year-old sister had been staying with the family. Chip had fallen hard for this fun-loving and affectionate young woman. Perhaps it was only natural curiosity that led him one day to sneak into her room and pull out her bra and panties. Then his mother walked in, whereupon she beat him mercilessly, screaming that he was bound for hell.

One can understand the boy's confusion. Sexual excitement and longing for love are bad. Really bad. To avoid punishment and shame, he must be good. Being good means being alone, feeling empty and always performing to please. As Chip grew into puberty these conflicting emotions grew as well; as did the split within his soul. Today, alone and facing another divorce, he seems ready to come to terms with himself, his choices and especially, his God. Hopefully, he will learn that the Lord does not abandon his children who fall short. With time, he works with us to pick up the pieces as he brings healing and hope. That is the message of this chapter.

In the Genesis narrative, we discover that the design for sexuality carries communal and generative purposes. Having defied this order, humans fall into themselves, away from each other and from sex as love or procreation. Misunderstanding God's design, we turn to self-centered strategies to deal with our "sexuality"—that catchall term which bundles identity, erotic drives, and longings for love. Born in sin and nearly drowning in lies and temptations, we stumble. We wrestle with impossible possibilities as we look to sex and sexuality to rescue us from the despair of life in a body. Restless and under clouded vision, we fall into holes. All kinds of holes. The following pages identify the more common pitfalls, none of which is new. And, most importantly, none of which is beyond hope.[106]

Abortion

In 2020, Coloradans had the chance to approve a measure to limit late-term abortions. Pro-life groups had worked long and hard to put this opportunity before the public. Without such a statute, babies could be killed right up to the moment of birth. No other event so starkly represents "terminal sex," a repudiation of the Creator's intention that men and women come together to bring life. The measure failed. Why? *Deception*, intrinsic to every type of sin, seems particularly necessary to shroud this activity. According to Lila Rose, many voters believed the lies that late-term abortions are rare, and "they must not be bloody, gory or evil. They must be life-saving, humane, medical treatments. But nothing could be further from the truth."[107] It is also not true that such proce-dures do little harm to the mother. She needs to process the

---

[106] One does not suggest that sexual relationships may be disordered without touching nerves as well as touching realms of real human pain. It would behoove any writer discussing delicate issues of private lives to do so with both sensi-tivity and humility. The New Testament both enjoins believers not to judge non-believers and lumps each of us in the same category as having resisted the grace and will of God. In addition, the issues are complex and surrounded by an ever-growing and cacophonous pile of studies and opinion pieces. It is thus beyond our scope to trudge too deeply into the weeds of every issue. Sociology and psychology are soft sciences and are subject to researcher bias and the fact that the objects of study tend themselves to be moving targets. Methodology can be problematic. Many issues of experimental design and choice of statistical tools can be questioned and disputed. Acknowledging my own blind spots, the following propositions and observations are thus offered in a spirit of humility and with the hope that the reader, if struggling with any of these issues, may find insight and a hope for greater wholeness.

[107] "Do Coloradans know the evil they voted to continue?" November 5, 2020. https://www.liveaction.org/news/coloradans-evil-voted-continue/?inf_contact_key=a7ad2ecefbf180996259eab4cb8b2b734dfbc39d7283b2cb89d518 9540b69330

trauma and God's grace can heal her grief, fear, and guilt. Several resources are available to facilitate such healing.[108]

Abuse

This category includes a range of troubling behaviors, from domination, hostile criticism, various forms of sexual harassment to sexual battery and rape. Why do people mistreat each other? How is it that hostile behavior is directed at the very people we are supposed to love? Some have observed that love and hate are not very far apart. Even Ruth Graham, the wife of the great evangelist, when asked if she had ever considered divorce quipped, "Divorce? Heavens, no. Murder? Many times." The truth behind her tongue-in-cheek comment lies in the fact that those closest to us carry the most power to disappoint us.

Cases of domestic violence illustrate the saying, "hurt people hurt people." I recall trying to explain this to a woman who had a history of hooking up with abusive men. As is often the case, she was a sensitive and kind person and had fallen into the pattern of what has been called "the broken wing syndrome." Being unsure of her own value and carrying a need to be needed, she would find herself drawn to immature men. These suitors could not fly well on their own. Lacking self-awareness, they failed to realize that the strong attachment they felt for the woman carried an unconscious demand that she prop up their self-esteem. In time, of course, she would tire of this project and express her own thoughts. This would activate in the man a psychic emptiness which he would interpret as betrayal. To him, this profound hurt could only be ameliorated by controlling behaviors or anger. These actions would often elicit her anxiety and self-doubt, causing her to

---

[108] For example, https://www.rachelsvineyard.org/; http://www.silentno-moreawareness.org/search/index.aspx; https://www.surrenderingthesecret.com/find-help/

respond with compliance. While an immediate crisis might be averted, the development of trust and mutual love remain elusive. Cycles of control and abuse, unless confronted, tend to perpetuate themselves.

Adultery

In decades past, it was predominantly men who cheated on their wives. Now, women have caught up. Regardless of who initiates the affair, the faithful partner invariably experiences a tragic betrayal. Cheating shatters trust, along with self-esteem. The one who steps out of the marriage to engage in an emotional or sexual relationship with a new person, on the other hand, experiences an exhilarating sense of being alive or perhaps really understood for the first time. Invariably, this is a fantasy. The conflict may be intense for the "cheater" who perceives his current marriage as terrible and the affair as wonderful. The split is exaggerated as the paramour is idealized while the spouse is devalued. The problem for the faithful partner who wishes to save the marriage is exaggerated by the fact that, upon discovery of the affair, he or she must deal with shock, depression, and anger—conditions which hardly make it easy to compete with the interloper. Affairs do not usually lead to long-term commitment. Less than 10 percent survive into a stable new relationship. Generally, the deception behind the temptation to cheat lies in the combination of secrecy, episodic intensity, sexuality, and mutual flattery. These become confused with intimacy. With time and hard work, marriages disrupted by adultery can be restored, healed, and even strengthened. Prayer, reading, and professional counseling are essential tools that can offer guidance and hope.[109]

---

[109] See as examples of helpful literature, Dave Carder, *Anatomy of an Affair: How Affairs, Attractions, and Addictions Develop, and How to Guard Your Marriage Against Them;* Janice Spring, *After the Affair: Healing the Pain and Rebuilding the Trust When a Partner Has Been Unfaithful.*

Avoidance

Not only are there fewer weddings these days, but many find themselves avoiding relationships altogether. Avoidant behavior is often related to anxiety. Whether from discomfort with the opposite sex or some other reason, many seem less inclined to see themselves partnering with another. As Bloom already observed in 1987, students are more apt to talk about individual goals than dreams of a white picket fence with little kids running around.[110] Some young folks seem to have given up altogether and label themselves "asexual."

Child molestation and pedophilia

"I discovered when I was about 10 or 11, I had this attraction to young boys. I could never tell anybody. When you have to lie for so many years about who you are, it becomes pretty easy." This statement issued from former elementary school teacher and captured pedophile, Erik Toth, in an interview with USA Today.[111] Notice the phrase "who you are." He identifies himself with a sexual proclivity. Justification follows. In the interview, he acknowledges that sex with children could be harmful but then refers to "research" that suggests that such activity may not be harmful and that the willingness of the child is a key. Of course, the idea that a child can give willing consent is absurd.

Deeply concerned about the harm caused by childhood sexual abuse, historian and filmmaker Steve Humphreys, documents his search for the extent and causes of such behavior. He finds Scotland Yard's pedophile expert, DC

---

[110] Allan Bloom, *The Closing of the American Mind: How Higher Education Has Failed Democracy and Impoverished the Souls of Today's Students* (New York: Simon & Schuster Paperbacks, 2012).

[111] Go inside the mind of FBI's most wanted pedophile. *USA Today*, October 7, 2014.

Jonathon Taylor, who states, "Ten years ago, paedophilia was reaching epidemic proportions. The problem is it's just gotten bigger and bigger."[112] Estimates of the number of child abusers in Britain alone range from 50,000 to an incredible 250,000. Up to 80 percent of such abuse occurs within the family or extended family, making it extremely difficult to detect.[113] Not all adults who are sexually attracted to children abuse them, of course. Humphreys decided to find pedophiles who have never been arrested and deny acting on their urges. His interview with "Eddie" is instructive. Eddie, 39, relates that it was during a difficult time when he was in his twenties, that he discovered he was a pedophile. In his words, "That was when I first recognized or rather, came to the conclusion that, it was fair to say, I am a pedophile… That's not at all to say that that's the only thing I am, but it does play a large part in who I am as a person." He goes on to say that he wishes he did not have this attraction; it is difficult for him, although he is also attracted to women of all ages. He would like help to overcome his feelings and wished that help were available to pedophiles before they come in contact with the law. Here we notice both the tendency to identify oneself with one's sexual proclivities on the one hand and the hope or wish to figure out how to overcome them on the other.

In California, licensed therapists are required to report to law enforcement should a client reveal that he has accessed child pornography. Unfortunately, such a law may deter some from finding the help they need. In Britain, a group of volunteers called "circles" meets with sex offenders who have served their time. This group offers accountability and support. They claim a 70 percent success rate.[114]

---

[112] The Paedophile Next Door, 1915. "Free the Children" https://www.youtube.com/watch?v=Ft9QKPku6ho
[113] Ibid.
[114] Ibid.

Cohabitation

Many adults today have grown up living through the pain of their parents' divorce. Remembering the fighting and the inconvenience of being shuttled from mom's house to dad's, they look askance at the institution of marriage. We can understand why "shacking up" has become a pervasive substitute in recent years.

The problem for these commitment-shy partners is that cohabiting individuals are more likely to break up and more likely to rebound to someone new. In addition, they live with uncertainty. *Am I in or out?* Their children suffering from insecurity is of course an additional concern.

Prostitution, Promiscuity, and Pornography

Why is prostitution invariably considered taboo, if not illegal? Why have societies everywhere limited sexual encounters? Beyond those already discussed, I think there are several reasons, the first of which is that the natural outcome of sex happens to involve procreation—a fact mostly forgotten these days. While the proliferation of the pill has facilitated this amnesia, there are other reasons as to why chastity has been an ideal in most cultures. Foremost of these is the fact that sex implies an intimacy and union that in fact does not exist outside of the protection of marriage. Without knowledge and commitment, it is "just sex." You don't really matter to me and I don't really matter to you.

As campus psychiatrist, Grossman worried, random hookups often bring tragic consequences. If the impersonal sex found in the college scene tends to divorce sex from personhood, the totally anonymous sex saturating the Internet invites a complete severing of persons. The excitement and arousal are entirely solitary. Not uncommonly, men addicted to chat rooms and other types of porn find themselves unable to have sex with a real woman.[115]

Consider also the intrapsychic consequences for the model. To continue this line of work, she must divorce herself from natural shame. Her real name, real thoughts, and real emotions must be split off from her performance. In the documentary, "My date with a porn star," three men who had been compulsive consumers of pornography, experience the industry firsthand. Initially, they are as excited as kids with a bag of trick-or-treat candy. They soon, however, sober up to the harsh reality of the business. As one man put it,

> Doing that would make me feel exploited. I don't know. I'd just stay in the shower for five hours washing myself... These people. It's like they've got immunity to care—about other people's feelings, about love and all that. It's like they don't respect themselves. It's weird. I can't explain it. It's absolutely disgusting and heartbreaking.[116]

Breaking the cycle of sex addiction

Addictions are cyclical in nature. One stage leads to the next, leaving the addict stuck in a downward spiraling loop. In 1983, Dr. Patrick Carnes, in his book, *Out of the Shadows*, broke the cycle into four stages: Fantasy (Preoccupation),

---

[115] See the summary statement of 50 authorities summarizing empirical evidence: "The social costs of pornography: a statement of findings and recommendations," (Princeton, N.J: Witherspoon Institute, 2010).

[116] https://www.youtube.com/watch?v=2UYoSja7fwI&index=3&list=PLITcq_JwVbFW6A6Ol9ClWVS5RQg5HDuX7

Ritualization (The Bubble), Compulsive Sexual Behavior (Acting Out), Despair (Shame).[117]

The easiest place to intervene is in stage one. As such, in treatment and twelve-step recovery groups, sex addicts try to learn what their triggers are and to develop healthier coping mechanisms. If the cycle can be stopped in stage one, then stage two never arrives. If, however, the cycle moves forward into fantasy and then ritualization, it gathers momentum like a boulder rolling down a hill. Then acting out sexually (and the consequences that follow) becomes almost inevitable.[118]

Recent research highlights the dangerous power of sexual conditioning.[119] The deleterious effects of pornography are particularly evident in the adolescent brain. According to the Medical Institute for Sexual Health,

---

[117] Patrick P. Carnes, *Out of the Shadows: Understanding Sexual Addiction (3rd Edition)* (Center City, MN: Hazelden,1983). See also, Kevin B. Skinner, *Treating Pornography Addiction: The Essential Tools for Recovery* (Provo, Ut.: Growth Climate, Inc., 2005).

[118] Robert Weiss LCSW, CSAT-S is Senior Vice President of Clinical Development with Elements Behavioral Health. A licensed UCLA MSW graduate and personal trainee of Dr. Patrick Carnes, he founded The Sexual Recovery Institute in Los Angeles in 1995. He is author of *Cruise Control: Understanding Sex Addiction in Gay Men* and *Sex Addiction 101: A Basic Guide to Healing from Sex, Porn, and Love Addiction*, and co-author with Dr. Jennifer Schneider of both *Closer Together, Further Apart: The Effect of Technology and the Internet on Parenting, Work, and Relationships* and *Always Turned On: Sex Addiction in the Digital Age*. He has developed clinical programs for The Ranch in Nunnelly, Tennessee, Promises Treatment Centers in Malibu, and the aforementioned Sexual Recovery Institute in Los Angeles. He has also provided clinical multi-addiction training and behavioral health program development for the US military and numerous other treatment centers throughout the United States, Europe and Asia. For more information you can visit his website, www.robertweissmsw.com.

[119] C.K. Atkins, "The Role of Pavlovian Conditioning in Sexual Behavior: A Comparative Analysis of Human and Nonhuman Animals" *International Journal of Comparative Psychology,* Volume 17, Issue 2.

pornography has emerged as an overwhelmingly pervasive and addictive form of sexual involvement that often drives other risky sexual behaviors. High-speed internet is delivering vulgar distortions of sex to our children at alarmingly young ages. Gaming devices and smartphones have become the secret portals of entry into the immature brains of our youth.[120]

The principle of neurogenesis, called Hebb's rule, can be summarized neatly: brain cells that fire together wire together.

When sexual excitement is induced in a young person, whatever stimulated that sexual excitement becomes connected to that sensation. Dopamine and the "reward circuit" are very active in this "molding" process, producing the desire to repeat the activity that brought the initial pleasure. When that stim-ulation comes from pornography, the young person naturally begins to seek out more pornographic stimu-lation. As the porn user becomes desensitized to their current pornography, the individual seeks out more "thrilling" and more "deviant" sexual acts to view in order to bring the same sexual pleasure that was first experienced.[121]

On the other hand, cells that stop firing together even-tually loosen their connection. Unfortunately, although the sex addicted brain does "heal" in this way, it is a difficult and much longer process to "unwire" those connections. Does it not, therefore, make sense to protect kids from viewing porn

---

[120] https://www.amazon.com/Pornland-How-Porn-Hijacked-Sexuality/dp/0807001546
[121] Ibid.; also, Raised on Porn | Documentary Film - YouTube

in the first place? Porn filters can be an important tool.[122] Happily, awareness of this harmful drug is growing.[123]

Transgenderism

Despite the growing acceptance of the proposition that gender is nothing more than a culturally derived reality and despite the common language that a child is merely "assigned" a gender at birth, bodies in actuality are either one or the other. The logic of gender activists stands out as curiously contradictory.[124] On the one hand, those wishing to normalize the transgender phenomenon argue that gender dysphoric children are born this way. The statement is often quoted, "I have a female brain in a male body." On the other hand, many young people claim they are "gender fluid." A teenager may experiment—behaving and dressing as a male one day and a female the next. As is typical for adolescents, peer pressure plays a role. This is evidenced by the new term, "rapid onset gender dysphoria."[125] In Sweden, researchers discovered a 1500 percent increase in gender dysphoria from 2008 to 2018.[126] The dangers associated with this disorder are particularly serious. Dr. Andre Van Mol has compiled warnings and guidelines for physicians who are called upon to evaluate or treat gender-confused patients. Discussing the practice of prescribing puberty blockers or cross-sex hormones, he

---

[122] For example, "Covenant Eyes," Screen Accountability™ | Covenant Eyes

[123] 20 Must-Know Stats About the Porn Industry and Its Underage Consumers (fightthenewdrug.org) October 8, 2021.

[124] See, Ryan T. Anderson, *When Harry became Sally: Responding to the Transgender Movement* (New York: Encounter Books, 2018).

[125] Littman L (2018) *Rapid-onset gender dysphoria in adolescents and young adults: A study of parental reports.* PLoS ONE 13(8): e0202330.https://doi.org/10.1371/journal. pone.0202330

[126] https://www.thelocal.se/20200213/sweden-sees-sharp-rise-in-gender-dysphoria-among-teenagers?inf_contact_key=64de19c4811c1b929793c08f757878fbd18a532c4142cb79caf2b269de1401fa

states, "The short- and long-term risks and permanent conse-quences of a minor undergoing transition are sobering."[127] These include permanent sterility, the removal of reproduc-tive organs, and the possibility of too little genital material for sex reassignment surgery. Less drastic consequences include weight gain, balding, loss of bone density, as well as cancer and cardiovascular disease. Testifying before the California Assembly as it considered a bill that would force foster parents to affirm without question a child's wish to transition genders, endocrinologist Michael Laidlaw bluntly summarized what was at stake in this so-called "affirmative care:"

- Powerful, dangerous hormones to block kids' normal puberty.
- High-dose, high-risk sex hormones with deadly blood clot and cancer risks.
- Hazardous surgeries for boys to turn the intestine into an imitation vagina while destroying their penis and removing their testicles.
- Breast binders and mastectomies to destroy teenage girls' healthy breast tissue, and ovary and uterus removal, ensuring infertility forever.

Such drastic interventions on children are performed under the rationale that transforming a body to match subjec-tive experience is necessary to reduce suicidality; in fact, such interventions may make it worse.[128] A study in Sweden, a highly affirming LGBT country, found that the suicide rate among those having completed gender—reassignment

---

[127] "My Child is Transgender. Make Her a Son." *Guidance for the Doctor*. Andrè Van Mol, MD | December 28, 2017.

[128] Transition as Treatment: The Best Studies Show the Worst Outcomes. Paul Dirks, The Public Discourse, February 16, 2020 https://www.thepublicdis-course.com/2020/02/60143/

surgery was nineteen times that of the general population.[129] Clearly, regret after surgery is not uncommon and suicidal depression is significantly higher than in the normal population.[130] On the other hand, almost all children and teens who identify as transgender reclaim their natal gender by late teens and early twenties.[131] Further, the literature consistently shows that children expressing gender non-conformity also experience unusually high rates of psychopathology and/or developmental disorders that ought to be addressed.[132]

Beyond the popularity of being "gender fluid" or the phenomenon of rapid onset gender dysphoria—which can legitimately be dismissed as artifacts of media hype and progressive indoctrination—we wonder about those children

---

[129] Dhejne C, et al, "Long-Term Follow-Up of Transsexual Persons Undergoing Sex Reassignment Surgery: Cohort Study in Sweden," journals.plos.org, Feb. 22, 2011.

[130] "The prevalence of suicide attempts among respondents to the National Transgender Discrimination Survey (NTDS), conducted by the National Gay and Lesbian Task Force and National Center for Transgender Equality, is 41 percent, which vastly exceeds the 4.6 percent of the overall U.S. population who report a lifetime suicide attempt, and is also higher than the 10-20 percent of lesbian, gay and bisexual adults who report ever attempting suicide." www.williamsinstitute.law.ucla.edu/wp-content/uploads/AFSP-Williams-Suicide-Report-Final.pdf See also, *The transgender suicide myth exposed: What should really terrify parents is the mutilation of their child's healthy body.* Michael Cook | Feb 14 2020 https://www.mercatornet.com/conjugality/view/thetransgender-suicide-myth-exposed/23295?inf_contact_key=71bc03aba47850bd8b-fbfc40d15455781b0a3f0fd3ee5d9b43fb34c6613498d7

[131] See "Childhood Dysphoria and Desistance" in *When Harry Became Sally: Responding to the Transgender Moment.* See also, Singh,Devita Bradley,Susan J. Zucker,Kenneth J "A Follow-Up Study of Boys With Gender Identity Disorder." In *Frontiers in Psychiatry,* March 29, 2021. https://www.frontiersin.org/article/10.3389/fpsyt.2021.632784

[132] For example, "Two years of gender identity service for minors: overrepresentation of natal girls with severe problems in adolescent development" *Child and Adolescent Psychiatry and Mental Health* | Full Text (biomedcentral.com), April 9, 2015; "*Mental Health of Transgender and Gender Nonconforming Youth Compared With Their Peers*" | *American Academy of Pediatrics* (aappublications.org), May, 2018.

and young adults who deeply and persistently feel troubled about their natal gender. Important research and theory continue to be necessary such as is illustrated in the following paragraph written by a University of California epidemiologist, Hasci Horvath:

> In my opinion—which is based upon extensive research, as well as my own 13-year-long experience in pretending to be a woman—GD is only superficially concerned with one's sex. It's more a disturbance of identity... Patients have whatever mental illnesses they may have, or that develop while in the ruminations and hypomanic states that typically precede "coming out as trans." I propose that GD is a moody, brooding syndrome that accompanies these mental illnesses. People with GD have cultivated an idealized vision of themselves as the opposite sex. At a critical point of rumination, after the patient has sufficiently disparaged his or her actual life and idealized life as the opposite sex, he or she realizes that body parts of the opposite sex may be obtained through the services of doctors (Raymond, 1979; Billings, 1982). Actually transforming into the opposite sex starts to seem feasible. The self-conception "splits" in two, and idealization becomes identity. Having negated any value in their actual male or female presence in the world, and now feeling themselves to actually be the self-generated persona, patients perseveratively ask themselves, "What's stopping me?" "Feasibility" seems to trigger the split. Here begins the acute phase of GD.[133]

---

[133] The Theatre of the Body: A detransitioned epidemiologist examines suicidality, affirmation, and transgender identity by Hacsi Horváth December 19, 2018 by 4thwavenow

Horvath makes the deadly accusation that those in the medical community who automatically affirm a child's self-conception are, in fact, colluding with mental illness, reifying delusions.

We must face the fact that gender confusion is impacting young people in epidemic proportions. How do pastors and parents respond? Mark Yarhouse and Preston Sprinkle are two Christian leaders who offer thoughtful and sensitive guidance to those who would lovingly counsel gender dysphoric persons.[134]

Paraphilias

Other sexually anomalous behaviors illustrate the degree to which humans can descend into sensual obsession. These include such behaviors as exhibitionism, voyeurism, fetishism, and even bestiality. Sidestepping the moral dimension, researchers have attempted to categorize such sexual orientations in terms of either "unusual erotic target preferences" or "unusual sexual activity preferences."[135] For example, a paraphilia may be understood either as an unusual object of sexual arousal, such as a nonconsenting person or an inanimate object, or an unusual activity, such as the experience of giving or receiving humiliation, as in sadomasochism. The concept of "erotic target location errors" (ETLEs) focuses on how some persons form erotic peripheral targets such as

---

[134] For example, see YouTube videos, Mark Yarhouse: Gender Identity & Christian Faith [Biola University Chapel] - YouTube and Identity, Teens & Gender | Preston Sprinkle & Helena Kerschner - YouTube; see also, Mark A. Yarhouse, *Understanding Gender Dysphoria: Navigating Transgender Issues In a Changing Culture* (Downers Grove, Ill.: Inter-Varsity Press, 2015).

[135] Freund, K., Seto, M. C., & Kuban, M. (1996). Two types of fetishism. *Behaviour Research and Therapy*, 34, 687-694.

clothing or feet or even their own bodies.[136] Classical conditioning has been suggested as a possible mechanism for understanding the development of such paraphilias. Salu has proposed a model of general sexual arousal along similar lines of behavioristic learning that implicates in particular, the role of the amygdala.[137] When we consider how deeply ingrained a conditioned fear or other behavioral responses can be, it is not a big leap to imagine how people can declare that they just cannot help what they feel or to what they are attracted. We also know that during orgasm, there is a heightened sense of learning in which an associational bond between stimulus and response takes place.[138] Freud coined the term, "polymorphous perversity," to describe the fact that persons could experience a kind of sexual pleasure "...in a variety of ways in the entire body, beyond the narrow range of genital stimulation that is consonant with reproduction."[139] A more recent descriptor is "poly sensuality." These terms simply highlight the fact that the human body is capable of responding sensually in different ways and areas. As Freud understood, as a child matures, shame, disgust, and moral training help narrow the focus of arousal to the genital zones—a necessary development to normal heterosexuality.

Therapists who treat adults who have been sexually abused as children recognize the common reality that these patients may have enjoyed the sensations of being fondled or otherwise

---

[136] Anne A. Lawrence (2009) Erotic Target Location Errors: An Underappreciated Paraphilic Dimension, *The Journal of Sex Research*, 46:2-3, 194-215, DOI: 10.1080/00224490902747727

[137] "The role of the amygdala in the development of sexual arousal.." The Free Library. 2013 *The Institute for Advanced Study of Human Sexuality* 24 May. 2019

[138] Genaro A. Coria-Avila, PhD,1,* Deissy Herrera-Covarrubias, PhD,1,2 Nafissa Ismail, PhD,2 and James G. Pfaus, PhD3, *The role of orgasm in the development and shaping of partner preferences.* Socioaffect Neurosci Psychol. 2016; 6: 10.3402/snp.v6.31815.

[139] Polymorphous perversity, Encyclopedia of Sex and Gender: Culture Society History COPYRIGHT 2007 Thomson Gale

inappropriately touched. A kind of sexual learning or conditioning may have taken place. Scharff's presentation of the case of mother-daughter incest provides a simple example of such learning. The mother would snuggle behind the child, fondle her genitals and rub her vulva against the patient's buttocks. The patient later remembered "... doing the same to her teddy bear as her way of masturbating."[140]

Invariably, despite any kindness by the adult abuser, patients describe violation and shame at having their sexuality awakened prematurely. Proponents of comprehensive sexual education might argue that it is only the abusive violation that causes shame. They might even insist that the fact that children experience such arousal only proves that they are naturally sexual and that such sexuality ought to be encouraged and celebrated. Such fallacious reasoning can be traced to Alfred Kinsey, to be discussed later. At this point, let it suffice to note that a wide variety of sexual experience and sexual targets can be conditioned. More importantly, as in other areas of learning, repetition and reinforcement strengthen associations between stimuli and response patterns. Conversely, as previously discussed, without these elements, neuronal bonds weaken and extinction follows. What this means is that, while particular sexual proclivities may appear to be fixed, they are malleable. That which was learned can be unlearned. Change is possible!

Psychiatrist Aaron Kheriaty laments the popularity of the movie, "50 Shades of Gray" which glamourizes BDSM— bondage, discipline, dominance, submission, sadism, and masochism. He warns that experimentation with sex and aggression or sex and humiliation leads to a fusing of neural networks that ought to remain separate. Emotionally charged experiences, as with addictions, with repetition, become

---

[140] J. S. Scharff & D. E. Scharff, *Object Relations Therapy of Physical and Sexual Trauma* (Northvale, NJ: Jason Aronson Inc., 1994), 229.

hardwired in the brain. Again, we encounter Hebb's principle, "neurons that fire together, wire together." Human beings have separate neural networks related to anger and aggression on the one hand and different neural networks or brain maps related to anxiety and anxiety-provoking experiences. The neural networks related to sexual behavior represent an altogether distinct experience. Once aggression becomes linked to sexual arousal or fear, fusion and confusion occur in the brain. Problems such as the inability to become aroused without violence follow such experimentation.

Patients also build up tolerance. With sexual behaviors, one needs to push the envelope just to get aroused. The aggressive, domineering, or painful behaviors must become increasingly intense or dangerous in order to "work."[141]

According to Kheriaty, BDSM experimentation represents the kind of cavalier, emotionally detached sexual encounter so prevalent on college campuses today. He urges wisdom and careful reflection when deciding about sexual choices.

Because there is an addictive and compulsive component to sexual learning, those struggling with paraphilias often face guilt, shame, and even fear of prison time. Therefore, it is essential to underscore that help is available. Medication and group therapy are helpful. Generally, outcome research indicates that cognitive behavior therapy is most effective in the treatment of these kinds of sexual disorders. The goal is to decrease inappropriate sexual arousal. Strategies include covert sensitization in which deviant fantasies and behaviors become linked with aversive images. For example, a man who is aroused by picturing himself undressing a child activates this image, then imagines a loud knock on the door followed by police who handcuff him, and so on. Satiation, orgasmic reconditioning,

---

[141] Aaron Kheriaty, *Hooked Up and Tied Down: The Neurological Consequences of Sadomasochism.* In **Public Discourse,** February 17th, 2015.

social skills training, and cognitive restructuring are additional strategies in the cognitive-behavioral toolbox.[142]

Unfortunately, a caveat must here be introduced regarding the "research" and public advocacy of heretofore respected professional organizations. For example, the American Psychological Association has instituted a task force on "consensual non-monogamy." The stated goal is to promote

> awareness and inclusivity about consensual non-mo-
> nogamy and diverse expressions of intimate relation-
> ships. These include but are not limited to: people who
> practice polyamory, open relationships, swinging, rela-
> tionship anarchy and other types of ethical, non-mo-
> nogamous relationships... This task force seeks to
> address the needs of people who practice consensual
> non-monogamy, including their intersecting margin-
> alized identities.[143]

The task force believes that stigma may attach to consensual non-monogamous practitioners (CNM) and cause "minority stress" and that healthcare providers may engage in "micro-aggressions." The call is for therapists to avoid "monosexism"[144] and become more CNM affirming. Psychologist Laura Haynes notes that the APA has expressed sympathy to other paraphilias such as sadomasochism and bondage. She writes,

> I think most Americans will be very concerned to learn
> this radical sex activism has hijacked the American

---

[142] Meg S. Kaplan, PhD, and Richard B. Krueger, MD *Cognitive-Behavioral Treatment of the Paraphilias.* Isr J Psychiatry Relat Sci - Vol. 49 - No 4 (2012)

[143] *American Psychological Association convenes task force on consensual non-monogamy.* The Alliance for Therapeutic Choice. https://a20ceadd-0fb7-4982-bbe2-099c8bc1e2ae.filesusr.com/ugd/ec16e9_d14438ab659e-4a7b9d3b79e05f64fc06. The full text of the task force can be found at: https://www.apadivisions.org/division-44/leadership/task-forces/

[144] Ibid.

Psychological Association and all our mainstream mental health professional organizations. They are no longer trusted sources of accurate scientific information about sexuality or gender. Unfortunately, they are radical political organizations at this point."[145]

Issues of same-sex attraction

In the past, people did not define themselves according to their sexual inclinations. It may be argued, in fact, that the terms heterosexual and homosexual are misleading, as if they represent discrete, natural categories rather than social constructs.[146] The dynamics around sexual arousal, sexual aims, and attraction are complex. The question of sexual orientation is deeply associated with lifestyle, love relationships, and personal identity. I would simply present the issue of mutability as a point of discussion. The public and professional discussion regarding the etiology and potential alteration of same-sex attraction is an area of controversy. The evidence, however, that sexual orientation is related to childhood and family factors and may be alterable is generally suppressed, misrepresented, or vilified. LGBT activism and media bias are dominant in this regard. Nevertheless, many case studies illustrate the fact that sexual attractions develop from both early sexual experience and early family dynamics.[147] For those experiencing "ego-dystonic" same-sex attraction (SSA), such knowledge can provide hope. Further, as most researchers

---

[145] Ibid.

[146] Michael Hannon, "Against Heterosexuality: The idea of sexual orientation is artificial and inhibits Christian Witness." *FirstThings.com*, March 2014. and "Sexual Disorientation: The Trouble with Talking about 'Gayness,'" *FirstThings.com*, Oct. 2013.

[147] See, *Shame and Attachment Loss: The Practical Work of Reparative Therapy* (Downers Grove, Il.: Intervarsity Press,2009); *Reparative Therapy of Male Homosexuality; A New Clinical Approach* (Northvale, New Jersey: Jason Aronson Inc., 1991).

will acknowledge, no gay gene has yet been discovered.[148] Therapist David Pickup, summarizing extensive experience with homosexual males, writes:

> I've never seen a case yet in all the years of all my SSA clients (95% of my practice over ten years, and all of Nicolosi's reports of his clients) in which attachment loss, defensive detachment, gender inferiority and severely unmet needs for affirmation, affection and approval were not causal to homosexual feelings. Even though I have a very open mind to inborn causality possibility, this has never been conclusively proven in research. I've never seen a case of male homosexuality in which there was not a severe lack of attachment to primary male role models, therefore a severe lack of attachment to the subjective core male self, which results in the automatic objectifying and erotic "fulfill-ment" of maleness in another man's body. If a boy doesn't attach enough to his male self, he'll be looking for his maleness only within the bodies of other men as objects, which robs him of the subjective and joyful experience of manhood in his own body, mind and heart.[149]

Joseph Nicolosi's books provide thoughtful and extensive theory along with case studies exploring developmental considerations in same-sex attraction.[150] Etiological considerations

---

[148] NE & BK Whitehead. *My Genes Made Me Do It! Homosexuality and the Scientific Evidence.* Copyright © 2018 Whitehead Associates Fifth (revised) Edition, 2018.

[149] Private communication.

[150] Nicolosi, *Shame and Attachment Loss.*

should also include the role of early sexual conditioning.[151] So-called "conversion therapy" has been widely misrepresented as entailing insensitive spiritual practices (pray the gay away) or long discredited and abandoned behavioral aversive techniques. Canadian journalist, Michel Lizotte presents decades of empirically validated—but censored!—research supporting the efficacy of professional counseling for those wishing to alter same-sex attractions.[152] Such counseling entails highly sensitive and sophisticated client-centered approaches.[153] The editor of the *Journal of Human Sexuality*, Dr. Christopher Rosik, analyzed the methodology of three research papers purporting to find harm in counseling homosexuals hoping to change their orientation. He writes that these articles reveal the authors' bias rather than actually identifying harm.[154] Dr. Paul Sullins also debunked the methodology of studies purporting harm from counseling aimed at changing sexual orientation.[155]

Finally, a growing number of Christians have found that their relationship with Jesus led them to change their

---

[151] Christopher H. Rosik , Jul 24, 2015 Sexual Orientation as a Conditioned Response to Childhood Sexual Abuse: A Rarely Discussed Factor in the Scientific Literature https://a20ceadd-0fb7-4982-bbe2-099c8bc1e2ae.filesusr. com/ugd/ec16e9_3c53225f709740279fffa9f371096311 Hoffmann, H. (2012). Considering the role of conditioning in sexual orientation. Archives of Sexual Behavior, 41, 63-71. doi: 10.1007/s10508.012.9915-9

[152] https://www.lifesitenews.com/news/new-documentary-explores-the-promise-of-conversion-therapy-for-homosexuals?inf_contact_key=71bbe594ab-b7a1a49bb4e981fe4b080f09c74070ac2bf3cfa7869e3cfd4ff832

[153] Christopher H. Rosik, Ph.D. Recently Published Research Counters Claims of Widespread Harm and Ineffectiveness of Sexual Attraction Fluidity Exploration in Therapy (SAFE-T) https://www.therapeuticchoice.com/

[154] "A Critical Review of 2020 Research on Harms from Efforts to Change Sexual Attractions and Behaviors: Minimal Advancement of Science, Maximal Advancement of Agendas. "*Journal of Human Sexuality*, vol. 11, 2020.

[155] "Absence of Behavioral Harm Following Non-efficacious Sexual Orientation Change Efforts: A Retrospective Study of United States Sexual Minority Adults, 2016–2018," *Frontiers in Psychology,* February, 2022.

sexual orientation.[156] The following references offer further understanding.

"Effects of Therapy on Religious Men Who Have Unwanted Same-Sex Attraction," Paul L. Santero, PhD, Neil E. Whitehead, PhD, and Dolores Ballesteros, PhD. *The Linacre Quarterly* 2018 10.1177/0024363918788559. https://www.thenewatlantis.com/docLib/20160819_ TNA50SexualityandGender.pdf

"Sexual Attraction Fluidity and Well-Being in Men: A Therapeutic Outcome Study," *Journal of Human Sexuality*, vol. 12, 61-86, 2021. https://www.journalofhumansexuality. com/books

https://www.davidpickuplmft.com/rt-is-safe-t#!

"Mutable or immutable? Homosexuals are born that way, gay activists argue vehemently. How is it that so many have changed?" Robert R. Reilly | 27 May 2013 - See more at:

http://www.mercatornet.com/articles/view/mutable_or_ immutable#sthash.l1KRa1mM.dpuf

https://www.josephnicolosi.com/collection/2015/5/28/ an-open-secret-the-truth-about-gay-male-couples

Christine E. Kaestle (2019) Sexual Orientation Trajectories Based on Sexual Attractions, Partners, and Identity: A Longitudinal Investigation From Adolescence Through Young Adulthood Using a U.S. Representative Sample, *The Journal of Sex Research*, DOI: 10.1080/00224499.2019.1577351

---

[156] https://changedmovement.com/ See also, *Desires in Conflict: Hope for Men who Struggle with Sexual Identity,* Joe Dallas (Eugene, OR: Harvest House Publishers, 2003,revised).

Diamond, L.M. Curr Sex Health Rep, Sexual Fluidity in Males and Females (2016) 8: 249. https://doi.org/10.1007/s11930-016-0092-z

Sabra L. Katz-Wise, Sabra L. Katz-Wise, Sexual Fluidity and Related Attitudes and Beliefs Among Young Adults with a Same-Gender Orientation. *Archives of Sexual Behavior* July 2015, Volume 44, Issue 5, pp 1459–1470.

Increasingly, our culture demands acceptance of behaviors that not long ago, most folks considered deviant. Now, approval is required.[157] To resist is to be narrow-minded and judgmental. As individuals search for intimacy and the freedom to pursue what they deeply believe will satisfy, should conservatives or people of faith oppose them? It is difficult to shake off the monikers of bigot, sexist, homophobic, or even just ignorant. Could we be on the wrong side of history? Psychiatry professor Glynn Harrison writes:

> In the space of just a few decades the Christian moral vision, which had buttressed the ancient institutions of marriage and family for centuries, effectively collapsed. And most people today would think good riddance.... As if from nowhere, Christians whose views once occupied the mainstream of public morality suddenly feel *weird*. It's worse than that: they feel *guilty*. Guilty for holding views held to be degrading to the human spirit. Guilty that they belong to a faith accused of

---

[157] David Horwitz outlines the phenomenal success of the gay and leftist agenda to push past acceptance of alternative lifestyles to fundamental transformation of the culture itself. *Dark Agenda: The War to Destroy Christian America* (West Palm Beach, Fl.: Humanix Books, 2018).

heartlessly pushing the most vulnerable and marginalized out into the cold.[158]

The truth, however, is that our faith addresses the most profound human needs. Jesus came to offer "abundant life." So why speak against adultery, polyamory, pornography, or transgenderism? Simply, to offer hope to those who would break free from sexual bondage. Perhaps, as well, to post caution flags to the young and curious. This is not about nonacceptance of persons, but rather to affirm our fellow travelers on this planet on the level of their most profound need.

The following chapter dips into the psychology of the developing self. It argues that the most satisfying framework for building a stable identity and lasting experience of intimacy issues from a more traditional understanding of the family and community and especially, of motherhood.

---

[158] Glynn Harrison, *A Better Story: God, Sex and Human Flourishing* (London: Inter-Varsity Press, 2017), xiv – xvi.

CHAPTER 6

Belonging Together and the Primacy of Woman

Women are the mothers of humanity; do not let us ever forget that or underemphasize its importance. What mothers are to their children, so will man be to man.[159]

When Kim was little, she was daddy's girl—my special bundle of joy. We called her "fireball" because she was so full of life. When she was about three, she took a hard tumble, skinned her knee and, of course, started wailing. I was only a few feet away so I crouched down with my arms out as she headed toward me. Was I surprised as she raced right past me! Turning, I saw the reason. There was mom, a good five feet further. Well, I guess the extra yardage was worth it. "Umph. What's so special about her?" I thought. Actually, that is a good question and the topic of this chapter.

Reviewing the Genesis declaration, "It is not good for man to be alone..." we note the converse observation that it became good when Eve was created. Adam alone was incomplete. In the woman, he finds his perfect complement. He does not need to be reminded of her value. Neither does the football star who mouths the words, "I love you, Mom!" after snagging a touchdown pass. What, we ask, is so special about the female? Let us begin at the beginning—the earliest experience of the human being.

---

[159] Ashley Montague, *The Natural Superiority of Women*, 1952/1974.

The mother/infant dyad and the emergence of the self

In times past and in less analyzed societies, the importance of mothering was as self-evident as the assumption that an infant ought to be breast-fed. In the modern era, careful observers have verified these truths. They have also cataloged data and theorized about just what exactly goes on in the earliest experience of a child and how that experience impacts further development. The following is a survey of some of these careful observers of early life as they lift the veil on what is going on as a newborn becomes a person.

One of the most influential theoreticians of personality formation was Donald Winnicott. As a practicing pediatrician and psychoanalyst, he was intimately familiar with babies and their mothers. The driving question behind his theories had to do with how the self develops out of its relational matrix. This approach—now widely accepted—stood in contrast to Freud's presupposition that the structure of the ego developed more as an independent operation. In Winnicott's observations, it was apparent that an infant emerges from the womb in a state of unintegrated bits and pieces of experience. He wanted to know how do these come together? The answer: not by themselves.

> The mother provides experiences which enable the incipient self of the infant to emerge ... The infant's organization of his own experience is preceded by and draws upon the mother's organized perceptions of him. The mother provides a "holding environment" within which the infant is contained and experienced.[160]

---

[160] "D.W. Winnicott and Harry Guntrip," in Jay R. Greenberg and Stephen A. Mitchell, *Object Relations in Psychoanalytic Theory* (Cambridge: Harvard University press, 1983), 191.

The critical need of the baby to be held and nurtured is matched by what Winnicott termed "maternal preoccupation." In other words, a new mom possesses a readiness to respond to the child's internal experiences, a mindset which allows her to meet his needs, which may be incessant and quite demanding.[161] As the child repeatedly feels the inner press of hunger, wetness, or cold and as these discomforts are met with the well-timed arrival of the breast or some other form of ministration, a correspondence is formed from which the infant begins to grow a solid sense of self. This matching pattern initially appears to be an illusory and omnipotent sensation as if his demand and the object of satisfaction are identical.

> The necessity for maternal devotion is apparent. The mother's empathic anticipation of the baby's needs and her precise timing are crucial... The simultaneity of infantile hallucination and maternal presentation provide the repetitive experiential basis for the child's sense of contact with and power over external reality.[162]

As the infant grows, the mother continues to respond to the child as a mirror—reflecting his or her experience and fragmented movements in such a way that helps them organize and integrate that experience into a gradually more cohesive self. Winnicott also noted that it is not only necessary for her to respond in an attuned way to his needs and demands, but her ongoing presence is also required. We envision quiet periods of sitting or rocking. There are no demands to be fed or changed. In this quiet state with mother,

> The infant experiences needlessness and complete unintegration, a state of "going—on—being" out

---

[161] Fortunately, the postnatal mother is helped in this regard by her body's production of a flood of nurturing hormones, such as oxytocin.
[162] Ibid.,192.

of which needs and spontaneous gestures emerge. The mother's non-demanding presence makes this experience of formlessness and comfortable solitude possible, and this capacity becomes a central feature in the development of a stable and personal self.[163]

Of course, mothers have their own needs and problems. In time, the mother finds herself less preoccupied with her child, hence less immediately attentive. A child is then forced to deal with his separateness and to accept that the entire world is not shaped by his demands. Mother nevertheless continues to respond but with less instant attunement. As personality theorist, Heinz Kohut observed, normal parental lapses are necessary for children to internalize and develop their own ability for self-care.[164]

Winnicott argued that, beyond normal lapses, there are two types of failings in maternal care that have a devastating impact on a child's emotional development. These deficiencies are felt by the child as "… A terrifying interference with the continuity of his own personal existence."[165] These involve the inability to respond to his excited or needy states, on the one hand, and interference when in the quiescent, formless state on the other hand. In the first place, when there is a lack of correspondence between the tiny creature's physical demands and parental succor, the sense of self as having an impact on the world fails to develop. He may be forced to deny his own needs and wishes and/or to mold himself to whatever comes his way. In the second sense, when the mother repeatedly impinges on the child's quiet, needless state, she deprives him of his conversation with his own inner world and the creative initiatives he might make. This might happen when the mother's own desire to play with or excite the baby blinds

---

163 Ibid., 193.

164 "Heinz Kohut and Joseph Sadler," Greenberg and Mitchell, 354.

165 Greenberg and Mitchell, 194.

her to the child's signals that he is overwhelmed or already overstimulated.

In short, when an infant repeatedly is unable to call parental attention to his state of mind, his ability to organize and integrate his experience suffers. His inner world, as he grows, carries a residue of fragmentation.

> Out of necessity he becomes prematurely and compulsively attuned to the claims and requests of others. He cannot allow himself the experience of formless quiescence since he must be prepared to respond to what is asked of and provided for him.[166]

In such a case, the child's own gestures and needs become divorced from the way his mother responds to him. This leads to a split between a detached "real self" and the compliant "false self" which is based not on his own inner reality but on his mother's image of him. If the disconnect is severe or continuous, anxiety becomes associated with any expression of real feelings, which must be kept hidden. An anxious, overactive mind may develop involving the constant need to suppress any impulsivity or spontaneity arising from the child's private world. In addition, he or she will need to stay vigilant as they survey the emotional landscape in order to enact compliant behavior and attitudes.

Another influential observer of very young humans was Margaret Mahler.[167] After the initial weeks following the child's birth, the baby begins to embark on a journey toward becoming, in a way, his or her own person. Mahler labeled this a process of "separation—individuation" as development proceeds from the original undifferentiated

---

[166] Ibid.

[167] Margaret Mahler, "On The First Three Sub Phases Of The Separation-Individuation Process." In *Essential Papers on Object Relations* (Peter Buckley, Ed.) (New York: New York University press, 1986).

"normal—symbiotic" phase. The first sub-phase of separation-individuation is called "hatching" in which the child becomes increasingly aware of her surroundings. In the following months, the little one progresses from crawling to walking and discovers the power of locomotion in the sub-phase termed "practicing." Both excitement and fear invade the child's life as she experiments with new powers to distance from her mother and that warm and protective nest. Somewhere around fifteen to sixteen months, the child realizes that the world is big and can be dangerous. In the "rapprochement" phase, she now becomes more tentative and frequently turns back toward mother. She continues her exploration of the world and her own powers but in a more careful cadence. This is a period of slow stutter-step growth with continual checking back for refueling and encouragement. In other words, as children separate from their mother, they continue to remain attached to her.

In her book on character pathology, Althea Horner concurs with other observers that early positive experience with the mother is the *sine qua non* of healthy personality development.

> The self develops within the context of the maternal matrix, and the primary mothering person is viewed as the mediator of organization. The consistent and predictable presence of the good-enough mother throughout the early months of life serves to tie the infant's universe of experience together in a particular way. First of all, she prevents the traumatic emotional states that overwhelm the ego and impede organization. Then, it is through her that the body, impulse, feeling, action and eventually thought become organized as part of the self and integrated not only with one another, but also with external reality of which she is representative... When early development within

the maternal matrix goes well, the outcome is the achievement of a cohesive, reality-related, object-related self.[168]

This solid relational footing then fosters continual differentiation and separation as the child gradually internalizes maternal functions of care. British analyst Christopher Bollas fleshes out for us this idea of internalizing maternal functions. Not only does the baby depend on the mother for survival, but her very attitude toward the child is of crucial importance. "Her way of holding the infant, of responding to his gestures, of selecting objects, and of perceiving the infant's internal needs, constitutes her contribution to the infant-mother culture."[169]

In these rituals of attention—in taking him out of the crib, sitting him on her lap, smiling and feeding him—the mother builds an inner world of cumulative experience. Borrowing from Winnicott and Edith Jacobson's observations, Bollas describes this process as "symbiotic relating." A preverbal, existential "knowing" emerges from the rhythms of care in which the mother is experienced as a "process of transformation." In other words, the mother day by day actually transforms the child's world. She is experienced as a "transformative object." In distress, the young one cries, the mother appears and resolves the issue and all is well. In stillness, the baby coos or smiles or otherwise engages the mother. She in turn responds with openness and interest and so the child's "own emergent ego capacities—of motility, perception, and integration" are affirmed. An "idiom of care" is thus internalized as essential to the survival and the growth of the self. This

---

[168] *The Primacy of Structure: Psychotherapy of Underlying Character Pathology* (Northvale, NJ: Jason Aronson, 1990), 30.
[169] *The Shadow of The Object: Psychoanalysis of the Unthought Known* (New York: Columbia University press, 1987), 13.

internal relational map will affect all future relationships or, as Bollas puts it, "Ego structure is the trace of relationship."[170]

Finally, we consider Daniel Stern. His influential study *The Interpersonal World of the Infant* introduced in 1985 the concept of "RIGS" or "representations of an interaction that have been generalized."[171] Since then he has elaborated the concept with the term, "schema." This idea captures "what it is like to 'be-with-another-in-a-certain-way.'" Schemas include perceptions, images, feelings, thoughts, motivations and actions. To help us understand how early schemas are developed and how they influence consequent behavior, Stern offers the example of a depressed mother.

Most depressed mothers try not to let their feelings color their relationship with their infant. Nevertheless, they often present a face that is expressionless. They tend to avoid eye contact. This lack of animation and under-responsiveness evokes a kind of behavioral deflation or micro-depression in the infant. Such a response to the mother's failure to engage becomes associated with or triggered by the child's attempts to engage her. With sufficient repetition, this experience may become encoded as a complex schema that is re-enacted throughout the person's lifetime. We know that mothers who struggle with depression do at times respond positively. It would not be uncommon then for a little boy to learn that, on occasion, he *could* reanimate mother. By persistent attempts to make funny sounds or a funny face, he discovers that his mother might also laugh and be attentive—for at least a little while. As a young man, he may very well find himself drawn to women who at first appear distant and unavailable. Having learned the role of charmer or funny guy, he pursues her and finally wins her attention. Her laughter brings a short-lived exhilaration followed once again by a kind of empty loneliness.

---

[170] Ibid., 50.

[171] *The Interpersonal World of The Infant: A View from Psychoanalysis and Developmental Psychology* (New York: Basic Books, 1985).

In recent years, researchers have increasingly linked mental health with attachment theory. Attachment studies with infants and young children indicate that children become attached to the caregiver in several ways. These ways powerfully determine future emotional and behavioral reaction patterns. By the end of the first year of life, researchers have been able to discern that perhaps 60 percent of children have achieved a secure attachment to their mothers, whereas the remaining kids hold an anxious avoidant, anxious ambivalent or in the worst case, disorganized sense of attachment.[172]

Hopefully, at this point we have established the fact of the inviolable primacy of the mother in the establishment of the personality. From the outset, the human self is a self-with-others—a self *vis-à-vis* a significant other. Well before words appear, that most significant "other" is a female. As a child individuates a self away from that primal, undifferentiated fusion with the mother, he or she faces challenges and uncertainties by referencing back to its earliest experiences, held in "implicit memory." Inevitably, preverbal questions such as, "Am I safe? Am I loved?" are linked to the quality of early maternal care. [173]

---

[172] For a summary of the research see, *Sonkin, Daniel (2005)*. "Attachment Theory and Psychotherapy." *The California Therapist, Vol 17, #1, 68-77.*

[173] Recent neuroscience helps us better understand the process of memory. We consider two types of memory – explicit and implicit memory. Explicit memory is a type of memory involves the recalling events, data or facts.

Implicit memory is a form of memory that includes a number of components including: cognitions, emotions, behaviors, perceptions, mental models, bodily sensations, or skill sets. Implicit memory does not require conscious attention for it to have impact. During the first two years of life, most learning occurs through implicit processes. Many attachment-related memories are implicit. When we experience implicit attachment memories, there is just a sense of knowing or simply responding. These implicit memories are often activated by current events that fit a particular emotionally loaded theme. Take for example, John, who experienced much rejection from his alcoholic mother. When his wife announces she is going out with her girlfriends, he becomes sullen and withdrawn. She asks him what's wrong. He says, "Nothing." They argue, it escalates and she leaves angry and hurt. He himself is bewildered, not sure why he felt threatened and offended at her wish to leave for a few hours.

In summary then, the perhaps inconvenient truth is that in the foundational months and early years of a child's life, it is the mother who wields the most power to shape the emerging self and to help her children answer the core questions of their existence in affirmative ways.[174] What seems to go largely unrecognized in a culture saturated with equity indignation, is that the maternal bond to children represents *power*. This is the massive power to shape the core of a person for an entire life. Does this mean that if you have problems, just blame your mother? Of course not. As we grow, we continue to make choices. Nevertheless, as clinicians who work with troubled people understand, the most severe psychopathologies typically originate in very early childhood.[175] A psychotic or severely drug-addicted mother cannot help but provide inconsistent if not abusive attention. Conversely, a loving and available mother is more likely to launch a secure child into the world.

The influence continues

This ability to shape and influence begins with the power of life or death. She alone decides whether the child in her womb will come to full term. She decides to what degree she will invest her life in her child. This power also implies obligation and responsibility. As we have seen, each one of us on this planet faces the temptation to resist the boundaries that may limit the possibilities we envision for our lives. Such limitations may come directly from the word of God or indirectly experienced as natural order. I would posit that the degree to

---

[174] Of course, other caretakers such as nannies, fathers and aunties can be sources of bonding and attachment. However, it is the mother's voice and her body and the breast of her body to which the baby is most naturally and primarily attached.

[175] Siegel, Daniel (2012) *Interpersonal Neurobiology and Clinical Application of the Adult Attachment Interview.* Mindsight Institute, Mind Your Brain, Inc.

which a mother or potential mother understands that she holds within her body the potential to birth and launch new human beings and accepts her primacy in caretaking, to that degree her children will grow as secure and confident individuals. As she accepts and enjoys her role as the center of the world for her family, her daughter is far more likely to identify with her and embrace her own value as a female. Conversely, should her mother appear to love her job as much as her children, this daughter will inevitably both question her own value as an object of her mother's love as well as doubt the importance of mothering *per se*.

It is just as obvious that the boy's feelings about himself will on a most fundamental level be shaped by his sense of his mother's comfort in her maternal role. Again, if she is at home with her responsibility as life-giver and person-shaper, this will go well for his emerging masculine self. Deriving her own satisfaction from her ability to nurture and launch this boy, she has no experience of "penis envy" or to intrude in her son's bonding with his father. She lets them play catch in the backyard or mow the lawn together without pressure to show them that she too can throw and catch a ball. Instead, she experiences vicarious pride in his emerging masculinity. She knows that her value as life-giver is unique and that her son will never possess that capacity. She is sympathetic to his need to push away from her. She laughs when he acts silly knowing that it is still her attention that he craves. She knows better than to take offense when he disdainfully scoffs at frilly feminine things. On some level, she understands the difference between her own primary worth and any achieved or artificial worth that he will find in life. She understands that her son, as is true with her own husband, will have to work to attain a different kind of self-esteem. This is the fluctuating worth that is based on tenuous talents, occasional achievements, or just the luck of the draw. She also knows that it is she who possesses the greatest power to affirm and bless his manhood.

Launching heroes

Jungian analyst Irene de Castillejo writes eloquently about the feminine soul in relation to the man's ego which "…is far less strong than we like to think." She describes the perennial struggle "…of the son to break free of the Great Mother."[176] In doing so, he embarks on a great quest. To become somebody, to really be somebody of value. To be a hero.

> Heroes they *must* be. Without some form of heroism, a man hardly feels himself to be a man. It is the hero in man that makes him really male…Our delinquents… are the failed heroes—the ones who tried and couldn't find the right channel. Better rob a train than be a nobody. Better prove one's prowess in a gang war than remain an anonymous fool.[177]

And the woman is invited to help him become that hero.

> Many women have forgotten, in the modern emphasis on a career and economic independence, that woman has a role to play towards man which is inherent in her nature… Her role is still, as it always has been, to be a mediator to man of his own creative inspirations, a channel whereby the riches of the unconscious flow to him more easily than if she were not there.[178]

Although women are now successful in man's world, many have not understood that the male needs her affirmation and, in a way, can hardly stand alone much less stand strong. They have forgotten

---

[176] Irene Claremont de Castillejo, *Knowing Woman: A Feminine Psychology*, C.G. Jung Foundation, 1973, 47.

[177] Ibid., 46.

[178] Ibid., 54-55.

… how precarious men feel, and how much the particular man needs his woman to believe in him and to
welcome his vision with as much warmth and tender-
ness as she accepts his child… He looks to her for
recognition of his unique personalness… He needs to
be believed in, and his work, whether she understands
it or not, to be given full value.[179]

In her pursuit of full equality in the "man's world," the
woman has also forgotten what her own subconscious tells
her. That her femininity is analogous to the parable of the
wise virgins who kept their oil ready waiting for the coming of
the bridegroom. This is a "readiness for relationship."

While she has made so many advances into the wider
world of work—the world that used to be a man's
world—she has somehow failed to express her own
deepest self… Schools and colleges have grown up
throughout the centuries to meet the needs of growing
boys, and girls have fitted themselves into what was
already there. They have accepted without question
the masculine overvaluation of the thinking function
and of physical prowess. Girls have adopted the ability
to do mathematics as the test of intelligence and the
capacity for games as a criterion of bodily perfec-
tion. Many an inferiority complex stems from these
mistakes. … Her achievement of becoming a creative
being in her own right and a factor of importance in
the economic world, is of little avail if she deprives
man of her fundamental role of helping him to find
himself. Her task is twofold. If she fails to have oil
always ready in her lamp for the actual man, she fails
him in the essential role he asks of her. But it is more

---

[179] Ibid., 56.

than this. The oil is her feminine spirituality, the totality of her own psyche. It expresses an attitude of spiritual waiting, and tending, and readiness for the meeting with its opposite which is a prerequisite for inner wholeness. ... But if she can hold the oil ready within the lamp, then, when the masculine spark comes, there burns a flame which is alive, and lights our human world. This flame is love. Love is wholly beyond us. It alights upon us and illumines our lives *only* when the opposites meet.[180]

According to de Castillejo, Western women, in mimicking the masculine inclination to separate, discover, and initiate things for their own sake, have lost their cosmic connection and awareness of growing life. In doing so, they have "upset the necessary balance between the opposite poles."

Staci Eldredge agrees:

True femininity arouses true masculinity. Think about it—all those heroes in all those tales play the hero *because* there is a woman in his life, a true Beauty who is his inspiration. It's that simple and that profound. True femininity calls forth true masculinity. We awaken it, arouse it in a way that nothing else on earth is close to.[181]

A question of gender worth

De Castillejo and Eldredge understand that on the deepest level, the feminine soul is relational; her power to affirm finds itself finally in relation to the masculine. From birth onward, she is indispensable. As the being from whom both sexes

---

[180] Ibid., 56-57.
[181] John and Staci Eldredge, *Captivating: Unveiling the Mystery of a Woman's Soul* (Nashville: Thomas Nelson, 2005), 149.

emerge, her significance is, to borrow Gilder's term, "unimpeachable."[182] She holds this value close.

It is the message of the body itself, whether she bears a child or not. Her feminine worth is certain and corresponds to her calling to relationship, a particular kind of relationship—one that gives and nurtures life. Every day, her larger hips and breasts remind her of a capacity and calling that is profoundly social.

This value is both a calling and a limit, a high identity and a boundary. She is mother of all life yet she is not totally free, but bound to the rhythms of her biology. Every month, she is reminded of a purpose she may or may not wish to embrace.

In contrast to the female, the calling and worth of a man is invariably more tenuous. While he is not so bound by his body, so too, is the meaning of his life less bound. Horner writes that "the tasks of male development are far more formidable than those of female development."[183] Following earlier observers, she asserts:

> The boy must separate himself from the primary attachment to, and thus identification with, the primary female mothering object. He must disidentify himself from her and counter identify with his father to establish and secure his male gender identity.[184]

Ultimately, he is left with a burden and a question. "What can I give to the woman who has given life to me?"

In summary, we have determined that the source and center of the physical and psychological world of both boys and girls

---

[182] George Gilder, *Men and Marriage* (Gretna: Pelican Publishing Company, 1986), fifth printing, 2008.

[183] Horner, 116.

[184] Ibid., 116; see also R. Greenson (1968) "Disidentifying from mother: It's special importance for the boy." In *Explorations in Psychoanalysis,* 305 – 312. New York: International Universities Press.

is their mother. Her very body reminds her of this status and calling. Her primary role in the birth and launching of the self is self-evident: a simple, common knowledge before the onslaught of identity politics and groupthink. This status and calling is a personal one, reflecting the nature of a personal and relational God. We also note the more tenuous status of the male in the cycle of life. In God's original scheme, might he be a counterpart with equal value in the launching of persons?

CHAPTER 7

Belonging Together and the Primacy of Man

"Love your wives, just as Christ loved the church and gave himself up for her." —Ephesians 5:25

I'm mowing the lawn. As sweat drips down my neck, I remember that I do not like to mow the lawn. I mowed neighbors' lawns as a kid, but that was a long time ago. Furthermore, it is early Spring and, in my mind, weekly mowing is not yet indicated. As I nurture my annoyance, I also imagine a potential smile from the other one in the house who happens to care about such things more than I. Yes, I had other things planned for this morning, but there is something that feels right in making her happy. Picturing her as pleased, my resentment vanishes.

A little bit of sweat to make my wife happy. Is that my role? Maybe. Or better yet, how about real sacrifice? In 2008, Liam Neeson starred in *Taken,* a gritty movie about a former CIA operative who kills with surgical precision and many times risks his life. Why? To rescue his teenage daughter who had been abducted on a trip to Paris. The movie earned 220 million dollars and spawned two sequels. The total earnings? 929 million. In a similar vein, we see amazing killing skill and fearless self-sacrifice in Denzel Washington's two wildly popular *Equalizer* movies. Could these kinds of stories scratch a powerful itch?

As described in the last chapter, the place and function of the woman is one of implicit and unimpeachable value.

Whether the milk from her breast or the milk of kindness from her spirit, she is the source from which every self emerges. And, to which every male self would return. But how is he to return? Is there a special calling—a purposive entelechy by which he can bring some value commensurate to the life and personal sponsorship the female has given him?

The question before us, as anthropologist Margaret Mead noted, has been an issue in every community, viz., where does the male fit? After all, his contribution to the next generation, when considering the raw physicality of the matter, is limited to a matter of minutes. With the help of the local clinic, his participation can be completely anonymous. We wonder, beyond this brief act of insemination, is there any essential value he brings to the woman? She has her job to feed the children and the 911 call to protect her from burglars. What exactly is he good for? Does he, too, have a place and a purpose?

The shrinking male

In the not-too-distant past, manhood was associated with leadership. As the number of female governors, judges, and police chiefs has escalated, assumptions that men are to be the natural leaders have disappeared along with the cassette tape. So, is this a good thing? In the first chapter, we sat in on Mr. Pauling's high school class and watched the boys shrug as the girls dominated student council elections. Why do they do that? And why do they get most of the Ds and Fs and fail to pursue higher education the way the girls do? We also ask, "How is it that so many young men are so immature?" [185]

Unfortunately, immaturity and/or passivity are not the only problems with men. I can't count the times wives and

---

[185] See Kay Hymowitz, *Manning Up: How the Rise of Women Has Turned Men into Boys* (New York: Basic Books, 2011).

girlfriends have cried in my office because their lives have been devastated by husbands or fathers who should have behaved with honor. Too many report being molested as children. Too many must battle to make ends meet because the fellow in their lives is doing drugs or drinking away his paycheck. And then there are the violent ones, the ones who throw things and beat their girlfriends and wives. To hear these stories is to witness a failure of masculinity.

Whether the scene is one of violence or a simple refusal to show up, the male in the third decade of the Twenty-first Century is struggling. Christina Hoff Sommers traces current trends that boys have fallen far behind girls in education and earning power. She points to the impact of early feminist writers such as Nancy Chodorow who argued that traditional sex roles favored male domination. Not understanding the profound differences between the sexes, Chodorow equated the suppression of opportunities for women with traditions that relegated to women the care of infants and children. She also believed that traditional sex roles kept boys from developing their nurturing capacity. Sommers writes:

> Chodorow's call for the transformation of the patri-archal sex/gender system and her condemnation of the "capitalist world of work" do not resonate today as they did in the 1970s. Her theories of child development and construction of gender are dated. The female propensity for nurture appears to be more than an artifact of culture. The more we learn about the power of hormones to shape behavior, the harder it becomes to think of sex differences the way Chodorow thought of them.[186]

---

[186] *The War Against Boys*, 117.

Carol Gilligan was another powerful agitator for change. She echoed Chodorow's belief that boys needed to be set free from the demand to be tough and competitive. Masculine stereotypes impeded their development. Presumably, if they were more like their mothers and sisters, they would become less bellicose, patriarchal, capitalist, and war mongering. The data, however, overwhelmingly point to fatherless homes as the problem, not masculine sex roles.[187]

Parallel to the call for males to give up historically masculine inclinations, charges were leveled against the school system. The girls were shortchanged. Mary Pipher's *Reviving Ophelia* (1994) won wide recognition portraying girls as disadvantaged, silenced, and basically victims of oppressive male culture. Ironically, not only did these claims lack evidence, the opposite proved true. There was no bias against girls and the girls were flourishing in school.[188] Nevertheless, a broad-based campaign for gender equality grew deep roots and continues in full force today. Sommers blames the disingenuous yet impressive power of the feminist lobby, represented by such organizations as the American Association of University Women. Such groups appear to be highly invested in maintaining the notion that girls are victims of sexism while implying that being a boy is some kind of social disease. Sommers calls for changes in school policy to address the different learning style of boys while appealing to feminists to understand that if boys are in trouble, this cannot be good for girls.

Changes in educational policy are certainly important, for example, the call for single sex learning championed by Leonard Sax and others. However, the issues transcend school policy. A more insidious and pervasive ethos of division and

---

[187] "Effects of Fatherlessness on Children's development," https://downloads. frc.org/EF/EF14K18.pdf, accessed May 5, 2020. See also, Sommers, "The War Against Boys" *Atlantic Monthly*, May, 2000.
[188] Ibid.

derision has left the young male without a place in the family. Or vital sense of purpose to the world at large. Why have so many young men not stepped up to the plate? In a word, a culture dominated by sexual license and liberal social-constructionist views of gender has left him without significance. And without guidance. While a girl holds within her body and an organic awareness that she carries the capacity to bring life, a boy lacks that grounding. And the twin juggernauts of sexual profligacy and feminism have robbed him of spiritual and historical pathways by which to find a corresponding significance. He no longer can count on culture to grant him status in her eyes as provider, protector, or leader. Certainly not as a hero. Nor is he expected to be wise or exhibit self-control. Watching Ed Bundy stick his hand down his pants as he stares stupidly at the TV, what is he to think? Does he chuckle as Homer Simpson is schooled by his little daughter, Lisa? Or does a quiet shame creep into his psyche? What image of masculinity grows in his mind? Maybe he's good for laughs. Perhaps so, but today, we find little in common discourse that offers him an honorable calling to which he *as a man* might aspire.

A vocation of love?

As we have considered the female's vital role in launching life, we also note that the driving force in all mothering is love. Her loving nature reflects our relational God. Ought not the man, equally designed to represent God on the earth, realize a vocation as relational? He, too, must find himself as he loses himself in loving and serving others. However, such a finding often seems more elusive for the male.

One might answer that need not be so. Perhaps, he needs to be set free from circumscribed gender expectations and just follow his heart. Be whoever and do whatever he wants. Unfortunately, some men have already chosen such a path.

Deadbeat dads. Fathers who quit their jobs and dwell in trailers to avoid paying child support. Or the twenty-five-year-old who lives in his parents' basement, works ten hours a week, and plays video games the rest of the time.[189] Of course, not all young men are so unmotivated and self-absorbed. Some do see themselves as relational, caring, and/or liberated from rigid sex roles. Nevertheless, as many frustrated "stay-at-home dads" discover, they come to the task from an inferior position. They are not the primary attachment figure, and they lack the softer voice, softer body, and patience of a mother. Moreover, a bottle is not the same as a breast. Furthermore, their ability to attune to a child's needs rarely matches her sensitivity and intuition.

How, then, is a man to live out his calling as God's loving representative? Furthermore, what role and self-understanding will bind him to the family? Such a role must be significant. In times of danger, it might be physical. (Honey, there's a noise at the front door!) In the past everyday world of survival, he brought home the bacon. Yet, even in traditional societies, these roles wax and wane. Their tentative quality becomes evident in times of accident or disability. Ultimately, the purpose of a man toward a woman and family must hold strong, permanent, and transcendent value. And convey a relational telos, a calling to love. We find such a vocation and status in the symbolic world. A spiritual directive offering meaning and purpose that is both commensurate to the value of the woman and meets her actual needs. Societies that enjoy stability, as we shall see in the chapters ahead, understand this necessity.

The ultimate test of any male/female relationship model or any sex role definition must never be about some ideal of

---

[189] "Half of male gamers age 18-25 would quit their job if they could support themselves as a professional gamer." In "The State of Online Gaming" *Limelight Networks*, https://www.limelight.com/resources/white-paper/state-of-online-gaming-2018/

demonstrable equality. The sexes are not equal in the sense that they are not the same. Such an ideal seems only to invite an endless swirl of envy, comparison, and competition. The real test must circle the question of blessing. Does the sexual modality foster mutual benefit? Defining sex never in terms of one gender apart from the other, the Bible presents just such a model.

The mystery of co-humanity

Like the woman, the man was never designed for self-centered ends. He was to be paired with a helpmate and was to husband her. Or, as the apostle Paul sums it up, he is to "love her as Christ loves the church and gave himself up for her" (Ephesians 5). Indeed, do we not find here a vital role for the male of the species? A calling to give of oneself, even in a sacrificial way. In this love, Paul also says, he "loves himself." But how does one love himself by loving another?

To answer, we look back to the beginning. At the origin, human life is not defined in static or individualistic terms. We do not properly exist as individual selves. We coexist. Karl Barth suggests the term "co-humanity." In the creation account, "we cannot say man without having to say male or female and also male and female. Man exists in this differentiation, in this duality."[190] Unlike the contrast between races or between child and parent or young and old, the sexual differentiation is the only structural differentiation in the life of living creatures. All other distinctions—bright or dull, strong or weak—are secondary to personhood and all other differentiations are relative. However, in every place and every experience, one is either male or female. There is no such thing as abstract humanity apart from concrete existence as male or

---

[190] *Church Dogmatics*, vol. 3, 286.

female. This "coexistence of man and woman is the original and proper form of this humanity."[191]

Theologian Helmut Thielicke agrees:

> The differentiation of the sexes is so constitutive of humanity that, first, it appears as a primeval order (Genesis 1:27; 2:18 ff) and endures as a constant despite its deprivation in the Fall (Genesis 3:16), and second, that to it is attributed symbolic value for the fundamental structure of all human existence... The creation of the woman from Adam's rib (Gen. 2:21ff.) parabolically suggests this constitutive character of the fact that man and woman belong together.[192]

In other words, the original relational template is sexual. As already noted, "The solitary Adam is not yet 'man'; he is still not the fulfillment of the creation of man."[193] Adam cannot fulfill or complete himself. Only the gift of the "other" brought completion. Therefore, loving Eve would only flow with loving himself.

Working together

Not only were the man and woman designed to love and fulfill each other, but they were also called to work together.

> Together they were given the mandate to populate and subdue the earth (Genesis 1:28). Male and female, different but "one flesh" designed to operate

---

191 Ibid., 292.
192 Thielicke, 3-4.
193 Ibid., 4.

in complementarity, harmony, and mutual benefit. A polarity of reciprocity.[194]

Biblically, there seem to be two kinds of activity that express God's work—two kinds of power, the power to initiate and the power to affirm. These essential powers can be discerned within the Trinity itself. God the Father ordains while God the Son sub-ordains.[195] Anderson somewhat awkwardly describes these as "the will to be" and "being willing."[196] God the Father enacts his divine power as he creates, as he wills into existence. God the Son, affirms this initiative. In his subordinate capacity, the Son expresses "the power of unfailing love, even as obedience unto death on the cross" (Phil. 2:8).[197] Each expression of God's love reveals his sovereignty. "The 'self-emptying' of Jesus is not an emptying of sovereignty but a manifestation of the sovereign God in reconciling the world to himself."[198]

The first chapters of Genesis tell of God's power of initiative, a mode of vision and creation. He asserts physical power and makes things happen. Then, in the action of creating beings like himself, he relinquishes total control. In creating man, he fashions beings who are in some mysterious way "like himself." He gives *them* power—the capacity to think, to reflect and to act.

God brings the animals to Adam to "see what he would name them." This is God waiting, ready to affirm. This is

---

[194] Michael Kuiper, "Male and Female Together: What the Ancients Understood," *The Human Life Review*, Fall, 2019.

[195] We think of the Holy Spirit as the active force, the immanent presence of God working out the will of God. None is inferior to the other, but the activity of each can be differentiated.

[196] *On Being Human*, 115.

[197] Ibid.

[198] Ibid. Anderson argues that the subordination of the Son represents an aspect of God's nature prior to the incarnation and thus remains an ontological reality, not a temporary modality designed only for the purpose of salvation.

God curious, expectant... enjoying Adam as he discovers his nascent powers. Sidestepping the charge of anthropomorphizing, can we not perceive a real relationship between Creator and creature? Like God, Adam is a real self, no simple pawn or robot. Of course, risk is involved. A free being may go his own way or turn away altogether. God in some mysterious way is not only not offended by Adam's ability to initiate, but is enriched (see Psalm 37:23). He is supportive. In a sense, he makes himself subordinate to Adam (What he called them, that was their name.). As other passages indicate, God functions as helper (*ezer*) (e.g., Ex. 18:14; Deut. 33:7). This is the power of affirmation. To help, to nurture. Before his ascension, Jesus promised to send another "helper," the Holy Spirit (John 14:16). A Spirit, incidentally, of immense power.

These two actions of love do not contradict each other. God leads and initiates. He also waits and watches, ready to celebrate, affirm or help. There is no conflict in this kind of agape love. These powers complement each other in a dynamic of purposeful, united creativity.

Imaging the Creator, humans come alive not in a self-contained fashion but in action toward each other, caring for and open to the influence of another who is different. Paul urges the Ephesian church to "submit to one another" (Eph. 5:21) and the Galatian church to "bear one another's burdens" (Gal. 6:2). Jesus himself declared that he had come "not to be served but to serve" (Mark 10:45). Here is, in James Olthuis's words, an "economy of love."[199]

> Here the movement of the other to myself is coincident
> with a simultaneous and voluntary movement of myself
> to the other. The desire of each evokes the desire of the
> other: mutual recognition, mutual yielding/receiving,

---

[199] *Knowing Other-wise: A Philosophy at the Threshold of Spirituality* (New York: Fordham University Press, 1997).

mutual delighting, mutual empowering. This is the oscillating rhythm of giving and receiving, the dance of identity and intimacy called love. In giving to the other, I, paradoxically, am being received, am enlarged and enhanced … In receiving the other, I expand, and, paradoxically, through my receiving, give.[200]

Sexual reciprocity represents the greatest possibility for such mutuality. Real intimacy entails a real meeting, not simply with those like yourself or who are extensions of yourself, but an encounter with one who is *essentially different.* Difference invites delight, the possibility of surprise—of enrichment beyond one's self-enclosed possibilities. Anderson writes that the fulfillment of personhood through sexual complementarity follows God's own nature.

As an intrinsic and essential differentiation, each gender is only finally able to fulfill itself in its potential in relation to the other. This relation is not fixed in the sense in which we declare that a man is thus and thus and only thus. Nor is it fixed in the sense that every man must relate to every woman in any particular way. Nevertheless the "concept of a hierarchical modality" is clearly discerned in the doctrine of the Trinity as well as in the New Testament teaching on headship and submission.[201]

In some way—perhaps deliberately unspecified—the man carries a different, more active role toward the woman, who is more receptive, affirming. In contrast, a symmetrical or partnership model has come to dominate Western attitudes. This view maintains that roles ought to be interchangeable, that persons should be free to be themselves, not cast into some pre-formed or archaic set of behavioral prescriptions. This view, wishing to honor individual distinctions, essentially

---

[200] Ibid.,146.
[201] Anderson,118.

denies sexual distinctions. This model seems not to consider a possible correspondence between the dynamics within the godhead and the interplay between the sexes. Any genital differentiation is merely incidental—of little consequence where it really matters: the pursuit of the true self. Politically correct, but not very sexy. As Mark Regnerus concludes from data in the *Archives of Sexual Behavior*, marriages have not only declined, but since the nineties, Americans are having much less sex. He concludes, "Men and women are not attracted to sameness, but to difference. We long for what is missing in ourselves. Needing each other makes us want each other."[202]

Although sex roles are not to be absolutized, an ordered equality emerges within the Trinity itself; therefore, ought not the ultimate in some way inform the provisional?

Working together requires a leader

I didn't think I was driving in an unsafe manner. The motorcycle cop who pulled me over for going forty-two in a twenty-five mph zone had a different view. He explained that the neighbors were concerned for their children and had complained of speeders. Hence, he had been posted—hiding I would say—on the side of the road. I did not appreciate the fine, but have driven more slowly ever since. Clearly, in the wake of the riots and cries of "black lives matter!" not all encounters with police have produced such salubrious outcomes. Yet, authority has always been a necessary component of societal order and an intrinsic order in creation itself.

Several markers help us recognize legitimate authority. The first of these is vigilance. The police officer carefully monitors the street for problems. Further, he carries the burden of responsibility. He must act should he perceive illegal activity. In his mandate to protect others, such action might incur risk.

---

[202] *First Things*, October, 2017.

He also must possess knowledge of the law and, as his sidearm indicates, he carries the power to enforce it.

Scripture teaches that the man is to be the head in the home, the authority.[203] Piper and Grudem unpack the passages found in Genesis, Ephesians, Colossians, 1 Peter, Titus, and 1 Timothy. A definition of headship emerges as a calling and obligation for men to grow into a mature masculinity "…a sense of benevolent responsibility to lead, to provide for and protect women in ways appropriate to a man's different relationships."[204] As editors of the 572 page scholarly study calling for a "recovery of biblical manhood and womanhood," Piper and Grudem are troubled by what they discern as a breakdown of divine order between the sexes. They write:

> We are concerned not merely with the behavioral roles of men and women but also with the underlying nature of manhood and womanhood themselves. Biblical truth and clarity in this matter are important because error and confusion over sexual identity leads to: (1) marriage patterns that do not portray the relationship between Christ and the church (Ephesians 5:31-32); (2) parenting practices that do not train boys to be masculine or girls to be feminine; (3) homosexual tendencies and increasing attempts to justify homosexual alliances; (4) patterns of un-biblical female leadership in the church that reflect and promote the confusion over the true meaning of manhood and womanhood… We believe that what is at stake in human sexuality is the very fabric of life as God wills it

---

[203] Wayne Grudem, "The meaning of *kephale* ('head'): A response to recent studies." In eds. John Piper and Wayne Grudem, *Recovering Biblical Manhood and Womanhood: A Response to Evangelical Feminism,* (Wheaton: Crossway, 2006).

[204] Ibid., 36.

to be for the holiness of his people and further saving mission to the world.[205]

In this "saving mission," the recovery of the biblical status of men is pivotal. But one wonders: Can there be any proposition more provocative than the notion that the male of the species is designed to be the leader?

Is "headship" a useful term?

At this point, it is important to acknowledge the weight of emotional and ideological resistance we find today against the concept of male leadership. In God's design, however, hierarchies of authority have nothing to do with value or advantage. Only in a fallen world does there exist the assumption that authority or power is to be craved. We should also acknowledge a distinction between essential and absolute. While the functions of leader and follower are essential elements in the union of two persons, if they were fixed in an absolute way, why would Jesus declare there would be no marriage in heaven? Further, in the question of ultimate destiny, "there is no more Jew nor Greek, slave nor free, male nor female" (Galatians 3:28). Paul here does not deny differences but insists they are of no consequence where it really matters: as heirs of the Kingdom of God.[206]

But what about the question of competence? "Bennie can't run, fight, or count without using his fingers. So, let's make him the captain!" We might be accused of such logic were we only trying to answer Margaret Mead's question as to what to do with the males. As if merit or competence should

---

[205] Ibid., 35.

[206] See Michelle Lee-Barnwell, *Neither Complementarian nor Egalitarian* (Grand Rapids: Baker Academic, 2016). She notes, "… The passage does not speak of equality as much as unity, of being 'one.' Jew and Greek, slave and free, male and female are not 'isos,' 'equal,' but 'heis,' one" (p 86).

be irrelevant! Or we could agree with Steven Goldberg (*The Inevitability of Patriarchy, Why Men Rule*) and chalk it up to a biological determinism that drives men toward ascendant roles. Or perhaps we should follow the advice of King Ahasuarus in the book of Esther and issue a decree throughout the land that the husband be master in the home? Perhaps *design* is a better answer.

Engineers refer to the term "functional coherence" when designing systems to work together. Biblically, the man and woman bless each other in different ways. Ray Ortlund, Jr. argues that the first three chapters of Genesis "lay the very foundation of Biblical manhood and womanhood."[207] In these chapters, two propositions clearly emerge. The first is that both sexes bear God's image equally. The second is that in their union as "one flesh," the man is granted headship, a "primary responsibility to lead the partnership in a God-glorifying direction."[208] This second proposition rankles feminists who seem to assume that headship equals domination or privilege. Redemption in Christ, they argue, frees the woman from any subordinate status imposed on her after the Fall. In response, Ortlund notes that this order was established before sin:

> God did *not* name the human race "woman"... He called us "man," which anticipates the male headship brought out clearly in chapter two, just as "male and female" in verse 27 foreshadows marriage in chapter two.[209]

That the humans are both designated as "man" (*adam*, in Hebrew), is perhaps not a very convincing stand-alone

---

[207] Piper and Grudem, "Male-female inequality and male headship: Genesis 1 – 3. p 95."
[208] Ibid.
[209] Ibid., 98.

argument for masculine primacy. However, just as the Israelites were "chosen" not because of any innate superiority or capriciousness of the Creator, but for a larger purpose (see Genesis 12), so too, men are to be the authority for purposes *well beyond the orbit of their own inclinations*. John Piper summarizes headship in this way: "Headship is the divine calling of a husband to take primary responsibility for Christ-like servant leadership, protection, and provision in the home."[210]

Psychologist Larry Crabb agrees that God has created us to reflect his relational nature in particular ways. "Relational masculinity" is the power to make a difference in someone's soul for God's glory.[211] Crabb describes the man as moving into the world, penetrating so as to make a difference. He cites evidence that the Hebrew word for male (*zakar*) carries the meaning of remembering and acting—as if to make an impact, to leave a mark. Like God at the creation, Adam was to move and speak into the void of the world. We find the first example of this calling in Genesis 2:19 where God gives Adam the responsibility to name the living creatures. Eve was not yet created. Crabb reminds us that,

> Like God, man was called to speak into darkness, to move into the confusion of a completely unnamed kingdom of animals, and to assign everyone a name. In ancient Near Eastern culture, to name something implied the authority to define its character, to give shape to its nature, to fill a void with something that came out of the one who gave the name.
>
> Could it be that God intended men to behave like him by courageously moving into whatever spheres

---

[210] Manhood, Womanhood, and the Freedom to Minister | Desiring God, June, 1989.

[211] *Fully Alive: A Biblical Vision of Gender That Frees Men and Women To Live Beyond Stereotypes* (Ada, MI.: Baker Publishing), 2014.

of mystery they encounter and speaking with imagination and life-giving power into the confusion they face?[212]

Adam was also to remember the command of God not to eat of the forbidden tree. And to act on that knowledge. But he was silent. He failed to speak the word of God to the serpent or to Eve. Remaining passive, he did not represent the truth he was given and failed to protect his wife from being deceived. "His disobedience did not begin with his eating but with his silence."[213]

In summary, we can abstract from our admittedly cloudy understanding of the Trinity two primary forms of self-expression, namely, that of initiative and response. Or, if you will, leader and helper. Each function carries the original purpose of responsibility to God and to the opposite sex. Each function in its original intention reflects a unity of ontological value and equally represents the very nature of God. Yet, in the Twenty-first Century as in every age since the Fall, we find ourselves far from the Origin. We live with two problems, both ancient and current—the male problem and the female problem.

The masculine dilemma

> *Masculinity is not something given to you,*
> *but something you gain.* —Norman Mailer

God designed the sexes to function as one. They belong together. The problem for the boy is that he must leave his primary attachment to the female in order to come back to

---

[212] *The Silence of Adam: Becoming Men of Courage in a World of Chaos* (Grand Rapids: Zondervan Publishing House, 1995), 65.
[213] Ibid., 97.

her as a man. He must bring to her some strength, some commodity that would complete and fulfill her. Here is the lurking question: How is he to find something so precious, so essential that might be commensurate to the life that she has given him?

Mark Batterson calls on young men to develop virtues. These include toughness, the desire to learn, willpower, true grit, vision, and moral courage.[214] Such character traits clearly aid a man's vocation of love. But love is difficult. Love requires action. Mature love is not static—but *ecstatic*, a dynamic pouring out of itself to another. Only God, however, possesses what philosophers call "aseity"—an existence of absolute self-sufficiency. God's love is self-generated, overflowing, and issues from his own being. But, a human must receive before he can give. Considering a future with a woman, the boy asks, "Who am I?" "What do I have to give?" "Where do I find it?" "How do I develop virtue?"

In his best seller, *Iron John,* Robert Bly analyzes a growing lassitude among men. Something is missing in the masculine soul. In contrast to the hard man of the fifties, beginning in the seventies, men have become soft, sensitive, and nice. Too nice. Something is missing, where to find it? In traditional societies, older men initiated boys, taught them the ways of the world, helped them become tough and wise. "In our culture there is no such movement. The boys in our culture have a continuing need for initiation into male spirit, but old men in general don't offer it…"[215]

In a broadside against passivity, Bly plums the depths of the mythological tale about the journey of a boy prince as he discovers who he is as a man and potential king. A leader in the Men's Movement of the eighties, Bly deftly unpacks this Brothers Grimm story of how a young boy is bewitched

---

[214] *Play the Man: Becoming the Man God Created You to Be,* (Grand Rapids: Baker Books, 2017).

[215] *Iron John* (NY: Addison-Wesley, 1990), 14.

to follow Wild Man into the dark forest. There he is challenged, wounded, mentored, and finds courage. A fierce, warrior energy is awakened as he is initiated into knighthood and wins the heart of a princess. Bly sees no conflict between fierceness and wisdom, boldness and higher purpose.

Wild and wise

John Eldredge agrees that contemporary men are soft and lack confidence. In his best seller, *Wild at Heart,* Eldredge notes that many men have grown up with harsh, rejecting fathers or no male role model at all. Male mentoring is essential. Bly is right, men initiate men and without such, they tend to be lost. They know neither their strength nor their calling. They are more tame than wild. Timid, they fall prey to addictions. Self-conscious, they look to the woman for affirmation—as if to tell them who they are.

We agree with Eldredge's wife, Staci, that a woman arouses masculinity. But she is not the one to confer it. It is one thing for a man to fight for a woman or struggle to provide for her. But when he depends on her for validation, does he not fall into the same sin as Adam? Allowing Eve to take the place of God? Eldredge thinks so:

> Look at all art, poetry, music, drama devoted to the beautiful woman. Listen to the language men used to describe her. Watch the powerful obsession at work. What else can this be but worship? Men come into the world without the God who was our first deepest joy, our ecstasy. Aching for we know not what, we meet Eve's daughters and we are history.[216]

---

[216] *Wild at Heart,* 116.

A man needs a much bigger orbit than a woman. He needs a mission, a life purpose, and he needs to know his name. Only then is he fit for a woman, for only then does he have something to invite her into.... The masculine journey always takes a man away from the woman, in order that he may come back to her first with his questions answered.[217]

In the tale of Iron John, the boy must break from the feminine orbit. He must steal the key from under his mother's pillow to unlock the wild man from his cage. Could God be the ultimate Wild Man—the one who evokes mystery, danger? The one who beckons with dark purposes—adventures beyond meaningless and safe routines? Indeed, does Jesus not call men to radical departure? He certainly did not invite his disciples to a soft life, but to break away and follow him. To one, he said, "Foxes have dens and birds have nests, but the Son of Man has no place to lay his head" (Matthew 8:20). Shattering the objections of the man who first needed to bury his father, Jesus simply replied, "Follow me and let the dead bury their own dead." That was blunt, not very "sensitive." Where would Jesus lead them? The disciples soon find out. As Matthew records it, we next find them encountering a crazy, demon-possessed man. After that, they nearly drown in a life-threatening storm.

Jesus did not expect his men to become mature, bold, or wise at once. With sharp or gentle words, he trained them, tested them, and showed them how to wield the sword of the Word of God. Is this word not like a seed, that when planted, grows and bears fruit (Matthew 13)? We note with Eldredge that the man's body produces seed. To fertilize a woman, his organ must swell and hers must open. Could it be that when a boy is trained in the Word by godly men that

---

[217] Ibid., 114-115.

the seeds of fierce and wild wisdom grow within? Could it be that this Word, having first produced the fruit of Christ's own character, becomes also the seed by which to husband a wife, cultivating in her a life of fruitful blessing?

The feminine dilemma

Although the man is not to find his answer in the woman, he does need her help. But why should she help him? Is it not better to be the leader? To be first and not last? The Bible enjoins wives to be submissive to their husbands. *Submission.* The term itself is odious. It smells of fearfulness and weakness. It may evoke historical or personal stories of abuse. In a way, the notion of submissiveness is anathema to one's good sense. Such an attitude, however, deserves a second look for those who would see themselves as biblical Christians.

Laporte describes the doctrine of kenosis as foundational for an understanding of mature relationships.[218] This is the attitude found in Philippians 2 where Paul describes Jesus as emptying himself of the normal prerogatives and powers of deity. According to Laporte, a Jesuit theologian, such a stance of selflessness, represents the most profound model for the achievement of maturity, freedom, and intimacy. This foundational stance is

> ... a surrender of our prerogatives, real and imaginary, as we live with and for others. This surrender will lead us to discover and fulfill our true selves, like a grain of wheat in John 12 that bears fruit through dying to its self-enclosed reality as a grain.[219]

---

[218] Jean Marc Laporte, "Kenosis as a key to maturity of personality" In RC Roberts and MR Talbot (Eds.) *Limning the Psyche: Explorations in Christian Psychology* (Grand Rapids: Eerdmans Publishing Company, 1997).
[219] Ibid., 229.

To live as God's creatures and in his likeness is to love, and to love one lives outside and beyond one's self. To do so requires faith. And trust. In other words, in order to love the other—the one who is not self and therefore potentially alien to one's own needs requires confidence it will be okay. I will be okay and I will be safe. Loving requires vulnerability, a kind of risky submission to the will of the other. The mutual submission of Ephesians 5:21 invites a positive expectation between partners. For the one who leads, an expectation of affirmation is necessary. "What if I say, 'let's pray' and she laughs in my face?" Conversely, to wait and be ready to affirm requires confidence that the one in authority is wise and is *for me*. The dilemma for the female is far more severe. "What if he becomes angry and hits me?" "What if I postpone my career goals and he abandons me with two kids and no job?" Serious questions. It takes two to properly complete the circle.

The last chapter highlighted the power of the female to launch and nurture life. In the ancient world and in many cultures today, the idea that women hold "power" seems almost ludicrous. Even in America, women only gained the right to vote after a fierce campaign by brave suffragettes. In this century, women have gained great political power, but stories of physical, sexual, mental abuse, and neglect continue to be far too common. No doubt many of those who would tear down the "patriarchy" can offer personal as well as histor-ical rationale for their antagonism. And how many other women, less vocal, simply keep their distance? The #MeToo movement brought to light a toxic masculinity that had been in the shadows for decades. And even if a young girl has not been hurt by the males in her life, what is she to think when the behavior of such icons as Bill Cosby is unmasked for all the world to see?

In a sinful world, there can never be a guarantee that one's investment in the other person will be treasured or recipro-cated. This means we need a source beyond the partner. To risk love, we need to know we are already loved. As Laporte puts it, "The Christian recognizes that the only power in which we are able fully to achieve a love which affirms the mystery of the other as other is God's love."[220]

Without God's presence, loving is risky, like a trapeze artist without a net. This is self alone. Today, the young breathe the atmosphere of individualism. No wonder marriage rates are down. Trust is elusive. Submission for many is out of the question. Young women have good reason to look askance at motherhood and homemaking. Can she find a trustworthy man? How long can she wait with "oil in her lamp"?

Sexual union after the Fall: Song of Songs

In Genesis, God is pleased with the design for the humans (1:31). In Genesis 2, we hear the voice of the man who also celebrates that design (2:23). *Bone of my bone, flesh of my flesh!* Representing the very nature of God, this man/woman modality pulsates at the center of humanity and is to be freely embraced. Barth writes:

> For it is here first and decisively that we have to see and learn what is meant by freedom of heart for the other, and therefore what constitutes the humanity of all other encounters. Genesis 2 is imperious in this respect.[221]

The Song of Songs counterpoints the Genesis picture. Here the woman speaks. In her voice, we discern an affirmation and exuberance for the man that is surely as strong as when Adam encountered Eve. Here, the "freedom of heart for the other" can hardly be missed.

---

[220] Ibid., 233.
[221] Barth, 293.

Let him kiss me with the kisses of his mouth—for your love is more delightful than wine (1:2) ... My beloved is to me a sachet of myrrh resting between my breasts. ... I delight to sit in his shade and his fruit is sweet to my taste. Let him lead me to the banquet hall and let his banner over me be love (1:2, 13; 2:3-4).

Situated in the middle of the Bible, this book represents a continuity of the theme that the sexes belong to each other. That they are designed to complete and fulfill each other. Clearly, these poems show the capacity that each sex has to awaken something deep in the other.

Complementarity: A survey of biblical texts

As noted, not all believers agree that the word of God teaches a complementary sexuality or that the primary relational template is sexual. Some argue that the Bible ought to be demythologized. Elements of oppressive patriarchy ought to disappear along with the King James Bible. Teachings that the man is the head of the house reflect the work of myopic writers who were simply bound by their times.

Nevertheless, biblical references to sexuality do seem to conform to a sweeping and consistent revelation. An inescapable theme emerges, viz., that there is something terribly vital in the sexual order. From the first chapter of Genesis in which God creates man "male and female" to the book of Revelation with its rich imagery of Christ and the church as his bride, one discerns a mystery. Clearly, there is a correlation between spiritual and fleshly realities.

At creation, God both identifies and solves the problem of the man's incompleteness. Alone, Adam was not yet fully man. So God fashions a "suitable helper" (Genesis 2:18, 20). Together, the man and woman constitute the image of God and represent his very nature to the rest of creation.

In response to the first man's loneliness, God does not make another man. Rather, he designs an *ezer kenegdo*, a helper or counterpart to complement him. We know that men often help each other, work together, and share common goals. But in this case, the ideal resolution to the man's predicament as "not good" to be alone is to fashion a being who is different and thus one who fits perfectly.[222]

In imaging God, the man and woman represent in some way the dynamics of the Trinity. As we have seen, Jesus, in his servant and subordinate role, is no less God than is the Holy Spirit or God the Father. So too, for the woman to be declared a helper, implies no less dignity. The word helper, *ezer*, is typically translated as "help" and is elsewhere used to describe God in his action as savior, rescuer, or protector. The word also describes those who provide assistance as to a king.[223] Leupold writes,

> Her position in reference to man is defined as first "a helper," literally, "a help," *ezer*... Her position is further defined by the expression "like him," *keneghdo*, literally, "as agreeing to him," or "his counterpart." She is the kind of help man needs, agreeing with him mentally, physically, spiritually.[224]

Such language cannot easily be dismissed as the artifact of nearsightedness in the ancient writer. In his treatise on biblical complementarity,[225] John Piper writes that in addition to Genesis 2:18-23, passages in Ephesians 5, Titus 2:5, and

---

[222] Kuiper, *The Human Life Review*, "Male and Female Together...".
[223] https://markfrancois.wordpress.com/tag/krister-stendahl/
[224] *Exposition of Genesis*, volume 1 (Grand Rapids: Baker Book House, 1950), 129-130.
[225] Barth, 163.

1 Peter 3:1-6 exhorting wives to be subject to their husbands reinforce an original and natural hierarchy. The differentiated roles described in these passages cannot be traced to the fall into sin. In Ephesians, Paul ties his teaching that the husband is the head of the wife to the relationship between Christ and the church. Peter links his call to the wives to be submissive to "the holy women of the past" (v.5).[226]

Matthew 25: What do the righteous do?

This passage does not address the sexes directly but in the context of this book, a curious observation surfaces. In the chapters preceding the crucifixion, Jesus teaches about the second coming, the signs of his return and the future judgment. One event will echo the nightly task of shepherds in those days: the separation of the sheep from the goats. These are the righteous and the unrighteous. We note the particular activities Jesus describes as quintessentially righteous:

> For I was hungry and you gave me something to eat; I was thirsty, and you gave me drink; I was a stranger and you invited me in; naked and you clothed me; I was in prison and you visited me (25:35-36). (NASV)

To feed and clothe the hungry and thirsty? To show hospitality? While these godlike, righteous behaviors are not gender specific, they certainly reflect what a mother does. And surely give the lie that caretaking, whether as a homemaker or in other capacities, is to be scorned as unimportant!

---

[226] Manhood, Womanhood, and the Freedom to Minister | Desiring God.

Letter to the Corinthians

No other passage lays out the issues as directly as in 1 Corinthians 11:2-16. Two terms emerge as instructive: head (*kephale*) and glory (*doxa*). The hierarchical thrust of Paul's teaching appears unavoidable. The head of the woman is man, the head of man is Christ and the head of Christ is God (v.3). Furthermore, the man "…is the image and glory of God; but the woman is the glory of man" (v.7).

Throughout the epistle, Paul had been addressing problems in the Corinthian church. In doing so, he both praised and castigated the young Christians while instructing them in godly doctrine. These new believers had come to faith from a cosmopolitan background, not unlike that of San Francisco. Corinth was a busy and wealthy seaport, known internationally for its games, luxuries, and ship building, as well as its literature. And temptations of every kind. The place was openly preoccupied with sex. Even street signs were shaped like genitals. Barnes writes that Corinth "became eminent among all ancient cities for wealth and luxury and dissipation."[227] The principal deity of the city was Venus, the goddess of love or, more accurately, licentious passion. Beautiful women would act as courtesans, prostitutes before the altar of Venus.

As Paul addresses various problems, he weaves in higher, transcultural principles with specific applications. For example, enjoining them to avoid prostitution, he points out that the believer's body is not his own but belongs to Christ and that marriage is a becoming one flesh. Therefore, while other sins are outside the body the one who practices sexual immorality sins against his own body (6:16-18). In Chapter 11, Paul discusses worship traditions and the covering of one's head. While we may safely consider the specifics as

---

[227] Albert Barnes, *Notes on the New Testament: Explanatory and Practical, I Corinthians* (Grand Rapids: Baker Book House, 1949), iv.

bound by current traditions, most scholars understand trans-cultural reasoning to be authoritative. The surface issue had to do with the wearing of a veil. Paul writes that every woman who prays or prophesies with her head uncovered dishonors her head, even as if it were shaved (v.5). How could this be important? Apparently, some women were flaunting their independence. These,

> —on pretense of being inspired, had prayed or proph-esied in the Corinthian church, and cast off their veils after the manner of the heathen priestesses. ... The question seems to have been whether, since she was inspired it was proper for her to retain the marks of her inferiority of rank, and remain covered; or whether the fact of her inspiration did not release her from that obligation, and make it proper that she should lay aside her veil, and appear as public speakers did among men.[228]

In response, Paul writes that the woman should cover her head because the head of every man is Christ and the head of the woman is the man, and the head of Christ is God. What does Paul mean by the word "head" (*kephale*)? Grudem reports that the word means *authority* or *leader* throughout both the New Testament and extra-biblical literature.[229]

Karl Barth's notes on this passage are instructive. Barth reminds us that this young church tended to be prideful and oppositional, and had challenged Paul's apostleship. Paul's concern here, as elsewhere, is for liturgical order.

> An enthusiastic attempt was being made to introduce equality where previously the custom had been both

---

[228] Ibid. 200 – 201.
[229] Wayne Grudem, "The Meaning of Kephale ("Head"): A Response to Recent Studies," in *Recovering Biblical Manhood and Womanhood.*

at Corinth and in other Christian communities that in their gatherings for worship the man should be uncovered and the women covered. We may well imagine that Gal. 3:28 ("neither male nor female") provided either verbally or materially the main argument in favor of abolishing this outward distinction and therefore against Paul, who had given this dictum but now favored the keeping of the tradition (v.2).[230]

According to Barth, Paul's summary in verses 11 and 12 is key. "However, in the Lord, neither is woman independent of man nor is man independent of woman. For as the woman originates from the man, so also the man has his birth through the woman; and all things originate from God." Here, we see absolute equality as affirmed in Genesis 2.

Yet only an inattentive enthusiasm could deduce from this that man and woman are absolutely alike, that there can be no question of super– and subordination between them, and that it is both legitimate and obligatory to abolish the distinction between the uncovered and covered head in divine service.[231]

As elsewhere in the letter, Paul is concerned that they understand that God is not the author of confusion but of peace. And peace requires order. Distinctions must be observed and these include true super- and sub- ordination.

Paul is trying to show that the observance of this relative, indirect and human order is necessary because it rests on an absolute, direct and divine order, so that the denial of the one means the denial of the other.

---

[230] Barth, 309.

[231] Ibid., 309 – 310.

The curious thing about the angels in v. 10 is most simply explained as follows. The angels are generally the bearers and representatives of the relative principles necessarily deposited with the work of God, and they are specifically bearers and representatives of the indirect human orders necessarily deposited with the divine work of salvation. They cannot, therefore see these orders violated without sorrow.[232]

So, what exactly does this order look like? What does this mean that Christ is the head of every man and the man is the head of the woman and God is the head of Christ? For one thing, Barth notes, the sequence obviates any notion that these relationships are on a scale, as if the relation of Christ to the man is just as the man is to his wife. Further, all subordination is grounded in submission to God.

Both superordination and subordination are primarily and properly in Christ... Whatever may be the *exousia* (authority) of man in relation to woman, it is legitimate and effective only to the extent that primarily and properly it does not belong to him but to Christ, and can therefore only be attested and represented by man. Conversely, Christ is the sum of all humility before God, of all the obedient fulfillment of his will. He is the one who according to Philippians 2: 6f., Although he was in the form of God did not count it his prey to be equal with God, but emptied himself, and took the form of a servant... He is thus the sum of all subordination, and stands relatively much lower than woman under man. And whatever may be her relationship to the *exousia* of man which she lacks, it is sanctified, ennobled and glorified by the fact that her

---

[232] Ibid.

subordination is primarily and properly that of Christ and can only be attested and represented by her. ... So sharply and clearly is it determined and limited on both sides by what is primarily and properly the affair of Christ! His is the superordination and His the subordination. His is the place of man, and His the place of woman. And what place is there to speak of little or much? There is assigned to each that which is helpful and right and worthy. ... The basic order of the human established by God's creation is not accidental or contingent. It cannot be overlooked or ironed out. We cannot arbitrarily go behind it. It is solidly and necessarily grounded in Christ, with a view to whom heaven and earth and finally man were created.[233]

Kevin Davis notes that Barth is careful not to ground the distinctions between male and female in natural typologies, for example, that all men are rational or dominant or all women are intuitive or emotional. Rather, true personhood and freedom for each sex is found in Christ. The calling of each, however, is not the same task or privilege. Nor can male and female be interchangeable as each is designed to fulfill the other. Davis explains:

Each finds in the other the fulfillment of the human image in God insofar as each is oriented to overcome this opposition—this otherness—in a union of perfected love and fidelity. Barth explicitly identifies this gendered identity of the human as the image of God in man... As the covenant of grace, the image of God in man involves a distinct sequence, an A and B,

---

[233] Ibid.

where A is wholly self-gift and B is wholly receptive of this gift.[234]

This order is a preceding and a following, each orientation finding its origin and motivation in the love of Christ. Any primacy of the man as leader or initiator can only be embraced in humility and as a call to service. Any authority is for the purpose of blessing and fellowship; and the woman is to actualize that fellowship as she is receptive to his self-giving initiative.

Paul follows his teaching on headship with the concept of glory (*doxa*) (v.7). The man does not cover his head since he is the image and glory of God. The woman is the glory of man. We note that Jesus taught his disciples that they reflect the glory of God by bearing much fruit (John 15:8). This is the fruit of love (v. 12). In this sense, it would appear that as one represents God and the glory of God, one exudes his nature—his heart and loving intention. So, too, the man is a direct expression of God in Christ who, in love for the world, "emptied himself, taking the form of a servant..." (Philippians 2:7). This is sacrificial leadership. And the woman, in receiving and affirming that loving initiative, honors him by helping complete his godly agenda, which also includes serving her, giving himself up for her well-being.

Servant leadership: A note to the Ephesians

Created to represent God's loving nature, are we not most fully human as we approximate that nature? Love pouring out of self into that which is not self. We understand that God's nature is communal, existing as a union of differentiated persons as Father, Son and Holy Spirit. A union of equal

---

[234] "Gender and theology series: Karl Barth on Man and Woman." January 2, 2013, Gender and Theology series: Karl Barth on Man and Woman (wordpress. com)

persons, functionally, hierarchically ordered. An essential attitude for such intimacy is submission. After calling everyone
to submit to one another, Paul specifies,

> Wives, submit yourselves to your own husbands as you
> do to the Lord. For the husband is the head of the wife
> as Christ is the head of the church, his body, of which
> he is the Savior... Husbands, love your wives, just as
> Christ loved the church and gave himself up for her
> to make her holy, cleansing her by the washing with
> water through the word, and to present her to himself
> as a radiant church, without stain or wrinkle or any
> other blemish, but holy and blameless. In the same
> way, husbands ought to love their wives as their own
> bodies. He who loves his wife loves himself. After all,
> no one ever hated their own body, but they feed and
> care for their body, just as Christ does the church—for
> we are members of his body. For this reason a man
> will leave his father and mother be united to his wife,
> and the two will become one flesh. This is a profound
> *mystery*—but I am talking about Christ and the church.
> (vv. 22-32)

Paul describes the connection between the headship of
Christ and the church and the headship of the husband and
the wife as a mystery, unknown in the previous covenant. In
expounding on Paul's use of the word head (*kephale*), George
W. Knight III points to Ephesians 4:15 in which Christ as the
head of the church marshals his authority and power to "cause
the growth of the body for the building up of itself in love."[235]
Here again, we find the motivation and design for leadership
is love.

---

[235] "Husbands and wives as analogues of Christ in the church: Ephesians 5:21-
33 and Colossians 3:18-19." In *Recovering Biblical Manhood and Womanhood: A
Response to Evangelical Feminism.* p. 170.

First Peter 3:1-7

Probably written during the time of Nero (54-68), Peter's first letter addresses believers across multiple provinces. During this period of great persecution, he reminds them of their true purpose as strangers and exiles who demonstrate the Gospel to a lost world. As a way of bringing others to faith, such a calling may very well involve suffering for the sake of Christ. Similar to the kenosis passage of Philippians 2, Peter urges a mindset of renunciation. Christians ought to be respectful and submit to governing authorities. Servants ought to adapt such an attitude toward their masters. They should be submissive, even to the ones who are harsh. The word, to submit (*hypotasso*) means to voluntarily and deliberately stand under another's authority.[236] This is done "for the Lord's sake" (2:13) and includes suffering unjustly, even as Christ bore our sins for our sake (2:21-24).

In Chapter 3, Peter addresses marriage partners. "In the same way, wives are to be submissive to your husbands" (3:1). This is so, even if the men are unbelievers because such behavior will win them without words or debate. Peter describes this attitude as issuing from the inner self, not gaudy outward adornment but the beauty of a "gentle and quiet spirit" (3:4). To buttress his argument, Peter recollects the "holy women of the past," including Sarah who obeyed Abraham (3:5-6).

Husbands, on the other hand, must show honor to their wives, living with them "in an understanding way" or literally, "according to knowledge." Barnes writes:

In accordance with an intelligent view of the nature of the relationship... The meaning evidently, is that they should seek to obtain just views of what Christianity enjoins in regard to this relation, and that they should

---

[236] Kostenberger and Kostenberger, 245.

allow those intelligent views to control them in all their intercourse with their wives.[237]

We note here that Paul is not the only apostle to assume a hierarchical view of marriage. In addition, Peter's argument is also based on transcultural principles. He references Jewish history and presents his appeal as a matter of great ultimate purpose, viz., the very progress of the work of God in the world.

Clearly, as Barth saw, the hierarchical relationship does not begin with the man. As Jesus reflected the glory of God, he lived out the Father's agenda, not his own. As the husband reflects the glory of God, he does not live out of his own will but receives his marching orders from Christ. Further, he loves his wife "as Christ loves the church." He does not seek the woman as an object of his own satisfaction, nor his primary resource. Sorry, Righteous Brothers, she is not designed to be your soul, nor your inspiration. Nor are you designed to look at her and declare, "without you, babe, what good am I?" Such expressions of dependency tend to turn off most women or worse, lead to control or abuse when she fails to live up to her messianic role. On the other hand, the man who first seeks guidance and strength from his Maker finds true inspiration for his life. As he pursues God, he grows in discipline, becoming more *like* God. His confidence and creativity swell; his love of people grows along with a desire to give of himself in the service of others. Finally, he is able to hold a woman, to bless and care for her. Having achieved a mature masculinity, he no longer must be held. He now can complete the cycle; he is the knight who returns with strength and purpose—gifts commensurate to the sponsorship he has received.

Having determined that the man and woman belong together and that the sexual power of each is designed to

---

[237] Barnes, 162.

nurture and bless the other, we next consider divergent social and cultural pathways by which humans in this world either approach or retreat from this ideal. The question to ask is this: Do we encourage attitudes and customs that bring the sexes together or do we embrace a culture designed around the demands of the individual self?

CHAPTER 8

Traditions of Connection or Competition

Nevertheless, in the Lord woman is not independent of man, nor is man independent of woman. —First Corinthians 11:11

I watched "Jason" shake his head and grit his teeth as he described the events of that morning. Considering the potential for abuse, I wondered about his ability to contain his anger. "I don't know what to do with that kid. I tell him he needs to get up and get to school and he tells me to go f— myself." Hearing this report, I myself am frustrated—it's just another version of the same scenario. I say, "You really need to get his mom on board. Has she looked at the material I gave you about parenting teens?" He tells me the same thing he told me last week, that she is always at work and doesn't want to deal with it. She gives her thirteen-year-old anything he wants.

This man was doing his best to parent kids who were not his own. Not married to the mom, he had little status even as a step-parent. Clearly, the son missed his dad, resented Jason as an interloper and carried unremitting anger toward his mother. They were not Christians and I didn't discern an opening from that framework. I did tell him this setup was nuts. He agreed.

No family or society is free from faults, free from the influence of the Serpent, that spirit of division. Nevertheless, certain customs seem to better foster harmony and the guidance of children than others. The thesis of this chapter is that, in contrast to current trends, traditional family patterns more closely align with God's original intention as well as nature itself.

As argued in the last chapter, Scripture reveals the trinitarian nature of God as differentiation within unity—a dynamic mystery. Imaging this differentiation and oneness, the sexuality of Adam and Eve binds them together. As they would enact their different powers to love and promote the potential of the other, they would each enhance their own nature as well. Further, their need and desire for each other vouchsafe a trajectory toward fruitful propagation and rule (Genesis 1:26-28). They would together enact their calling to "fill the earth and subdue it."

To divide and conquer

That humans would live, thrive and propagate, however, was never on the agenda of the Enemy. The third chapter of Genesis describes the serpent as "more crafty" than any of the other creatures. In questioning Eve, he subtly impugns the word of God in its determination that Adam be first. It was to Adam that God commanded not to eat of the tree of knowledge of good and evil. And it was to Adam he gave the commission to work the garden and take care of it (Genesis 2:15). Longman points out that the Hebrew word for "take care" is *shamar* and is more appropriately translated as "to guard."[238] Bypassing Adam, the serpent subverts his authority, weakens him. Adam allows this and Eve is left unprotected. Speaking directly to Eve, the deceiver invites her to assume that she alone is the arbiter of the Word of God. Repudiating

---

[238] Tremper Longman III, *Confronting Old Testament Controversies: Pressing Questions About Evolution, Sexuality, History, and Violence.* (Grand Rapids: Baker Books), 2019, 213.

her responsibility and role as a support to her husband, she acts without consultation.[239]

Such an inversion of the original order carried disastrous consequences. The human project is now laced with conflict. Now, knowing themselves to be the deciders of good and bad, they cannot be trusted. As we saw in Chapter Two, after defying the single limit that would guarantee their life's potential, they must now know further limitations. In the curses, God seems to address each at the point of their unique honor and obligation. Because "you listened to your wife..." (Genesis 3:17), Adam's honorable designation as first (Hebrew, *rosh* also meaning *head*) is now to be accompanied by anxious toil. At the point of her honor as a helper and life-giver, Eve must suffer pain during childbirth and her subordination will be colored with conflict (verse 16). From communion to division, from self-together to self-alone. Tainted by sin and self-will, they are thrust from Eden. The serpent appeared to have won the first round.

A penultimate world

From the garden to the farm so to speak, they did not die at once. And God did not abandon them; nor did he surrender his original plan that the humans be fruitful, fill the earth and domesticate it. The free food was gone but they did eat. Just as a farm demands toil, it also holds promise of bounty and beauty. A penultimate goodness remained, a "common

---

[239] Paul twice indicates that it was Eve who was deceived (I Tim. 2 and 2 Cor. 11). This hardly means she was the greater sinner. As David Mathis notes, the primary responsibility was Adam's. He was not deceived but stood by and allowed the serpent to subvert God's order when he "...first approached and spoke to *the woman* (3:1). Then the woman, rather than the man, spoke to the serpent (3:2), and she ate first (3:6). But it was the man God first confronted (3:9). *How Man and Woman Fell Out of Order,* June 26, 2020 https://www. desiringgod.org/articles/why-did-satan-target-eve

grace." Van Til offers a definition for this postlapsarian goodness as that which first

> ...restrains the destructive process of sin within mankind in general and (2) enables men, though not born again, to develop the latent forces of the universe and thus make a positive contribution to the fulfillment of the cultural mandate given to men through the first man, Adam, in paradise.[240]

This tangible goodness prepares the way and foreshadows an ultimate goodness. To understand eternal love and redemptive discipline, one must taste temporal love and temporal frustration.

It is in this sense of penultimate goodness that we contrast patterns and consequences of traditional as opposed to progressive lifestyles. The task is to identify practices that approximate the gifts of God at the origin. We ask, to what degree does a community acknowledge a supreme being. To what degree are natural laws affirmed and are the sexes brought together? Ultimately, to what degree is life itself promoted and cherished?

While the motivation of particular individuals may be obscure, we can, perhaps, examine the fruit of certain social and familial patterns.

Assessing sexual telos: Generative pathways vs. terminal sex

The intention of this study is not to argue that progressives are bad and traditionalists are good. Nevertheless, some activities reflect greater penultimate value than others. Some traditions

---

[240] "Common Grace" in *Baker's Dictionary of Theology*, E. F. Harrison, Ed., (Grand Rapids: Baker Book House, 1960) 131.

more closely approximate the Creator's intention for mankind than do others which seem to sponsor division.

Jesus declared that "by their fruit you shall know them…" (Matt. 7:20). Although the issues are complex, the fruit cultivated by radical feminism and sexual libertarianism leaves a bitter taste. To put it bluntly, the taste of death—or at least the prevention of new life. Many feminists seem to eschew sex with men altogether. Pornographers and the sexually promiscuous promote sex with self or with a condom. No sex or prophylactic sex. In contrast, societies that survive for generations tend to evidence certain markers that we would do well to cultivate. We can thus differentiate attitudes toward sex as being "terminal" as in sex for its own sake, with neither the goal of attachment to another, nor reference to children as a natural outcome; or, we can discern a purposive or "generative" sexuality. In broad terms, these categories overlap with traditional, conservative attitudes as opposed to more liberal viewpoints which tilt toward individual freedom and rights.

In comparing fruit from a generative view of sex as opposed to a terminal one, we consider several categories. These include issues of personal identity, boundaries, and the coming together of the sexes.

The quest for identity

The concepts of self-image and self-esteem have long generated much interest in psychology. Occasionally, I ask clients to write what comes to mind when answering the question, "Who am I?" Other questions quickly follow: "Am I okay? What would I like to change?" It goes without saying that positive self-esteem is to be preferred.

On the point of self-esteem, a secularized culture crosses swords with biblical faith. Those who do not believe in a creator must fall back on their own self understandings; they must make their own meaning, generate their own system of value to achieve a positive self-concept. Without God, self-esteem can be as fickle as a basketball as it rolls around the rim and decides not to fall into the net. Christians, on the other hand, believe they "fall short of the glory of God," and understand the futility of generating one's own value. The believer can relax. "My identity and worth depend on someone greater than me."

The dialogic nature of identity formation

Christians understand that our real identity is in Christ. Yet, in our quest for penultimate wisdom, we also believe a healthy self-concept can prepare the psychological soil for the seed of the Gospel. What are the ingredients for such? Borrowing from sociologist, Philip Rieff, Senior Fellow at the Institute for Faith and Freedom, Carl R. Trueman explains that a child's identity emerges from the dynamic interplay between his or her unique individuality and the community. The order of this dialogue between self and culture is important. The culture stands outside and in most ways above the individual. Culture provides values and purposes *in response to which* the individual self finds satisfaction. Trueman writes:

> This is an important point: culture directs individuals outward. It is greater than, prior to, and formative of the individual. We learn who we are by learning how to conform ourselves to the purposes of the larger community to which we belong.[241]

The "dialogic nature of identity" refers to the need to interact in society in ways that both fit with one's individual

---

[241] *The Rise and Triumph of the Modern Self: Cultural Amnesia, Expressive Individualism, and the Road to Sexual Revolution* (Wheaton, Ill.: Crossway, 2020), 44.

feelings as well as the larger community.[242] Individual inclinations must be validated by society as well as nature itself. An individual child develops conclusions as to who they are in ongoing encounters with family and community expectations and standards. My older sister, for example, was a gifted musician. She practiced for hours and was rewarded by becoming the pianist for her college choir. My mother hoped I, too, would develop musically. When she discovered I could not carry a tune to save my life, she gave up on her wish that I join the church choir. When I failed to make the basketball team, my options for building a confident self-esteem further wavered. Disenchanted with school, I found some acceptance among the drug and alcohol crowd. This kind of *ad hoc* subculture provided only temporary satisfaction, ultimately more misery than mastery. Legitimate cultural ideals and customs, on the other hand, have always sponsored healthy, prosocial identities to which the young may aspire.

Today, we are witness to a profound reversal of this order. Traditional codes are oppressive. Established culture is nothing; it is the individual self that matters. In many ways, outward institutions have become the servant of the individual, rather than the shaper of mature citizens. We see this in the university. Trueman argues that educational institutions are no longer places for the formation of individuals but "platforms for performance, where individuals are allowed to be their authentic selves precisely because they are able to give expression to who they are 'inside.'"[243] Students go to perform not to be formed. In many schools, external reality itself is questioned and objective truths are just constructs by the powerful to overpower the weak.

The triumph of such individualism can be seen even on the dance floor. In decades past, dancers would practice

---

[242] Ibid., 70.
[243] Ibid., 49.

specific steps. Careful choreography was the goal. Today, random shuffling, often with hardly a glance to the partner, characterizes much that passes for dancing. A recent segment of "Good Morning America" highlights the loss of traditional codes: Amid loud applause, an eleven-year-old boy prances out dressed in full drag queen regalia. The sexualization and exploitation of this boy who calls himself "Desmond is Amazing" is truly disturbing. Ironically dressed as a woman, his advice to other children is "be yourself always." I was heartened, however, by the overwhelming number of concerned comments that followed the video.[244]

When the individual self is king, that self inevitably lacks grounding. One cannot walk on air. The dialogic nature of identity formation requires outside support. When traditions and natural boundaries are repudiated, the search for affirmation intensifies. The need to belong and the need to be validated. As sexual mores and traditional dreams of marriage and family lose their power to guide or inspire, the young are thrown back into themselves. "Who am I?" and "What is my life all about?" For many, the answers are as hazy as smoke. We begin to understand the powerful pull of identity groups.

Life without limits

We saw in Chapter Two that the original prohibition was designed both to protect and to guide us to freedom. Liberty within limitation. After the original limit not to know good and evil was violated, other limits have always worked to promote penultimate good. Boundaries protect against disorder and enhance well-being.

As a people, we have come not to like limits. I recall a speaker on the radio as he described a graduation ceremony for kindergartners. Aside from the question as to whether such

---

[244] The 11-year-old trailblazing drag kid 'Desmond is Amazing' - YouTube

a ceremony was appropriate, he became quite bothered as the little ones sang, "We've got the whole world in our hands. We've got the whole wide world in our hands…" Actually, this is not true and the sooner they learn that the better.

In May, 2021, the US Senate rejected a proposal by Republicans that would limit research involving the inter-mixing of human and animal genes. Apparently, the demo-cratic senators who would lift the ban believe that science itself should be unbound. In a disturbing commentary, L.A. Marzulli suggests that such crossbreeding, which results in bizarre creatures called "Chimeras," represents the spirit of the age, a spirit of mass confusion and defiance of all boundaries. This defiant and demonic spirit is depicted by the Baphomet symbol, a goat's head with a half male and half female body.[245]

Designed for union

While the defiance of limits produces division, God's design invites union—the integration of different parts and persons. Originally defined as a "one flesh" relationship, the term marriage denotes a pulling together, a unification of two different people. As a union of persons, marriage holds the potential for fulfilling deep, personal needs—beyond those of the body. As a transformative experience, each sex finds itself in losing itself in loving the other. Inasmuch as each sex reflects God's nature as creative and loving, as male and female come together, they actualize each other's nature—a gender specific entelechy. For example, as the man repudi-ates narcissistic demands in order to love and protect his wife, she comes alive. In response, she enacts her own feminine nature and affirms his masculine initiative. As she makes him feel important, like a hero, his love deepens. The initial lust he felt for her body morphs into the experience of bonding

---

[245] PP&S Report- The Spirit of our Age - YouTube, July 2, 2021.

with her soul. Conversely, as she grows more confident in his attention, she becomes freer to live out feminine longings to connect with and take care of others. Motherhood emerges as the precious potential it was designed to be.[246]

Sex roles

As conversation around the topic of design has faded from public discourse, so has the implication that the two sexes should fulfill or complement each other. Sex roles are assumed to be sexist, archaic and in some way, misrepresentative of the true nature and potential of an individual. They are offensive and confining. While charging into this minefield, we pose a few questions: Might there be a reason why every culture in history has assumed some role differentiation? Could certain sex typing match real differences? Further, might not sex roles actually be necessary for the development of healthy self-esteem and confidence? Finally, is not some form of sexual differentiation necessary to lay the groundwork for enacting the Genesis mandates that male and female belong together in the great vocation to fill and domesticate the earth?

In the not-too-distant past, children's books happily depicted little girls helping mommy bake a cake and little boys helping daddy wash the car. What's wrong with that? Obviously, such role distinctions ought not to be absolutized. Yet, they both imply a correspondence with a natural femininity orienting a daughter toward a potential future as mother and nest maker while summoning a son toward a larger role that would also bless the family.

For many, however, all differentiation of sex roles is offensive as if difference itself implies abuse.

---

[246] See "The High Calling of Wife and Mother in Biblical Perspective" by Dorothy Patterson in *Recovering Biblical Manhood and Womanhood: A Response to Evangelical Feminism, op cit.*

Difference may cause disadvantage. Adept at high-lighting instances of male oppression, equity feminists work to eliminate male advantage. To them, difference must imply inequality—of size and power or wealth and privilege. Inequality produces oppression. The struggle for gender equity is thus equated to battles against racism, classism, or ageism.[247]

Since difference is dangerous, the possibility of sexual complementarity must also be resisted. Elizabeth Elliott notes that words like masculinity and femininity have been expunged from current discourse. "We have lost our bearings in a fog of rhetoric about something called equality, so that I find myself in the uncomfortable position of having to belabor to educated people what was once perfectly obvious to the simplest peasant." [248] Reflecting on the way indigenous peoples of South America expressed masculinity and femininity, she writes,

> The femininity of woman was a deep-rooted conscious-ness of what she was made for. It was expressed in everything she did differently from men, from her hairstyle and clothes (if she wore any) to the way she sat and the work she did. Any child knew that women wove hammocks and made pots and caught fish with their hands, cleared underbrush, planted crops, and carried by far the heaviest loads, while men chop down trees and hunted, caught fish with nets and spears, and carried no loads at all if there was a woman around. Nobody had any complaints. These respon-sibilities were not up for grabs, not interchangeable,

---

[247] Kuiper, 49.

[248] "The Essence of Femininity: A Personal Perspective." In eds. John Piper and Wayne Gruden, *Recovering Biblical Manhood and Womanhood: A Response to Evangelical Feminism* (Wheaton, Illinois: Crossway, 2006) 395.

not equal. Nobody thought of power or prestige or competition…

Once, in the bumbling way of foreigners, I "brought down the house," as it were, by picking up a man's eight-foot spear and pretending to be about to hurl it. They died laughing. If they had not taken it as a joke, I would have been in serious trouble. Women had nothing to do with spears. Their power did not lie in being equal with men but in being women. Men were men and women were glad of it.[249]

We notice in the story that the different expectations provide a pathway for each sex to contribute. In the West, an egalitarian "partnership" model tends to dominate. Inasmuch as this view denies essential differences, couples find themselves forming matches around nonessential characteristics: shared goals and values, likes and dislikes, and so on. While these elements are important, they shift and change. The basis for attraction is more tenuous. "The connection remains only as long as goals are shared and a parity of contribution and reward is perceived."[250] Traditional societies, on the other hand, have always understood that,

A certain self-esteem is granted by virtue of belonging to one sex and not the other. Fundamentally, this status is an essential value *to* the opposite sex. The corollary assumption is simply that "I am not so special in that I can complete myself. I need what the other can give." As such, each sex carries a unique power to satisfy the other. At its most primal level, this essential

---

[249] Ibid.
[250] Kuiper, 47.

power represents a generative value with its potential for production of offspring.[251]

Anthropologist David Gilmore studied a broad sample of cultures from hunter-gatherers to post-industrial societies. Noting that manhood has never been something easily defined, he wanted to uncover commonalities among various expressions of masculinity. Among his conclusions were the following: "All societies distinguish male and female and provide institutionalized sex appropriate roles for adult men and women."[252] These roles become anchors or identities offering a kind of stable self-concept and esteem to both sexes. Further, he discovered that

> manhood ideals make an indispensable contribution both to the continuity of social systems and to the psychological integration of men into their community. I regard these phenomena not as givens, but as part of the existential "problem of order" that all societies must solve by encouraging people to act in certain ways, ways that facilitate both individual development and group adaptation. Gender roles represent one of those problem-solving behaviors.[253]

Gilmore found that in every culture, masculinity is a precarious thing, something not given automatically, but a thing to be achieved. A "primeval oneness with mother" must be overcome. "To become a separate person the boy must perform a great deal. He must pass a test; he must break the

---

[251] Ibid., 49.

[252] *Manhood in the Making: Cultural Concepts of Masculinity* (New Haven: Yale University Press, 1990), 9.

[253] Ibid., 3.

chain to his mother."[254] Differentiated gender roles provide pathways for such achievement.

In contrast, an ideology that denies the complementarity of differentiated sexuality is, in the final analysis, no sexuality at all. It has become increasingly popular to deny that there is such a thing as masculine or feminine. Or any design or necessity that they fit together. Singer Celine Dion has even popularized a line of children's clothing that eschews pink and blue in favor of black-and-white outfits.[255] Homosexual psychologist and advocate of non-binary sexuality, Ken Corbett would free individuals from a kind of "gender straight jacketing." He agrees with queer theorist, Judith Butler that societal constructions of gender roles tend to cause a painful dislocation between a child's inner reality and the performance expectations impinging on that reality. Cultural norms that imply that a boy ought to like baseball or play in a rough-and-tumble way, for example, are hurtful, spoil his imagination and in a way, diminish his humanity. In his opposition to the "normative regulatory regime," Corbett writes:

> We have been too quick to presume gender to be a coherent internalization and identification, as opposed to a complex and enigmatic series of internalizations and identifications that may "cohere" much less than has traditionally been assumed.[256]

The coherence Corbett refers to juxtaposes a kind of inner identity with external gender roles. It is true, for some, the discord between typical sex role expectations and one's private interests and inclinations can indeed be painful. My older

---

[254] Ibid., 28.

[255] Exorcist priest warns of Celine Dion's clothing line for kids: 'definitely Satanic.' *Kansas Star*, Nov. 28, 2018.

[256] *Boyhood: Rethinking Masculinities* (New Haven: Yale University press, 2009) 134.

brother was six feet and four inches tall and could not bounce a basketball without hitting his toes. He would become irritated when people just assumed he was on the team. He wrote poetry and played the cello, thank you very much! Although he did not "fit" so well some of the stereotypes in the sixties, the culture still affirmed that boys were boys and girls were girls and that they naturally would come together as provider and homemaker, father and mother. Indeed, my brother did become a father and provider as a counselor and college professor.

In the wish to bring correspondence between a child's inner feelings and public gender expression, equity ideologues make the fatal mistake of ignoring the greater need to adjust one's subjective feelings to fixed reality. They would have a child deny biology—that immediate and ever-present reality of his or her own genitals. To these partisans,

> Gender is merely "assigned," a figment of cultural imagination. Unfortunately, children now find themselves deprived of such cultural constructions that in fact honor real biological differences. Not only are they cheated of the self-esteem and security of knowing that they have value to the other sex, but find themselves pitted against that sex.[257]

Complete or compete?

YouTube videos depicting adolescent boys and girls in competition wrestling provide a disturbing case in point. Since high school programs are forced to include girls, spectators are treated to a spectacle of pubescent angst. As noses collide with crotches, sweaty, desperate fingers grasp for hand holds inches away from genitals or breasts. Hardly an enlightened

---

[257] Kuiper, op cit.

celebration of equality, such a scene scores a low point in the drive for equality. How under the myth of gender sameness is the boy to develop an attitude of protection, provision, or self-sacrifice to a wife or to any woman? "She doesn't need me for anything. And she's trying to be better than me." Quite literally, the teenage girl who wrestles boys wants nothing more than to slam him and hold him down. As one observer pointed out, the boy loses either way—as a bully if he hurts her and a weakling if he loses.

> The girl loses as well, having relinquished her femininity to masculine pursuits. Thrown together in a contest of strength, each is forced to deny physical differences, repudiating nature and nature's goals. The boy sees she is out to take his little trophy, his symbol of masculinity. The girl, having been disabused of her status as life bearer, now tacitly repudiates her own body, coveting the hard shell and aggressivity of the boys around her. Supplanting dreams of home and family, colorful ribbons and plastic trophies steal our children's imaginations.[258]

Progressive ideology requires that children be free from any sex role constraint. And gender activists, in their wish for coherence, paint an ideal in which one's body ought not to oppose one's inner experience or "real self." Each of these attitudes, while understandable in one sense, ultimately produces a host of discordant sequelae. These include chronic conflicts between the sexes, low birth rates, aborted or abandoned children, and premature and painful medicalization of gender-confused children too young to give informed consent.

Psychological adjustment, on the other hand, has always been about adjustment to reality. Those who would repudiate

---

[258] Ibid.

a binary understanding of gender hold that one's internal self-perception trumps biological reality. This view not only contradicts decades of psychological wisdom but centuries of common sense. As in the mental disorders, body dysmorphia or anorexia nervosa, a strong conviction about one's body doesn't make it true. When your three-year-old son prances out in his sister's dress and declares he is a girl, you might chuckle for a moment, but you do not reinforce such a fantasy. Why not? Because little selves, just like big ones, must learn to adjust to reality and not vice versa.

Sex roles affirm the natural value one gender holds toward the other. In marvelous synergy, each sex actualizes the deepest nature of the other, calling forth life and purpose. On the other hand, a philosophy of gender sameness repudiates any special contribution one sex might make to the other. Equality activists thus delegitimize the woman's special ability as nurturer in the home at the same time they would dethrone a man from the status of wage earner. Does this attitude not deprive girls today of their ability to celebrate their natural and essential value as females? Inasmuch as she understands that boys are not being groomed to provide for women and children, is she not forced to think first about money and career? When her mother returns to full-time work leaving her six-month-old sister to daycare, the message is loud and clear: the need for a mother is simply not that significant.

Fathering has lost status as well. Having grown up in an environment of media male bashing and surrounded by a parade of role models as funny perhaps, but insignificant, a young dad may not know how to engage his children. He is often not even near them. Certainly, he may not grasp the truth of his own significance in childrearing. At best, he may see himself as merely a poor substitute for mom.

If the sexes are to find fulfillment in each other, they must experience a reciprocity of gender roles. They must realize they are not complete in themselves and so value what the other brings. When a society affirms inherent worth to each gender, real meeting and mating become possible. As the man approaches the woman, he does so with confidence because he knows he has something she needs and that she will affirm him in his action toward her. As she, in turn, considers his advances, she understands that she is precious to him. If his approach is immature or self-seeking, her own self-confidence allows her to resist his demands. She knows that what he really wants is not just her body but her approval. Valuing the distinctives of her own gender, she can afford to be selective. At the same time, she carries an undeniable wish for connection, for a man who brings something she lacks, something uniquely masculine.

Stepping back and stepping up, helping and leading

Peter Kreeft suggests that the ultimate law of being is agape love. As expressed in the Trinity, such love is "ek-static." "God eternally leaps out of himself into himself. Each person of the Trinity is eternally engaged in the ecstasy of self-giving."[259] God's very existence thus enacts a kind of self-forgetful joy. "So extroverted that his extroverted consciousness is another Person, so outside himself that he is a second self, and then so outside themselves in love that they are the Third, the Spirit."[260] Jesus calls us to a similar self-forgetfulness—a finding of self by losing self (see John 10:10; 12:25; Matt. 10:39). While Kreeft's language might seem a bit obscure, have we not each felt a certain joy and freedom as we have focused on the needs of another?

We have suggested that the masculine carries a predominant impetus to initiate while the predominantly feminine capacity is to affirm. Each of these actions mirrors in some

---

[259] *The Heart's Deepest Longing*, 147.
[260] Ibid., 154.

way the actions of the Persons of the Trinity. Each mode reflects the divine nature as self-giving love. Love that is purposive, never static. Adam and Eve—a dynamic union working toward a common goal. In pursuit of this original goal to be fruitful, fill the earth and subdue it, love and service to the other goes without saying.

Loving cooperation requires a certain degree of humility. *I cannot do everything, do not know everything and have some need of you.* Along with humility, a good measure of self-denial completes the circle. *Submission* to the other's needs. To step back and away from self long enough to appreciate the other and the willingness to sponsor the other. To do so also requires the belief that as I give of myself to bless another, I too will be blessed.

High school football cheerleaders understand that they lose nothing by cheering on the boys. They don't covet the boys' ability to push and shove each other to the ground. They know they already possess what the boys want. By celebrating the masculine aggressivity of "their" boys, they know they hold a kind of special power to bless and affirm the budding manhood sweating on that muddy field. The cheerleader who leads the chant, "Make noise for our boys!" can do so because it fits within her "incorporative" nature.[261] By "taking in" their success, she herself gains. She is aware of her boyfriend's furtive glance in her direction immediately after catching a pass. Knowing on some level, she has helped sponsor his achievement, she shares his pride.

An implicit male dependency remains a subconscious reality within both sexes. The cheerleader knows this deeply; the more solid she is in her own femininity, the more easily she can step back and allow the boy to find his manhood. As she knows he needs her, she knows he will love her. Whatever

---

[261] See Erik Erikson, *Childhood and Society*; See also, Erikson, E. H. *Identity: Youth and Crisis* (New York, NY: W.W. Norton), 1968.

masculine powers he develops he shares with her because he knows he did not develop them without her. She in turn comes to trust that he will direct those powers to bless her. Or, as Staci Eldredge put it, "true femininity calls forth true masculinity."[262]

Indeed, as the boy sees her cheering him on, he feels empowered. He is excited by her attention. He comes to love her more deeply as he experiences her encouragement and admiration. Quickened in spirit, he marshals his physical power and energy. He corrals it, sublimates it to long-term goals. He *steps back* from immature and impulsive demands for self-gratification. He loves her not for her body but for herself because it is that soulish part of her that sees his soul and recognizes his strivings to be significant to her. I recall the first time I won my event at a high school track meet how I raced to tell my girlfriend and how excited she was for me. Did her response feed my adolescent narcissism? Possibly. Did it cost her anything? Not if we understand the power of affirmation. I would've done anything for that girl. Indeed, under a cloud of romantic love and with visions of family, young men have always stretched and sacrificed themselves for the love of a woman. As a teenager, he *steps up* to spend long and exhausting hours on the football field. Or practices skateboard tricks into the night to impress a girl next morning. In a few years, he steps up to endure grueling boot camp so he can become the soldier who will protect her and perhaps die for her. Or he steps up to invest years of long hours so he can be the doctor or the scientist who will cure her ills.

The boy/man steps up—becomes well socialized and emotionally mature—because in the first place, he wants to. He wants to do so because the pursuit of self-giving actualizes his deepest nature which is to love—to come back to the source and to give life to that source. To serve the female

---

[262] Op cit.

in this way gives him significance. Furthermore, he steps up because he can. He has the mental and emotional power and the stamina to do these things because the men and women in his life have sponsored that manhood. His father had stepped up to play with, teach, and discipline him. His mother had stepped back to honor his father in his masculine role—one she did not attempt to co-opt. His sisters stepped back to allow him to build a fort in the backyard with his friends while they were content to do their own thing. Aware that only women hold the power to bring life into the world, they did not need to covet whatever activities the boys were pursuing.

When the uniqueness and value of each gender is understood, loving complementarity enhances individual wholeness. In contrast, when a society roundly repudiates traditions that have included complementary sex roles and fails to embrace biological certainties, deep human needs for significance and connection suffer. When young girls lack role models in the media or education that value motherhood and instead are flooded with heroines who are governors, cops, soldiers, doctors, and lawyers, how are they not to assume that these intensive, high demanding careers are *the only* ones to strive for? How would they not also begin to doubt their private inclinations toward home and children?

Generative modes

While sex roles ought not to be rigid or experienced as punitive, different expectations for boys and girls have always provided gender affirming pathways that correspond to each sex's potential to affirm the generative nature of the other. Sex roles—if not too rigid or confining—provide pathways that facilitate identity, meaning and purpose. These not only help children negotiate the complexities of their ever-changing bodies and uncertain place in the world, they point to the next generation.

Erik Erikson, in his classic study, *Childhood and Society*, describes in detail the normal developmental trajectory of boys and girls in their early years. By the time a boy is three or four years old, he is more independent and active. His behavior is more "intrusive." At this "phallic" stage, he is well aware of differences between the sexes. He pulls away from his mother and pokes and prods with toy swords. Girls also become aware of sexual difference and they too experience greater locomotor restlessness and social intrusiveness. However, the young female's natural inclination is to more receptive, inclusive activity. At this stage, both sexes develop an emerging awareness of some meaning inherent in sexual differentiation beyond simple choice of toys or dress.[263] This is

> ...a rudimentary generative mode, representing the dim anticipation of the fact that genitality has a procreative function... That boys and girls are differentiated not only by differences in organs, capacities, and roles, but by a unique quality of experience. This is the result of the ego's organization of all that one has, feels, and anticipates. It is never enough, then, to characterize the sexes by the way they differ from each other, although such difference is counterpointed by cultural roles. Rather, each sex is characterized by a uniqueness which includes (but is not summed up by) its difference from the other sex; a uniqueness which is founded on the preformed functions of the future inseminator and the future child-bearer, in whatever system of distribution of labor and cultural style. Here

---

[263] Differences in preferences appear early, girls preferring dolls and boys' trucks. Jadva, V., Hines, M. & Golombok, S. Infants' Preferences for Toys, Colors, and Shapes: Sex Differences and Similarities. *Arch Sex Behav* **39**, 1261–1273 (2010) doi:10.1007/s10508-010-9618-z

the modes of intrusion and inclusion are polarized in the service of production and procreation.[264]

This is a period in which children pay special attention to their same-sex parent. Child psychologist Haim Ginott put it simply: "To fulfill their biological destiny, boys must identify with their fathers and girls with their mothers."[265] When that parent is warm, affectionate and involved, children are much more likely to identify with that parent. This is especially so when both parents support each other in their complementary roles.

As the boy helps dad in various tasks and perceives that his mother values those tasks, he comes to believe he too can bring value to a woman. As a girl identifies with her mother, she grounds her own being in nothing less than the survival of the species. She understands the centrality of feminine power to affirm and nurture the lives of others. While every child may not grow up to become a father or a mother, they learn there is meaning to be unfolded in relation to the other sex. There is something purposive about belonging to one sex or the other.

In a culture in which self is primary and motherhood is disparaged, mistrust, insecurity, and isolation have become the norm for many. As Mary Eberstadt points out, after sixty years of the sexual revolution, children raised in daycare and too soon separated from mothers, the absence of fathers and the press of identity politics, we should not be surprised that our society is falling apart. We have forgotten that we are communal creatures born to belong to family. Tragically, this is happening throughout the Western world.

---

[264] Erikson, 91.
[265] *Between Parent and Child* (Avon Books, 1969), 199.

In post-revolutionary societies, the old ways of knowing who I am and what I'm for (i.e., by reference to family, extended family, and real-life larger communities) are growing weaker for many people and no longer exist for some. ... Systemwide familial dislocations are now having repercussions at every stage of human life, as shown by new data about the steep rise in psychiatric problems among American teenagers and young adults; decades of empirical evidence about the harms of fatherless homes (a literature as well-known as it is ignored); the "loneliness studies" now proliferating in sociology, spotlighting the increasing isolation of the elderly in every Western nation.[266]

Adrift from the moorings of family, tradition, and faith, individuals in the Twenty-first Century must find themselves by themselves. Inevitably, they are thrown back on their own subjectivity. As more come to realize the self cannot complete itself, perhaps a willingness to consider certain traditions will grow. The next chapter highlights just a few ways culture can enhance the lives of men and women.

---

[266] *Primal Screams: How the Sexual Revolution Created Identity Politics* (West Conshohocken, PA: Templeton press, 2019), 10-11.

CHAPTER 9

In Celebration of Old Ways

*Blessed are those who find wisdom. Her ways are pleasant ways,
and all her paths are peace.* —Proverbs 3

We sat in awkward silence for several minutes. Finally, Noah, 23, shrugged his shoulders, shot me a sheepish look and said, "Gee, Doc. I guess I just don't really know." I resisted the temptation to react. So, I simply grunted, thinking, "This is his pain, let him feel it." My hope was that the uneasiness might motivate him. That any self-consciousness might stimulate self-reflection. But he did not seem to feel any discomfort. After all, his situation wasn't so bad; so, when I had asked him what he thought was important in his life, why should he feel uncomfortable that he had no answer? Why trouble about a job when you have everything you need at home? Why trouble about a driver's license when mom gives you rides? And, when tension between mother and son became too great, he would stay at his father's house, which wasn't so bad, either. His father mostly left him alone except when they would smoke a bong together.

The helplessness I felt with Noah reminded me of a different kind of frustration I had experienced with Joni. She had originally come to see me for help with depression. After only a few sessions, we discovered the source of her unhappiness. She desperately wanted to be married and start a family. This attractive thirty-five-year-old was likable, intelligent, and responsible. I could not understand why she could not find a mate. However, as she talked about the various men she encountered, it soon became clear. She found them content with low-wage jobs and happy to spend weekends watching movies or playing video games. She figured it was unwise to try to change them, but was unwilling to wait for them to grow up.

Considering these two vignettes, one wonders how much a troubled culture has influenced their situations. How is it that boys are not becoming men? And what will become of a society filled with immature, unconfident males? Warren Farrell states, "Boys are falling behind girls in almost every single academic subject including reading and writing which are the two biggest predictors of success or failure..." Boys who do poorly in those subjects are much more likely to drop out of high school. Sperm counts have dropped by 50 percent in recent years and IQ scores by 15 percent. Only 39 percent of university students are boys and the number who say they do not like school has skyrocketed by 70 percent since 1980. One causal factor is clear: the lack of dads in the home. In fact, one in three kids in the US and the UK grow up without a father.[267]

The question of rules and authority... Do we need a dad?

We have discussed the vital role of boundaries in fostering well-being: the implementation of laws and limits. As was true at creation, humans continue to be obligated to submit to boundaries—prohibitions not necessarily to their liking. On the other hand, as Genesis taught us, submission to proper authority holds the promise of life. Such an external force may appear as a natural, physical limitation—a boundary as to what is possible and what ought not to be pursued. It only took one sprained ankle to tell me not to jump off the roof

---

[267] The Four Dos and Don'ts of Divorce | Warren Farrell | The Jordan B. Peterson Podcast - S4: E:41 - YouTube, accessed August 19, 2021.

again. Appropriate limits to constrain our desires may also appear as legal, moral, or spiritual law. Or the weight of tradition, custom, or taboo.

To be effective, each of these should not be perceived as arbitrary, but should make sense on some level. Consider the traditional authority of the father. Do not his larger size, stronger arms, and deeper voice imply some differentiated role or power? When such a man is also kind and involved, a natural assumption of authority becomes a sensible fit within the family structure.

On the other hand, such reasoning is anathema to many. One wonders what kind of unhappiness the protesters of patriarchy must have accumulated to leave them so embittered. Clearly, when authority is perceived as abusive, resistance will follow. Whatever the motivation, we cannot help but sound a loud alarm. Decades of progressive indignation have now so infiltrated the public sphere that boys and young men are, as Helen Smith puts it, "on strike." She worries that as boys refuse to grow up, our culture will rapidly become fatherless.[268] There can be no doubt, if a society fails to develop mature men and celebrate fathers, it will not survive. How is this so?

Chana Ullman, adducing multiple studies on the father's role in child development, notes that social adjustment, academic performance, identity, and sex-role adaptation in both boys and girls are facilitated when fathers exhibit warm involvement in their kids' lives. Summarizing, she writes,

> Three related functions can be identified as a special, though certainly not exclusive, arena of the father. First, insofar as he tends to be perceived by the child as the stronger adult figure, the father endows laws and

---

[268] *Men on Strike: Why Men Are Boycotting Marriage, Fatherhood, and the American Dream – and Why It Matters* (New York: Encounter Books, 2013).

constraints with authority, inhibiting impulses and imposing a meaningful structure on behavior. Second, as the traditional mediator between the family and the outside world, he promises protection from external dangers, assuring the child of her or his own individual ability to cope with them. Third, as a different "significant other" within the family orbit, the father offers a necessary counterpart to the mother-infant relationship, aiding the differentiation of the separate sense of self.[269]

Let us consider:

- A father is the spiritual leader, representing a bridge of authority between the concerns of daily living and the ultimate world of heaven.
- A father protects the innocence of his daughters. Potential suitors must face his scrutiny, whether they approach through the front door or the portals of the internet.
- A father provides for his family. Too many unmarried pregnant women no longer can trust the man to give her the security that would allow her to relax and enjoy her young ones.
- A father teaches his children, trains them in mental and moral knowledge. Today, men too often are considered to be ignorant or bad or both.[270] Last week, I hazarded a foray into television programs aimed at children. Within the first minute after clicking the

---

[269] *The Transformed Self: The Psychology of Religious Conversion* (New York: Plenum Press, 1989), 50.

[270] McGuire, op. cit., cites a Brigham Young University study finding that 40% of fatherly behavior in media aimed at tweens depicted them as buffoons. In addition, half of the children's responses to their fathers involved "negative behaviors like eye rolling or walking away." 116

station, I was greeted with a scene in which a bright twelve-year-old asked her dad what she should do. He simply made a foolish shrug and said "I'm sure you will figure it out honey. You always do."

- A father models ethical, moral behavior. In contrast, the media typically portrays him as self-centered and lawless.
- A father represents and enacts positive initiative, prosocial assertiveness, loving leadership. In the Twenty-first Century, masculine initiative is maligned and assumed to be toxic.
- A father channels his sexual drive, inseminating only a future mother.
- A father models maturity, thoughtfulness and self-control. Too often, we find ourselves surrounded by grown-up boys. A Peter Pan culture.

Dating and waiting

I was fifteen when I ventured on my first real date. To tell the truth, it was a bit of an ordeal. I had to walk across town to pick her up; then together, we traipsed back several miles to the movie theater. After that, I had to walk her home again. Not an easy endeavor, but it spawned some benefits. The first of which was a personal decision to grab my driver's license on the day of my sixteenth birthday! More importantly, we had a chance to talk and get to know each other. Incidentally, our parents knew and approved of this rendezvous.

These days, many don't really go on dates. They "hang out." Or they hook up. In short, if they get together at all, it's through shortcuts. On the other hand, the old-fashioned ritual of going on a date requires a certain amount of thought, preparation, and planning. These, in turn, require a certain amount of maturity. And distance. The girl is not immediately available at the boy's beck and call. He must wait for her answer. To do so facilitates frustration tolerance. And she retains her dignity, the mystery of her femininity.

Typically, conservative parents set sixteen or seventeen as an age requirement for dating. Some discourage dating altogether in high school. They suggest instead that young people get to know each other in a group context. Church youth groups have been excellent venues through which adolescents can ease into friendships with the opposite sex.

Can we solve the Lois Lane syndrome?

In discussing what makes a man attractive to a woman, Jordan Peterson and Warren Farrell discuss a common phenomenon in the dating world today. As you may recall, the mild-mannered and sensitive Clark Kent and Lois Lane worked closely as reporters for a big-city newspaper. Despite spending much time with Clark, Lois had no interest in him. On the other hand, she fell madly in love with Superman. But then, she also came to realize that Superman was tough and not emotionally responsive! So, which is it? Here is a similar scenario: A cheerleader's boyfriend wants to have a heart-to-heart talk. He has decided that football is dangerous and a waste of time. According to Peterson and Farrell, the common reaction is to drop him and go for the next guy on the team.[271]

Eggerichs is correct when he abstracts from Ephesians 5 the principle that women have a special need to feel loved while men require respect.[272] ("To sum up, each one of you is to love his wife as himself and the wife is to respect her husband." v. 33) How is that to happen today? For decades, young men have been told to *stand down*, the implication being that they should be more like girls and that masculinity is toxic. Many, such as Noah in the vignette, have taken that

---

[271] *The Four Dos and Don'ts of Divorce*

[272] Emmerson Eggerichs, *Love and Respect* (Chicago, Il.: Thomas Nelson, 2012).

advice and now Joni cannot find a man. Meanwhile, young women have been told to *stand up*, so to speak—groomed to pursue achievement and high-powered careers. Peterson observes that we tell three lies to young women: "There's nothing more important than your career. There's nothing more important in your life than your career. There *should* be nothing more important in your life than your career." Men, however, do not readily fall in love with women who are their bosses, have higher degrees or make more money than they. In short, women are deprived of the love they long for and men fail to receive the respect they crave. In other words, the changes we have seen in Western culture do not make the sexes very attractive to each other.

Old fashioned complementarity

Are the old ways the sexes related to each other really so bad? One might ask, "Are you crazy? Do you seriously wish to turn the clock back?" Well, maybe a little. I recall listening to a woman describe her terrible childhood and being fascinated to learn what helped her survive. She would watch TV. Shows from the sixties and seventies pictured loving families, men who were wise and kind. Women who loved their children. Of course, without some dysfunction, "Leave it to Beaver" or "Ozzie and Harriet" would not be funny. Yet, the fundamentals of family were there and my client held onto them like a lifeline.

We have seen that in profound ways, feminine power resides in the power to affirm masculine power, a power essentially designed to represent the loving initiative of God. In her role as launcher of persons and chief cheerleader, she celebrates her son's need to differentiate himself from her, to see himself as strong in her eyes. When believing he possesses some calling and some masculine capacity that she needs and values, he stretches himself. He grows in discipline as he decides to delay gratification to pursue some important dream. Whether the goal is to attain Eagle Scout, first string on the football team or valedictorian, it must be seen as special to the female. Hard work, the development of frustration tolerance and the ability to hold in mind long-term goals are necessary for maturity. As boys grow into well socialized men, they will love women, who in turn affirm them. Real masculinity is both fostered by the female and enacted in her service. A well socialized man is a gentleman, a scholar and a soldier. He is a soldier because he is willing to fight for his family; he is a scholar because he studies life—whether that life be on the street, in the factory or in the library—in order to provide for his family; he studies the Word of God—a word which enjoins him to study the woman (1 Peter 3:7); he is a gentleman because he respects the woman, listens to her, allows her to go first, pulls her chair out for her, and shows her kindness in numerous ways. A well-socialized man will die for a woman but will never ask her to sacrifice her life for him.

In addition, a well-socialized man does not keep his wife under his thumb. He understands that as her children grow, she has many years ahead of her. Having himself gained a footing in the world, he is well placed and ready to sponsor her in whatever wider dreams or career goals she might entertain.

We understand that after the Fall, no family can do better than simply approximate wholesome life patterns. Nevertheless, some scenarios seem likely to promote satisfying relationships. These involve conferring unique roles and values to each gender. The goal? Enhanced self-esteem, personal security, and meaningful destiny for each family member.

Everyone a mother or father

Do we really want to fit everyone into the "happy days" of the 1950s? Not every couple has a child. Nor does everyone get married or have that desire. Yet, if gender is not accidental and there exist essential differences between the sexes, it follows that unmarried people will also find their deepest nature lived out in primarily feminine or masculine modes. Inasmuch as each sex is born with an essential nature oriented toward the other and carries an innate potential toward generativity, their sexual proclivities predate marriage and will be felt regardless of marital status. Thus, the single man retains an impulse to differentiate himself from the female as well as to serve and protect her. The single woman continues to hold a special orientation to support, empathize, and seek connection. As she lives for God, she offers support and nurture to those who need such comfort and will find herself doing so even if she pursues a traditionally masculine career. Single men as well live out their masculinity as they initiate new ideas, pursue leadership roles in the church, and the mentoring or fathering of others. Without absolutizing specific roles and behaviors, we can affirm, as does the New Testament, that single persons can come fully alive living out their sexuality knowing neither physical sex nor a spouse. This "gift of celibacy" may offer greater freedom and fulfillment as the apostle Paul himself experienced. The Roman church recognizes both a high calling for those with such a gift as well as the understanding that God does not want us isolated, but that we belong together. Married or not, we are family. We are not mere persons alone, but sisters and brothers, mothers and fathers.[273]

The troubling changes described in this book have not appeared overnight. While conservatives within the church still extend a special position to the man as head of the family, the forces that would deprive both sexes of any special, generative role have been operating tirelessly for many years. The next chapter describes several observers from outside the

---

[273] Piper offers helpful insight to single believers as they live out their uniqueness as males or females. *Recovering Biblical Manhood and Womanhood.*, 36-46.

church who have, years ago, sounded the alarm that the family in the West is in trouble.

CHAPTER 10

Secular Prophets and the Road to Sexual Suicide

Does not wisdom call out? —Proverbs 8:1

I f you are a fan of Saturday Night Live, you will recall the "church lady" played by Dana Carvey. Dressed in an old-fashioned skirt and wearing a gray-haired bun, he appears as a prune faced old spinster who disdains various expressions of sexual freedom. Quite funny at times, but the message is unavoidable: Christians are judgmental, repressive, and unreasonable prudes. Old-fashioned values ought to fade away with old people. It is true that religious people hold more conservative views and tend to oppose the more relaxed sexual mores of recent decades. And while the portentous tone of this book is biblically based, it is nevertheless important to consider the insights of *secular* thinkers who have expressed concerns about the direction of Western culture.

J. D. Unwin: Sexual constraint leads to societal flourishing

A reluctant prognosticator of societal decay, this Oxford anthropologist spent the bulk of his career examining some eighty cultures and six civilizations. Published in 1934, J. D. Unwin's 600 page *Sex and Culture* was only a "summary" of his life's work.[274] Unwin was not a religious man, but a

---

[274] London: Oxford University Press, 1934.

rationalist who held to strict principles of scientific inquiry. His driving question was to examine the relationship between sexual freedom and cultural flourishing. In his preface, he makes it clear he has no ax to grind, no thesis to prove. He was simply curious to test the suggestion made by analytical psychologists that civilizations are always built up by social regulations that "forbid direct satisfaction of the sexual impulses...[and promote] compulsory sacrifices in the gratification of innate desires."[275] Initially, Unwin had questioned the Freudian concept of sublimation in which sexual energy is diverted to other more socially valuable ends. In the preface to his finished work, he shared his surprise and seemed almost apologetic in his conclusions, which "the evidence appeared to force upon me."[276]

Unwin discerned four cultural categories in terms of the degree to which architecture, art, engineering, literature, and the like flourished. These ranged from the relatively inert "zoistic" "dead cultures" which simply focused on people's immediate needs and wants to the highly productive, energetic "rationalistic" cultures. He analyzed each of these in terms of the degree of sexual restraint in premarital and postmarital relations. Prenuptial expectations ranged from complete promiscuity among the young to strict rules of chastity whereby virginity before marriage was enforced. The postnuptial categories ranged from absolute monogamy to absolute polygamy.

Kurt Dunston summarizes his most significant findings:

- Effect of sexual constraints: Increased sexual constraints, either pre- or post-nuptial, always led to increased flourishing. Conversely, increased sexual

---

[275] Ibid., in https://archive.org/details/b20442580/page/n9/mode/2up

[276] Ibid. preface, *Sex and Culture*.

freedom always led to the collapse of a culture three generations later.

- Single most influential factor: Surprisingly, the data revealed that the single most important correlation with a flourishing culture was whether pre-nuptial chastity was required or not. It had a very significant effect either way.

- Highest flourishing of culture: The most powerful combination was pre-nuptial chastity coupled with "absolute monogamy." Rationalist cultures that retained this combination for at least three generations exceeded all other cultures in every area, including literature, art, science, furniture, architecture, engineering, and agriculture.

- Effect of abandoning prenuptial chastity: When strict prenuptial chastity was no longer the norm, absolute monogamy, deism, and rational thinking also disappeared within three generations.

- Total sexual freedom: If total sexual freedom was embraced by a culture, that culture collapsed within three generations to the lowest state of flourishing—which Unwin describes as "inert" and at a "dead level of conception" and is characterized by people who have little interest in much else other than their own wants and needs. At this level, the culture is *usually conquered or taken over by another culture with greater social energy.*

- Time lag: If there is a change in sexual constraints, either increased or decreased restraints, the full effect of that change is not realized until the third generation.[277]

---

[277] "Why Sexual Morality May be Far More Important than You Ever Thought," *The Orthodox Church of Tomorrow* December 2, 2019 By Fr. John Peck https://frjohnpeck.com/why-sexual-morality-may-be-far-more-important-than-you-ever-thought/

Dunston also notes that,

Prior to the sexual revolution which began in the late 1960s, prenuptial chastity was still held in strong regard by Western culture. But, starting in the 1970s, pre-marital sexual freedom became increasingly acceptable. By the early 2000s, the majority of teens were sexually active, to the extent that remaining a virgin until marriage was regarded with disbelief if not ridicule.[278]

Unwin's predictions are disturbing. Cohabitation has become the norm while commitment has dropped sharply;[279] belief in God has decreased since the 1960s and a rise in superstition seems to have filled the gap.[280] Rational thinking has been replaced by subjectivism. We experience now a postmodernism that is better characterized as "post truth."[281] Dunston writes:

Unwin's three main predictions—the abandonment of rationalism, deism, and absolute monogamy—are all well underway... Thanks to the rationalist generations that preceded them, the first generation of a society setting aside its sexual restraints can still enjoy its new-found sexual freedom before any significant decline in culture, but the data show that this "having your cake and eating it too" phase lasts a maximum of one generation before the decline sets in... and it

---

[278] Ibid.

[279] "More cohabitation, less commitment?" *Medical Institute for Sexual Health*, Sept., 2018. https://www.medinstitute.org/articles/more-cohabitation-less-commitment/

[280] https://www.pewresearch.org/fact-tank/2016/01/21/americans-spirituality/

[281] "Why Sexual Morality May Be Far More Important Than You Ever Thought," op cit.

appears that our civilization is following the same, well-travelled road to collapse.[282]

On the other hand, let us remember: As a people come to realize their need, God is always ready to heal their land (Second Chronicles 7:14).

Carle Zimmerman: The rise of atomism and the drift toward Nihilism

In 1947, distinguished Harvard professor of sociology, Carle Zimmerman produced his magnum opus, *Family and Civilization*. This work is still honored today for its comprehensive investigation into the history of the family and the correlation between types of family and the viability of civilizations. In his introduction to a recent republication, Alan C. Carlson writes, "The book stands as an extraordinary feat of research and interpretation. It sweeps across the millennia and burrows into the nature of otherwise disparate civilizations to reveal deeper and universal social traits."[283]

Beginning in antiquity, Zimmerman studied Greek, Roman, Russian, Chinese, Hindu, and Muslim cultures. He discerned three main types of families from strong to weak. The weakest family structure is the "atomistic" pattern in which the state and the larger society hold significant power. In the "trustee" family, less common in today's world, strong bonds held the extended family and clan together. Government or societal influence was relatively weak. The "domestic" family represents a balance between family power and societal input. Early marriage, the importance of faith, childbearing, and a sacramental view of marriage characterize this type of family.

---

[282] Ibid.

[283] "Introduction to the 2008 edition," *Family and Civilization*, Carle C. Zimmerman (Wilmington, Delaware: Intercollegiate Studies Institute, 2008) p. ix.

Zimmerman described what he calls "familism"—"a system of life which must be built largely from within."[284] Many sociologists, enchanted by social progress but ignorant of history, have failed to grasp the pivotal role of familism. This is the profound power of the family to shape ideals, to build character, and to maintain a vital society. According to Zimmerman,

> The family gives more and requires more of the individual than do other social organizations. For long periods of youth, it gives everything without recompense, as if life itself brought with it certain inherent rights of birth in no way dependent on innate goodness or ability of the parents. Then for long periods it takes from the individual without direct accountable physical recompense. The person, as his role changes from family dependent to family head (parent) is demoted from King to slave... The psychology of this is interesting. Familism has to be motivated by the acceptance of ideals of behavior based upon a way of life and not upon the usual system of rewards and punishments in nonfamily society. As a result, it is easy for persons to escape the demotion of social freedom by a conscious avoidance of the family. Consequently, when familistic ideals are broken among the masses, we find whole peoples turning away from familism and extremely violent eruptions against this system.[285]

Familism is not only essential in character formation but profoundly affects all other aspects of culture. When civilizations were thriving, a strong familism fostered such qualities

---

[284] Zimmerman, 185.
[285] Ibid., 187.

as loyalty, self-sacrifice, and belief in God. Zimmerman concluded that,

> familism is the greatest single factor in cultural integration. The family contribution is a basic one... The basic habits and fundamental beliefs in a value system exist simply because the family exists, and are directed around familism. Thus, cultures are fairly well integrated about a system of values to the extent that familism is present.[286]

In disturbing contrast, the atomistic family pattern carries the least degree of familism and has always emerged as a correlate and precursor to societal decay. Instead of strong communal affiliations, the growth of individualism and statism would rise in dominance. Zimmerman also described a kind of Manichaeism that played a central role in the weakening of Greek and Roman culture. This was the hedonistic "eat, drink, and be merry, for tomorrow we die" mindset. He quotes Polybius's description of key factors in the decline of the Greek family. These included low birth rate, attitudes of pride, greed, and indolence expressed as a reluctance to take on the responsibilities of marriage and child-rearing. Zimmerman also cites Theodore Mommsen's *History of Rome*. Here again, the emergence of the atomistic family could be discerned.

> The increasing development of extrafamily sex life; the decay of the mores of the upper class families; the rise of sexual abnormalities; the increasing refusal of women to be sedate in an unsedate world; the emergence of purely romantic conceptions of love, which finally became dominant; the decline in the seriousness with

---

[286] Ibid., 194.

which adultery is considered; the purely formal adhesion to the moral code; the increased popularity and frequency of absolute divorce and separation... and, finally, positive social antagonism to the old domestic family system and the family among the whole masses of the people.[287]

In the West, certain philosophies taking seed in the Nineteenth Century fueled the rise of atomism in our day. These included an economic theory in which an unrestrained, greedy individual might "challenge every value in relation to his profit, loss, and gain in material consumption."[288] Further, the philosophies of Hegel, Marx, and social reformism cultivated the deification of the state while weakening the family. Such movements linked themselves with the evolutionary idea of history as unfolding in constant linear progress. According to Zimmermann,

> The 19th century idea of evolution, with its vision of unending goal-destined progress, had two very important effects upon the family. In the first place, the philosophy destroyed the concept of historical tradition for the 19th century. All any college student learned of social science and sociology from the 19th century to World War I was a theory of social relativism, the linear "evolution" of society through the 19th century, the need for challenging all social institutions including the family, and the possibility of continued improvement through the destruction of accepted values.[289]

---

[287] Ibid., 43.
[288] Ibid., 124.
[289] Ibid.

Zimmerman writes that every social movement from that time on, from economic theory to family legislation, carried the result of diminishing the strength of the family and tradition.

George Gilder: The sexual revolution and feminism as agents of cultural decay

In 1973, as the women's liberation movement was gaining speed, lone conservative intellectual George Gilder stepped on progressive toes with unpopular warnings that have proved prescient. His book, ominously entitled *Sexual Suicide*, argued that the only freedom that "sexual liberalism" would produce is to liberate men from their families. In his revised version in 1986, *Men and Marriage,* his worst fears were already being realized.[290] Now, thirty-five years hence, it would be well to review some of Gilder's salient observations.

In a nutshell, Gilder warned that were men to be deprived of some special status and dignity bequeathed by society simply by virtue of their being male, an unraveling of the social fabric would occur. Following anthropologists such as Margaret Mead, Gilder argued that while the role and dignity of the female are unimpeachable, the roles and status of the male are always fragile and tenuous. Life itself issues from the woman, who remains at the center of the most basic unit of life, the family. The position of the man, however, bounces precariously on the peculiarities and whims of any particular culture in which he finds himself. Mead states it directly, "The central problem of every society is to define appropriate roles for the man."[291] Historically, the role of provider and protector has given the male a solid sense of value and place in the world.

---

[290] Gretna: Pelican Publishing Co, 2008 edition.

[291] Margaret Mead, *male and female: a study of the sexes in a changing world* (New York: Morro, 1949). Cited in Gilder, 29.

Gilder argued that the male sexual rhythm, with its visual emphasis and demand for immediacy, has throughout history been properly sublimated in positive, productive work. A young boy would define himself as valuable in contradistinction to the young girl because he believed that she would need him in his capacity as protector and provider or "head" of the family. She, in turn, valued and accepted her unique sexual identity as life-giver and nurturer, knowing that such an identity and honor is hers merely by virtue of her body. Accepting her femininity, she had no need to compete with the male for dominance and so naturally confirmed to her mate his value to her as a man.

Aside from sexual intercourse, the male lacks obvious essentiality. Is he even necessary? In a sense, even this act is trivial. He has no say as to whether his child will even come to term or not. He may not even know for sure whether the child belongs to him. "The father is neither inherently equal to the mother within the family, nor necessarily inclined to remain with it. In one way or another, men must be *made* equal by society."[292] Regardless of whether a young dad holds a bottle or changes diapers, he will never experience the depth of sensation or fulfillment felt by the woman as she suckles her child. In less developed societies, the greater physical strength of men provided compensation. In more advanced cultures, men have counterbalanced their less critical connection to the family with their role as provider. "Money replaces muscle." As young women outpace men in earnings, even this connection grows increasingly tenuous.[293]

---

[292] *Men and Marriage*, 6.

[293] Some have argued that, via the social welfare state, the black man especially has found himself untethered to his offspring. In his research for Lyndon Johnson's war on poverty, Daniel Moynihan reported that ever expanding welfare programs harmed the black male's role as provider and contributed to increasing divorce rates, child abandonment and out of wedlock births.

Gilder further pointed out that in societies that survive, the delights of sexual knowledge were to be kept within proper boundaries. Traditionally, as a young man learned to submit his sexual drive to the sexual rhythm of the female, with its accent on long-term consequences, personal love, and commitment, he gained self-control, maturity, and confidence. In old England, the father of the bride would not give the hand of his daughter to a man who had not first built his own farmhouse. In this way, he demonstrated he was capable and worthy of being a husband and father. Sex with the female was the long-term prize of sweaty effort and the mastery of skills. Gilder warned that should the sexual revolution, in tandem with women's liberation, render this process archaic, the "sexual constitution" would be disrupted. The stability of the family and, indeed, society itself would be severely undermined.

Gilder noted that women take their sexual identity for granted. They seem not to understand male anxiety or why men need to prove their manhood. Why the pissing contests? Why the constant need to mark their territory? Nor have women understood that the "sexist" male may simply wish to protect his special contribution to the female. "Why can't men just be themselves?" The reason, writes Gilder, is that,

> Unlike femininity, relaxed masculinity is at bottom empty, a limp nullity. While the female body is full of internal potentiality, the male is internally barren (from the Old French *bar*, meaning man). Manhood at the most basic level can be validated and expressed only in action.[294]

Just sitting around and waiting leaves a man restless and insecure. His identity is dependent on action. This action

---

[294] Ibid., 9-10.

must be carefully channeled—for his own sake and for the sake of those he cares about. He must see himself as provider or protector—some role of significance to the female. Gilder summarizes a cross-cultural study of 190 different societies:

> If society devalues this male role by pressing women to provide for themselves, prove their "independence," and compete with men for money and status, there's only one way equality between the sexes can be maintained: Women must be reduced to sexual parity. They must relinquish their sexual superiority, psychologically disconnect their wombs, and adopt the short-circuited copulatory sexuality of males. Women must renounce all the larger procreative dimensions of their sexual impulse.[295]

Unfortunately, this secular prophecy has proven to be hideously accurate. The reduction of the female, at least in some quarters, has become extreme. A slide toward serious degradation. Rebecca Whisnant writes that a cursory sample of online pornography reveals that

> ...the humiliation of women is a virtual constant in contemporary mainstream pornography (Dines, 2010). Here a woman crawls on hands and knees; there a penis is shoved in her mouth sideways, distending the face, so that she looks ridiculous; and everywhere, she intones, "I'm such a filthy little whore."[296]

---

[295] Ibid., 5.

[296] "Pornography, Humiliation, and Consent," University of Dayton, August, 2016. Dr. Norman Doidge—author of the neuroscience book *The Brain That Changes Itself*—stated that hardcore porn "is increasingly dominated by the sadomasochistic themes . . . all involving scripts fusing sex with hatred and humiliation."

There is something more than just kinky sex here. Comparing such scenes with the sadistic humiliation and torture of Iraqi prisoners by U.S. soldiers at the Abu Ghraib prison, Whisnant discerns a viciousness that seems to motivate many porn videos. The popular Bangbus videos, for example, feature picking up (supposedly) unsuspecting young women, sexually molesting them and unceremoniously dumping them on the street.[297]

How is it young women submit to such objectification? In Chapter Eight, we examined the dialogic nature of identity formation—that a developing self interacts with cultural codes and natural boundaries. How many girls today, malnourished by a culture that questions everything, no longer assume any value as potential child-bearers? How many grow up valuing neither their femininity nor their dignity?

Abstinence: Is the female required to socialize the male?

As women have traded modesty and reticence for sexual freedom, they have simultaneously lost their calling—according to Gilder—to socialize men.

> In creating civilization, women transform male lust into love; channel male wanderlust into jobs, homes, and families; link men to specific children; rear children into citizens; change hunters into farmers; divert male will to power into a drive to create.[298]

Without such transformation, the impulsive sexuality of the male works against both women and culture. Female sexuality, on the other hand, has always involved greater discretion, a more careful selection of partners, more self-control,

---

[297] Ibid.
[298] Gilder, 5.

and consideration of future consequences. In every stable society it is the woman who grants or withholds sexual favors. And it is women who domesticate and civilize men. The male is the restless, hungry one. The seeker. She is the one who withholds or grants sex and love. It is therefore vital for her to require him to mature if he is to possess her body.

As Unwin and Zimmermann discerned, healthy societies require marriage as a prerequisite to sex. Marriage, in turn, appears to be a prerequisite for society itself to survive. Gilder quotes anthropologist Bronislaw Malinowski on the importance of marriage as well as the requirement of male maturity. The prerequisite for a man to gain a wife is "to prove his capacity to maintain the woman."[299] Margaret Mead states directly that the male role "in marriage in every known human society, is to provide for women and children."[300] Without a woman, man is at a loss, feels he is dispensable. But he must have ways to find her, to win her, and to feel that he is equal to her. If she abandons her natural reluctance and consideration of the long-term consequences of sex, she will inevitably lose her dignity as a woman. At the same time, she deprives him of the ultimate necessity to mature.

Indeed, have we not seen in recent decades how females have surrendered their natural reluctance for one-night stands? Too many women, in a kind of questionable "submission," have opted for the short-term rhythm of male sexuality with its demand for immediate gratification. This is the inferior pattern. Citing anthropologists Mead and Ashley Montagu and psychoanalysts Karen Horney and Erik Erikson, Gilder contrasts the more stable and secure femininity with the insecure and "questing masculinity." At the core of this male inferiority lies two facts. From birth, as described in previous

---

[299] Ibid., 15. Robert Briffault and Bronislaw Malinowski, *Marriage: Past and Present* (Boston: Parker Sgt., 1956), 50.
[300] Mead, *Male and Female*, 195.

chapters, the male child shares with his sister a primary bond with mother, but he must break that attachment. On some level, he forever carries the knowledge that he lacks the organic indispensability of the female. In addition, the boy finds within his body an unfocused energy. He is more aggressive, more impulsive. Lacking a vision of love and significance, he finds himself without a map. He is lost. Without a clear role and a growing tie to his father, he remains directionless, untethered to the family or the future. Unsure of who he is.

> Male sexual consciousness comes as an unpro-grammed drive. Nothing about the male body dictates any specific pattern beyond the repetitive release of sexual tension. Men must define and defend the larger dimensions of their sexuality by external activity… Men have only one sex organ and one sex act: erection and ejaculation. Everything else is guided by culture and imagination. Other male roles, other styles of masculine identity, must be learned or created. The most important and productive roles—husband and father in a durable marriage—are a cultural invention, necessary to civilized life but ultimately fragile.[301]

The heart of the matter is the basic and universal fact of the sexual superiority of women. Gilder argues that the female thus holds a special responsibility for maintaining civilization itself, whereas the male has no such natural agenda built into his body.

> Women domesticate and civilize male nature. They can jeopardize male discipline and identity, and civi-lization as well, merely by giving up the role… The essential pattern is clear. Women manipulate male

---

[301] Gilder, 8-9.

sexual desire in order to teach men the long-term cycles of female sexuality and biology on which civilization is based. When a man learns, his view of the woman as an object of his own sexuality succumbs to an image of her as the bearer of a richer and more extended eroticism and as the keeper of the portals of social immortality.[302]

Of course, men must be tamed, not neutered. Their aggressivity must be channeled in generative, prosocial directions. Is this the job of lawmakers? Gilder does not think so. The West already has many laws that are easily and often broken. Rather, some social role—one that excludes women—must be carved out for the boys in the family. Such a role must be affirmed by women, especially the mother. And the achievement of that role must be affirmed by women, especially a future wife.

A father's warm bond with his son and availability as a role model is, of course, essential. But what if the dad has not achieved that vital position in the family? What if he is distant, dishonorable, or absent altogether? Mom is still there. As she picks up the slack, she continues to love her boy. But what is he to conclude about his father? Even if his mother refuses to denigrate him, some tacit truth lingers: men must be bad. Or useless. The boy dares not lose his mother's approval but his curiosity and longing grow. He needs to identify with males; maybe he is bad or useless as well. Divided within, he is a pendulum from mother's good boy to lost bad boy. Fatherless, he searches for ways to father himself.

---

[302] Ibid., 13.

"No girls allowed"?

This brings us to the topic of boys' clubs or boys-only clubs. Gangs. Gilder highlights cross-cultural studies depicting how tribes and societies accept gang-like activities in their young men. Remember, the male does not have within his body inscribed behavioral inclinations. He is untamed, direction-less—"clueless," if you like. He needs guidelines, masculine roles. That is why he hangs out with other boys. He gains both confidence and information from his affiliation with other males.

Boys also learn better with other boys.[303] Do you remember the movie, "Dead Poet's Society"? Like the Pied Piper, Robin Williams's character created in his boys an enthusiasm for learning that was contagious. Gilder offers data that support single-sex learning. In the obsession with androgynous freedom ("gender is a cage"), liberal educators insist on merging the sexes earlier and earlier. By the time they are in high school, many boys, unless particularly bright or obedient, have long concluded academics is not for them. Having lagged behind since kindergarten, can we blame them? "Clearly in a losing game in masculine terms, the boys react in two ways: they put on a show for the girls and dominate the class anyway, or they dropout."[304]

To thrive as a culture, do we not prefer a man to be educated and civilized? Untamed and ignorant, he is dangerous. If a society fails to provide a boy with prosocial expectations, rites of passage, and cultural pathways that bid him to pursue

---

[303] More research is needed but a systematic review of studies supports the value of single sex classrooms in terms both of academic achievement and emotional maturity. See "Single-Sex Versus Coeducation Schooling: A Systematic Review—Final Report." US Dept. of Education, Executive Summary—Single-Sex Versus Coeducation Schooling: A Systematic Review (2005); see also, Sax, Leonard. "The Promise and Peril of Single-Sex Public Education: Mr. Chips Meets Snoop Dogg." *Education Week* 24.25 (2005): 34-45.

[304] Gilder, 117.

significance, he will flounder. Or he will fight. An angry, lost, and antisocial male is a blight to society. Masculinity itself becomes suspect.

The upshot of George Gilder's analysis is this: If women themselves and the society as a whole do not create or at least allow significant, viable pathways to masculinity but instead promote ubiquitous gender sameness, that society will suffer internal chaos. In addition, through declining birthrates, it loses viability altogether. Could we really be committing "sexual suicide"?

Allan Bloom: The tyranny of limits; openness is everything

The *New York Times* described the 1987 bestseller, *The Closing of the American Mind: How Higher Education Has Failed Democracy and Impoverished the Souls of Today's Students,* as, "that rarest of documents, a genuinely profound book."[305] Today, reading the twenty-fifth anniversary edition, the reflections of this now deceased professor are more relevant and disturbing than ever. His is a book about students, but more so, about culture and the direction of our culture. Impervious to the growing political correctness in academia, Bloom exposed a kind of intellectual hegemony in the university that continues unabated to this day. In his careful analysis of university culture, he identified two assumptions that must never be questioned: that truth is relative and everyone is equal. These twin convictions carry moral fervor. On the first assumption, Bloom writes:

> The relativity of truth is not a theoretical insight but a moral postulate... Relativism is necessary to openness; and this is the virtue, the only virtue, which all primary

---

[305] Allan Bloom, New York: Simon & Schuster Paperbacks, 2012.

education for more than 50 years has dedicated itself to inculcating. Openness ... is the great insight of our times.[306]

Students are indoctrinated to believe the danger is not a matter of falsity against truth, but intolerance. They must be open to every claim and every way of life. The only enemy is the person not open. Hard facts, traditions, absolutes, taboos, and social constraints—even nature—bow to the god of openness and freedom. All limits are "arbitrary and tyrannical. There are no absolutes; freedom is absolute."[307]

The consequences for personal relationships, writes Bloom, have been disastrous. Students lack dreams, passion, or concern for anything beyond themselves. The ideals of patriotism, family, and religion have faded into a self-centeredness in which everyone does as he pleases. Set free from the moorings of tradition and community, young people are...

spiritually unclad, unconnected, isolated, with no inherited or unconditional connection with anything or anyone. They can be anything they want to be, but they have no particular reason to want to be anything in particular. Not only are they free to decide their place, but they are also free to decide whether they will believe in God or behaviorists, or leave their options open by being agnostic; whether they will be straight or gay, or, again, keep your options open; whether they will marry and whether they will stay married; whether they will have children—and so on endlessly.[308]

---

[306] Ibid., 25-26.
[307] Ibid., 28.
[308] Ibid.

The other absolute, beside the absolute that there are no absolutes, is a deeply held belief in Equality. Everyone is just... persons. Distinctions must be eradicated, or at least not noticed. Everyone is the same. Since males and females are the same, sex with either sex is optional. The doctrine of relativity and openness, by the way, demands that you agree.

These overriding principles of openness and equality have carved a path into the American zeitgeist well past politics and education. These twin forces, feeding each other in a strange alliance, have penetrated the most intimate areas of sex and love. "The sexual revolution marched under the banner of freedom; feminism under that of equality."[309] The common denominator is separation, an uncoupling of the sexes from each other and from nature. The feminists declared that biology was not destiny and agreed with the sexual libertarians in separating sex from traditional boundaries, commitment and the natural telos of sex. Each celebrated abortion. For the feminists, freedom from pregnancy carried the additional gift of freedom from the patriarchy. The goal of uncoupling from male dominance overlapped nicely with the easy coupling of free love in the sixties.

Bloom observed how the sexual revolution equated happiness with sensuality and entailed a significant assault on modesty. As shame disappeared, sex became "no big deal," in other words, depersonalized. When sex is just sex and the person disappears, one body is as good as another. Or equal to another, just as women are equal to men, have equal roles, are equally self-sufficient, and have no great expectation for each other. Bloom also noticed that words such as "I love you" were rare. The phrase "I'll always love you" was never spoken. Respect for each other's freedom seemed to preclude both passion and commitment.

---

[309] Ibid., 98.

Ideologies not grounded in truth or nature invariably push against nature. In the obsession with equality, feminists demanded that men embrace an equal share of household duties and childcare. This meant that men must change their nature. "The souls of men—their ambitious, warlike, protective, possessive character—must be dismantled in order to liberate women from their domination."[310] Men must become caring, sensitive, and nurturing—or else they are stubborn and sexist. The lie still hovers as an essential postulate of the canon of equality: men and women are the same. In describing the silliness of regulations giving men paternity leave, Bloom, unafraid to call a thing a thing, quips, "Law may prescribe that the male nipples be made equal to the female ones, but they still will not give milk."[311] Nor is it the nature of fathers to have the same attachment to children, and when women attach themselves to their career as do men, is this not, Bloom wonders, a formula for neglect?

Robert Bork: An enfeebled, hedonistic culture?

A final secular observer to consider from the last century is judge and Yale law professor Robert Bork. Michael Novak suggested that Bork's *Slouching Towards Gomorrah* may be the "most important book of the 90s." In no uncertain terms, Bork argued that "modern liberalism" is driving the collapse of American culture. Over two decades ago, he adduced growing evidence that we were becoming "an enfeebled hedonistic culture."[312] In depicting the progressive changes since the sixties, Bork alluded to the "Durkheim constant." This phenomenon is the notion that,

---

[310] Ibid., 129.

[311] Ibid.,131.

[312] *Slouching Towards Gomorrah: Modern Liberalism and American Decline* (New York: Regan books, 1996), 2.

There is a limit to the amount of deviant behavior any community can afford to recognize. As behavior worsens, the community adjusts its standards so that conduct once thought reprehensible is no longer deemed so.[313]

Bork warned that a disturbing twist has followed this principle. Americans not only have become accustomed to behavior which in the recent past would have been censored, but traditionally normal and moral behavior has now become portrayed as oppressive. As Charles Krauthammer also observed, "As part of the vast social project of moral leveling, it is not enough for the deviant to be normalized. The normal must be found to be deviant."[314] Bork saw this turn of events as extremely dangerous.

As a function of "modern liberalism," radical educators speak as if meaning has no correspondence to reality. Professors dismiss long-held assumptions about truth or moral absolutes as mere social constructs. Without the tempering forces of authority, religion and tradition, forms of radical egalitarianism and radical individualism have invaded the American mind. The one demands equality of outcome while the other demands freedom from restriction. Bork predicted an inevitable road to cultural disaster as "radical egalitarianism becomes tyranny and radical individualism descends into hedonism."[315]

No modern movement, in Bork's darkly direct analysis, has been more fanatical and more destructive than radical feminism. "Totalitarian in spirit, it is deeply antagonistic to traditional Western culture and proposes the complete

---

[313] Ibid., 3.

[314] "Defining Deviancy Up," *The New Republic*, November 22, 1993, P. 20. Cited in Bork, 3-4.

[315] Ibid., 11.

restructuring of society, morality, and human nature."[316] Despite the fact that barriers to women's achievement have been dismantled, radicals are not happy. In the nineties, feminism had become like a religion all its own, preaching a distinctive doctrine of evil and redemption. Patriarchy is the cause of inequality and oppression; salvation is to be found in freedom from male dominance and traditional sex roles. Inevitably, the family itself, with its binding roles of mother and mothering, must be dismantled.

Nihilistic attacks on religion and the traditional family are next. Bork references the well-known Hite Report. In a caricature of family life as a nest of oppression, Hite argued that children have to humiliate themselves under their parents' power in order to receive love. Further, the family is nothing but a contrivance by the man so he could own his woman.[317] Religions that support traditional family structures fare no better. These, too, are male inventions designed to dominate women.

Already in the 90s, Bork understood the growing feminist hegemony and intimidation in education was nearly complete. In sociology, for example, in thirty-six of thirty-eight textbooks discussing sex roles, anthropologist Margaret Mead is misrepresented as having found genuinely matriarchal societies. In her review of Steven Goldberg's book, *Inevitability of Patriarchy,* she writes: "It is true, as Professor Goldberg points out, that all the claims so glibly made about societies ruled by women are nonsense. ... Men have always been the leaders in public affairs and the final authorities at home."[318]

Bork saw that beyond proselytizing for feminist revisionism and lesbianism in women's studies programs, the relentless agenda was not above sexual and racial discrimination

---

[316] Ibid., 193.

[317] See Shire Hite, *The Hite Report on The Family: Growing Up Under Patriarchy* (New York: Grove press, 1994).

[318] Cited in Bork, 211.

in faculty recruitment. White males need not apply. Aside from education, the military itself is a target for reforming society. One argument that feminists advanced for putting women in combat is that it is crucial for their self-esteem. Never mind that training standards must the lowered, that men are stronger and faster than women, that menstruation and pregnancies tend to impede the work of a soldier, that the Israelis, Soviets, and Germans had all concluded that women in combat was a bad idea or the fact that male soldiers invariably become distracted and attempt to protect their women partners. Regardless, the narrative of equality must be maintained.

Beyond the extensive damage to the military and education, what troubled Bork most was the effect on mothers and the family. His conclusions echo the concerns of other observers in the last century:

> Perhaps the most vicious aspect of radical feminism is that it necessarily criticizes and demeans women who choose to work primarily as mothers and homemakers. They are made to feel guilty and told that their lives are essentially worthless.[319]

The above writers expressed no particular religious view or faith and offered no particular belief system to protect or promote. Their observations, lacking an apparent ax to grind, are striking, insightful, and disturbing. The following chapter takes us on a deeper quest to investigate the kinds of motivation behind the anti-tradition ideologies and attitudes which have become so dominant today.

---

[319] Ibid., 223.

CHAPTER 11

The Search for Wholeness:
Public and Personal Theories

We are in the middle of an astonishing process…
Never before has there been an ideology that aims to destroy
the gender identity of man and woman and every
ethical standard of sexual behavior.[320]

Monday morning, 6:30. "Ugh. I don't want to go to school." Alex's first thoughts arrived with a racing heart and anxious stomach. Stressful memories of the boys' bathroom last Friday. Taunts and cruel words. "Move your skinny ass!" because he was thin and slow. He'd heard much worse, but mostly he was just ignored. The day has hardly started and this thirteen-year-old is miserable, beset with dread and a cascade of negative thoughts. "I don't fit in. No one likes me. I'm going to look like an idiot in PE today. I hate baseball… Well, maybe I can sit with Alyssa at lunch. At least I won't be at the table all by myself like a freaking loser. I wish I could be like Ben. But what if he catches me staring at him? I hate my body." Before his feet hit the floor, Alex is a nervous wreck.

Alex's experience of morning misery is nothing new. His troubling thoughts and feelings have plagued him since fifth grade. And they are very real. Or are they? Can we not, with sincere compassion, affirm that indeed, his agony is real. But what about some of the conclusions which in his mind seem

---

[320] Gabriele Kuby, *The Global Sexual Revolution*, 7, 10.

logical enough? "I don't belong. Real boys are good at sports. Maybe I should've been a girl. I must be gay..."

The last chapter presented a sample of serious scholars who warned that our culture is in trouble. In the following pages, we dig further into the suppositions that rattle behind the mistrust of tradition, authority and even the wisdom of biology. What kinds of motivation drive the sexual licentious and radical feminists? We divide them into private and public dimensions. In the first, as the story above illustrates, we discern deeply personal struggles. The need driving Alex is for relief. The second dimension, embodied in anti-establishment political and social movements, carries a more insidious agenda. Here, we find radicals who dress their ideologies in the garb of righteous rescue. As angels of light, they obfuscate the hostility endemic to their philosophy. Under cover of progressive advancement, they would dismantle the very traditions that have enabled Western culture to flourish.

Private theories in the search for personal transformation

Having defied the single boundary that would have vouchsafed near unlimited freedom, Adam and Eve must forge ahead under the shadow of death. They have lost that freedom to "just be." That integrated state of perfect union with God, oneself, and others has faded into an elusive dream, perhaps only an inchoate longing. Longing for...what? Peter Kreeft tells us the deepest longing is for heaven.[321] But we don't know that. We do know we want to feel different, to be free from the angst of having to judge every thought and action.

Alex lives in conflict—with other boys, with certain role expectations, and with his feelings. Conflict is painful and it is normal to seek resolution. In high school, I nurtured the dream of watching heads turn as I cruised down Main

---

[321] *Heaven: The Heart's Deepest Longing,* op cit.

Street in my '36 Ford. After months of cursing and bloody knuckles, I had to admit that the Chrysler Hemi engine was not going to fit and worse, I was not mechanically inclined. Eventually, it was a relief to admit it. In my case, the conflict was resolved in favor of reality. Alex, on the other hand, may come to relieve his tension by relinquishing a pretension to normal masculinity. But should he? Should he embrace the theory that he must be gay? Or, perhaps he would be better off as a woman? How does he choose? His feelings are *real* but what about his thoughts?

Developmental psychologist Lawrence Kohlberg presents the following snippet. Two little boys chat. Johnny is four and a half years old and Jimmy is just turning four.

JOHNNY: I'm going to be an airplane builder when I grow up.

JIMMY: When I grow up, I'll be a mommy.

JOHNNY: No, you can't be a mommy. You have to be a daddy.

JIMMY: No, I'm going to be a mommy.

JOHNNY: No, you're not a girl, you can't be a mommy.

JIMMY: Yes, I can.

Kohlberg notes that the constancy of sexual identity is typically uncertain in pre-school children. Therefore, Jimmy's difficulties in establishing gender identity should not be relegated to emotional problems. Rather, they may be understood as parallel to his cognitive development.[322] In other words, as his brain matures and he gains more experience with reality, appropriate adjustment will follow. We note that in this exchange, Jimmy is confronted with a conflict. As the two boys argue, his distress may intensify. Jimmy wants to be a mommy and feels this strongly. Capitulating to these feelings, his friends and family will ease his distress by agreeing with his theory. As he grows, his distance from the reality of his body grows and so does his theory. Under the sway of "affirming" ideology, he may soon convince himself he is a girl trapped in a boy's body.

In Chapter Five, we summarized an interview with Erik Toth, the school teacher arrested for molesting students. From boyhood, he also struggled. At some point in his life, he resolved the conflict between his desires and public morality by concluding his sexual inclinations represented his real and immutable reality. What followed was a theory that justified the notion that child/adult sex, if consensual, is not harmful.

Alex, Jimmy, and Erik. Each knows conflict—a battle within. To resolve conflicts, we resort to explanations—theories that explain and suggest a path forward. Kohlberg's story of Jimmy comes to us from a recent academic past still innocent of activist dogma when psychologists could label a thing abnormal without fear of public censure. A child's private and at times highly idiosyncratic theories of self could be challenged. Unfortunately, as subjective experiences have overpowered traditional wisdom in the public eye, the young are cheated. Both of the protection from public sanctions against deviant behavior as well as from religious or therapeutic remedies.

---

[322] Cited in Paul Henry Mussen, John Janeway Conger and Jerome Kagan, *Child Development and Personality* (3rd Edition), New York: Harper and Row, 1969. 502-503.

Public theories and the drive for transformation

In contrast to the private struggles of individuals, the broader cultural movements of radical feminism and the sexual revolution are maintained by comprehensive ideologies. These philosophies invite women not to want children, men not to protect them, the lustful not to wait, and everyone to love whomever they want. And to believe whatever they feel. The problem is never one's experience but the dominant standards that would deny that experience. These theories appear to relieve individuals from painful tension. Yet, they seem not so concerned about relieving private pain as they are about transforming society as a whole. Disguised as light, this is a dark agenda—deeply anti-establishment and anti-God. In the following pages, the insights of several thinkers help us uncover the sort of motivation behind the thought forms that would unravel honored traditions of faith and family.

Robert Bork refers to the radical liberalism of the sixties as a spirit of "antinomianism." This attitude of resistance to rules and regulation, tradition and religion is, in fact, not new. Its roots can be traced to the Enlightenment itself.[323] We look fondly on the advance of science in the 1700s. We embrace the importance of reason and the ideals of progress, freedom and tolerance. Religious intolerance and artificial moral restraints were exposed and the rights of individuals were promoted. The ideal of a smart and good society captured the minds of deep thinkers. Nevertheless, a troubling byproduct emerged, viz., a profound misunderstanding of the nature of man. "The Enlightenment optimists made a serious mistake about the nature of the individual human in whom they placed so much faith."[324] How so? Men such as John Locke, Adam Smith and Jefferson assumed that humans naturally carried within them-

---

[323] *Slouching towards Gomorrah: modern liberalism and American decline.* (HarperCollins, 1996).
[324] Ibid., 58.

selves a kind of moral decency and self constraint. They failed to realize that the positive qualities of rationality, honesty, and moral benevolence were not "timeless, natural qualities of the *individual*..." but are in fact qualities promoted and developed by society.[325] Unfortunately, a kind of adversarial relationship between the individual and society developed. The image of a liberated, freedom loving individual became constantly juxtaposed against the punitive restraints of law, religion and traditional morality.

Bork echoes T.S. Eliot's observation that liberalism is not so much a movement toward something as it is a movement against. "What liberalism has constantly moved away from are the constraints on personal liberty imposed by religion, morality, law, family and community."[326] In consequence, the dissolution of social standards invariably leads to an extreme individualism.

Print and other media pave the way. For example, *Time Magazine*, without a hint of irony or disapproval, nearly celebrates teenage gender confusion. In Park city, Utah, the extracurricular club called the Gay-Straight Alliance has set up a signup table.

> Sitting behind piles of rainbow-colored paper cranes—a hot fundraising item—the group leaders are counting the different identity labels they encounter. Sure, there's lesbian, gay, bisexual, transgender. But there are more. Way more... There's also a romantic, asexual, gender queer, two-spirit and on and on. ... "Some days I feel like my gender could be like what I was assigned at birth, but there are some days when I feel the opposite way," says Roland Little, an

---

[325] Ibid.; Robert Nisbet, *The Quest for Community*. (London: Oxford University Press, 1953), 225.
[326] Bork, 61.

18-year-old high school senior in Kentucky who identifies as gender fluid...[327]

We wonder, where will such subjective, hyper- individualism take us? Perhaps the *National Geographic,* January, 2017
issue that highlighted nine-year-old transgender kids should
win the prize for advancing an agenda of disturbance. What is
this preoccupation with normalizing what is abnormal? How
is it that the mercurial feelings of young children now bend
common sense and nature itself?

C. S. Lewis: Seeing through the smoke

As we saw in the last chapter, astute cultural observers began
shooting warning flares over seventy years ago. At that time,
C.S. Lewis, as a Christian, offered the most prescient and
elegant early description of a cultural decline already growing
in the West. Lewis had discerned an alarming tendency in
education to conflate emotional reactions with fact. Until
modern times, teachers and philosophers understood the
difference between a person's subjective sense of a thing and
the thing itself. The way we assess value to options or objects
has always been related to the way things really are. Not the
way we feel about them.

Lewis argued that within every great civilization there is
a sense of basic reality and an assumption of what is right or
good. Early Hinduism, for example, spoke of good conduct
as conforming to the *rta,*

—that great ritual or pattern of nature and super-
nature which is revealed alike in the cosmic order,
the moral virtues, and the ceremonial of the temple.

---

[327] "Beyond he or she: Our new generation is redefining the meaning of gender"
by Katy Steinmetz. Time, March 27, 2017.

Righteousness, correctness, order, the *rta*, is constantly identified with *satya* or truth, correspondence to reality. ... The Chinese also speak of a great thing (the greatest thing) called the *tao*. It is the reality beyond all predicates, the abyss that was before the creator himself. It is nature, it is the way, the road. It is the way in which the universe goes on, the way in which things everlastingly emerge, stilly and tranquilly, into space and time.[328]

Paul assumes the universality of natural law when he writes to the Romans that even the Gentiles who do not have the revealed law of God,

... do by nature what the law requires, they are a law to themselves, even though they do not have the law, they show that the requirements of the law are written on their hearts, their consciences also bearing witness, and their thoughts sometimes accusing them and at other times even defending them. (2:14-15)

Lewis calls this the "doctrine of objective value, the belief that certain attitudes are really true, and others really false, to the kind of thing the universe is and the kind of things we are."[329] Such assumptions of an undergirding reality and a corresponding natural morality are not only common to every enduring civilization but represent the absolute prerequisite to the viability of such cultures.

What Lewis called the innovator seventy-five years ago, we today would recognize as the progressive or postmodernist ideologue. This is the person who devalues natural order and questions traditions and taboos. That things really are true or

---

[328] *The Complete Works of C.S. Lewis*, 700-701.
[329] Ibid., 701.

false, good or bad. This is the nihilist, who proclaims that all statements of value are nothing more than personal opinion. Although writing at the height of World War II, Lewis was less concerned about war than he was about a rising moral relativism. Such thinking was already being manifested in the very places where thinking should be grounded in truth and reality, the academy.

The moral relativism saturating universities today seems to look askance at natural law or the idea of objective good. A utilitarian principle obtains in which one thing is as good as another: "Well, it works for me." As Lewis worried many years ago, science itself can become infiltrated with a secularist worldview: nature is just a matter of random events sans purpose or design. This modern view pictures man as highly malleable. Unfortunately, such a state leaves him a vulnerable prey to social engineering by the educational elite. Lewis wrote,

> Either we are rational spirit obliged forever to obey the absolute values of the *tao*, or else we are mere nature to be kneaded and cut into new shapes for the pleasures of masters who must, by hypothesis, have no motive but their own 'natural' impulses.[330]

It only follows that such a worldview carries great implications for a culture's understanding of sex and sexuality. Knippenberg writes that Lewis presented the West with an early warning:

> The body and the erotic procreative relationship between men and women are not mere nature, to be manipulated and embellished. They are not mere

---

[330] Cited in David J. Theroux, "Why C.S. Lewis Is As Influential As Ever," *Independent Institute*, August 3, 2015.

matter, to be shaped in any way that we please. They are, rather, an indicator of a larger order, something that offers us a clue to that larger order and that has to be understood in the light of it.[331]

Failing to embrace a larger order, progressives fall to an agenda to make their own order. Filled with the proud promise of ever-advancing technology, they defy tradition, declaring themselves in conquest of nature. Lewis put us on notice that human nature itself would be the last casualty of such hubris. Was he presaging some philosophy of transhumanism?

Jordan B. Peterson: Exposing cultural Marxism

Those whom Lewis called "the conditioners" would correspond today to the postmodernists. Trends already evident in the forties have, in the Twenty-first Century, become the dominant ethos in education. Yet, pushback is growing. In 2016, Canadian psychology professor Jordan Peterson skyrocketed to world fame when he refused to be bullied into using false gender pronouns. A brilliant debater, his YouTube lectures captured the attention of millions. His 2018 book, *Twelve Rules for Life*, quickly became a bestseller. His understanding of postmodernism and "the long arm of Marx" is especially insightful.

Peterson points to the influence of Marxist humanists as the theoretical engine driving the assault on patriarchy in college campuses. He highlights Max Horkheimer who developed "critical theory" in the 1930s. As did other leftist atheists, Horkheimer did not trust Western principles of economic freedom and the free market but saw them as disguising inequality, domination, and exploitation. As part of the Frankfurt School of social work, he believed that

---

[331] Joseph M. Knippenberg, C.S. Lewis in a Secular Core: Sex, Love, and *That Hideous Strength*. In Public Discourse, August 6, 2018, September 30, 2018.

sociology as a discipline of observation and analysis should give way to social change. The hope was to "… emancipate humanity from its enslavement." The aim was "… a full-scale critique and transformation of Western civilization."[332]

Postmodernists, such as Jacques Derrida, promoted a radicalized form of Marxism. Marx attempted to reduce history and society to economics, the oppression of the poor by the rich. Peterson summarizes the deadly fruit of Marxist theory. When communism was put into practice in the Soviet Union, China, Vietnam, Cambodia, and elsewhere, economic resources were brutally redistributed. Tens of millions died.

Despite the rumors of atrocities, many intellectuals continued to hold positive attitudes toward communism. Solzhenitsyn's book, *The Gulag Archipelago*, documented mass murders of political prisoners and demonstrated that the system could only survive through tyranny, lies, and slave labor. Nevertheless, Marxist ideas continued to be attractive. Sartre even denounced Solzhenitsyn as dangerous. How then, did the tragic costs of communism slip from academic attention? Peterson explains:

> Derrida, more subtle, substituted the idea of power for the idea of money, and continued on his merry way. Such linguistic sleight-of-hand gave all the barely repented Marxists still inhabiting the intellectual pentacles of the West the means to retain their worldview. Society was no longer repression of the poor by the rich. It was repression of everyone by the powerful.[333]

---

[332] *12 Rules for Life: An Antidote to Chaos.* (Canada: Random House, 2018), 306.
[333] Ibid., 310.

Deconstructing gender

According to Derrida, oppression is built right into language by the very categories we use to understand the world. Those categories or constructs are not real per se but subject to interpretation. Further, to *construe* or define the other is to do violence by binding the other's reality to our own definitions and should be "deconstructed." All distinctions are power based and designed to benefit those making such categories.

> According to Derrida, hierarchical structures emerged only to include (the beneficiaries of that structure) and to exclude (everyone else, who were therefore oppressed). … There are "women" only because men gain by excluding them. There are "males and females" only because members of that more heterogeneous group benefit by excluding the tiny minority of people whose biological sexuality is amorphous.[334].

Derrida is generally understood to teach that everything is interpretation. In other words, nothing is actually real. Any distinctions are based only on the exercise of raw power. It does not matter that there is overwhelming, multidisciplinary research demonstrating that biological factors powerfully influence sex differences; the postmodernists merely dismiss such science as another game of power. Facts take a backseat to ideology. The conviction that western society is pathologically patriarchal or that all hierarchies are based on power and aimed at exclusion is continuously affirmed despite the lack of evidence.

The theory of non-binary sexuality is a fitting example of ideology trumping nature. Gender is not really a real category, but merely construed. Nevertheless, an individual who desires

---

[334] Ibid., 310 – 311.

gender reassignment surgery is to be unarguably considered a man trapped in a woman's body (or vice versa). *The fact that both of these cannot logically be true is just ignored.* Or rationalized away with another postmodern claim: that logic itself—along with the techniques of science—is merely part of the oppressive patriarchal system.

While arguing there is no difference between the sexes, the neo-Marxist elites nevertheless continue to pound on the male. "As privileged beneficiaries of the patriarchy, their accomplishments are considered unearned. As possible adherents of rape culture, they are sexually suspect."[335]

Such pounding takes a toll. As we have seen, after decades of reviving Ophelia and ignoring Joe, young men are not stepping up to the plate. With ever fewer boys pursuing higher education, this cannot be good for women either. Women inevitably desire to marry a man of equal or higher status. Peterson describes his experience with high-powered female lawyers who, in their thirties, find themselves ready for marriage and children. With men lagging behind in education and with fewer high-paying industrial jobs, the question arises, where are they to find similarly high-achieving men who can support them in their wish for children?

Tradition and the "super theory"

Something disturbing has happened to classical liberalism. According to Polish philosophy professor, Ryszard Legutko, this once respectable ideology has morphed into a troubling super theory. A deeply illiberal set of ideas has become "… a comprehensive and obligatory way of thinking, that is enforced in modern society as a best regulator of human diversity and the only sure guarantee of freedom."[336] This highly

---

[335] Ibid., 297.
[336] "Why I Am Not a Liberal" (*First Things*) March 2020, 24.

self-confident approach to political and cultural life believes itself above discussion and ready to impose its will wherever dissent may arise.

In brief, the super theory holds that *openness* is the key to well-being and freedom. There ought, therefore, to be "room for every human desire and life plan." The goal of public life should be to maximize the freedom for everyone to "be themselves." Traditional thought forms and institutions are obstacles to this ideal. This is especially so for the disadvantaged of the world. Suffused with indignation, this theory requires that all boundaries and limits must be removed. Meanwhile, those who have been privileged must have some space taken from them so they can no longer dominate.[337] For the sake of justice and equity, an intentional social engineering is required to promote some groups and opinions while demoting others. Legutko writes:

> It becomes necessary to champion women and blacks and criticize white men and their "patriarchal" institutions, to restrain Christianity from cultural dominance, and to open public space for Muslim communities. These projects require a certain degree of coercion, or at least energetic persuasion, which is usually directed against entrenched ways of life, allegedly anachronistic beliefs, traditional divisions, supposedly sacrosanct norms, and so forth.[338]

Children should be taught inclusive language. History is to be taught as a story of discrimination and *thought crimes* must be identified. These include sexism, homophobia, binarism, to name a few. "All that must be monitored and eliminated...

---

[337] Ibid.
[338] Ibid.

from legal punishment to social ostracism, from education to browbeating."[339]

The family is a target. Far from being a pillar of the social order, marriage is but an archaic and oppressive institution. Such a tradition must be actively opposed. Those who would disagree are ostracized, lose their jobs, and shamed by twitter mobs.

To embrace the project of unhindered freedom to become whoever and whatever one wants, a "minimalist conception of the human self" is necessary. This is what Legutko calls a "thin self," one easily dominated, entitled, without strong convictions and open to anything. Anything, except boundaries.

> ... we should refrain from ascribing too much to human nature. We must forswear appeals to natural law, for such concepts put limits on what and who we can become. More broadly, historical, communal, or metaphysical dimensions need to be downplayed or repudiated... In this way, the liberal ideal of freedom, if put in practice by a society in a thoroughgoing way as the liberal super-theory requires, erodes the substantive basis for moral and political analysis. The perfectly liberal society is a thoughtless society.[340]

The truth is that it is rational thinking and the appropriation of realities associated with religious and cultural traditions that foster good moral character. And character sponsors freedom. Legutko argues that both Aristotle and Paul taught that real freedom requires character and self-control to resist being controlled by instincts, desires, whims, and impulses.

The super theory emphasizes a super individualistic view of humanity. Each person has the right to "be free to become

---

[339] Ibid.
[340] Ibid., 27.

whoever and whatever he wants."[341] A dangerous "mental trap," however, lurks behind such a promise. Liberalism offers such rights,

> ...only on the condition that people adhere to its increasingly intrusive regulations and, more importantly, embrace the entirety of its ideology concerning right and wrong, what to love and whom to hate.... the more one sees one's independence in liberal terms, the more one succumbs to ideological conformity: the more one thinks of oneself as a master bearing innumerable rights, the more one resembles the Aristotelian slave.[342]

Alternative views are disallowed. Without a solid sense of self forged by discipline, family, and tradition, an individual finds himself confused about his identity. Not knowing who he is, he becomes "like a wave of the sea, blown and cast about by the wind" (James 1). He becomes an underdog to his own subjectivity, falling prey to a "mystified view of himself as an already completed person awaiting only self-expression, recognition, and inclusion. He is an exemplary consumer and easily absorbs mass opinion."[343] In believing himself free from all that would bind and define him, he does not know that he is controlled by an intransigent liberalism that tracks down dissenters "accused of authoritarian crimes."

Sex and the super theory

Herbert Marcuse, an influential member of the Frankfurt School, was a powerful advocate of such liberalism and also a champion of unchained sexual freedom. Considered the "Father of the New Left" in the sixties, he believed that

---

[341] Ibid.

[342] Ibid.

[343] Ibid.

capitalist democracies become repressive, totalitarian and marginalize minorities. Liberation from such Right-winged repression included the battle for erotic freedom. Albert Mohler points out,

> In the second half of the twentieth century, Herbert Marcuse revisited Freud in his book *Eros and Civilization*, mixing his theories with those of Marx in order to develop a theory of sexuality as liberation. The whole problem, Marcuse thought, was the very restraint that Freud believed was inevitable and necessary, the repression that Freud saw leading to civilization itself. According to Marcuse, the only way to achieve liberation is to undo that repression, to reverse that restraint, and thus to unleash in society itself that infantile stage of pure sexuality–of polymorphous perversity.[344]

Shifting desires

The provocative literary critic, Andrea Long Chu is a trans woman who has recently undergone bottom surgery—an operation she did not expect to make her happy. In a *NY Times* interview just before going under the knife, she admitted that ever since she started taking hormones, her gender dysphoria is worse. Her honesty is both disarming and troubling. Chu told the times:

> Until the day I die, my body will regard the vagina as a wound; as a result, it will require regular, painful attention to maintain. That is what I want, but there is no guarantee it will make me happier. In fact, I don't

---

[344] http://www.albertmohler.com/2005/09/19/the-age-of-polymorphous-perversity-part-one/

expect it to. That shouldn't disqualify me from getting it.[345]

In an interview nearly a year later, she again exhibits remarkable transparency with Lila Shapiro, who reports:

She says she's feeling more miserable than she'd expected. "It is perversely vindicating," she adds with a wry smile. Dressed in a jumpsuit patterned with blue-and-white flowers, she brushes a curtain of curls away from her face with a flip of her wrist, revealing a tattoo of a geometric vulva on the underside of her forearm. "It's very dangerous to get what you want." It was "easily the most impulsive thing I've ever done," she says. "I was the happiest I've ever been," she says of the weeks after she transitioned. "It was like having a crush on myself."

Snapping out of her reverie, she sighs and adds, "Now I'm just in a sexless marriage with myself."[346]

In an essay in *First Things*, Angela Franks puzzles out this bright but frequently suicidal author and internet trans star. Franks directs our attention to the post-modernist French philosopher Giles Deleuze. Although not as well known as his contemporaries, Michel Foucault or Jacques Derrida, Deleuze, who threw himself out of a window in 1995, has had a profound influence among leftist deconstructionists. According to Franks, Deleuze's writings offer context to the kind of self-loathing and narcissistic nuttery Chu is famous for. It's all about desire. He argued that thinking and wanting

---

[345] Cited in Angela Franks, "Deleuze on Desire" (*First Things*) April, 2020.

[346] "The 26 year-old critic argues for a new understanding of gender and desire in her debut book, *Females*."

By *Lila Shapiro@lilapearl* Vulture.

should be allowed to spread haphazardly, like rhizomes. Repudiating not only Christianity but, in a way, the whole history of thought constructions, he reveled in an anarchy of desires. Everything is as the wasp and the orchid, naturally flowing and free to unfold without the strictures of class, identity, and meaning categories. The family itself is a factory in which the parents "transmit angst and irrational fears to the child and bind the child's sexual desires to feelings of shame and guilt."[347] Sexuality reflects a multitude of flows and certainly should not be limited to male and female gender roles.

Corresponding with the "thin self" of the super theory, Deleuze taught that the self is but a byproduct of desire. To think of oneself as an independent being is merely a bourgeois illusion.

> With this displacement of the subject, the inexorable mechanics of desire take center stage. The quasi-autonomous motor of desire forms things now in this way, now in that, legislating upon plastic matter. The body becomes a kind of prime matter, "a surface for the recording of the entire process of production of desire." With this sentence, Deleuze explains the tattoo phenomenon... thus, instead of a rational engagement with an intelligible—that is, already formed – material world, there arises the technical imposition of form on the passive surface of the body.[348]

One is reminded of the old sailor who ruefully comments on the garish breasts he had tattooed on his forearm forty years ago: "It seemed like a good idea at the time."

Considering the primacy of autonomous desire, the evacuation of meaning, and the power of technology to impose

---

[347] Wikipedia, *Anti-oedipus.*
[348] Franks, 40.

itself, one begins to comprehend the mindset that could lead an individual, without the moorings of faith or traditional morality, to engage in painful reconstruction of body parts. Why? Because I want to. My desire demands it. Franks recalls Pope Benedict XVI's lament that the technocratic mentality with its false promise of mastery and transformation plays an essential role in maintaining a culture of death. "He recognized that technology can 'become an ideological power,' able to blind the intellect to truth and obliterate wonder…"[349] The fact is that we are not designed to live by our own private meanings. We need a reality intrinsic to the thing itself.

Without faith in an ultimate reality, what do we do with our "fallen desires"? The lust of the flesh, the lust of the eyes, and the pride of life? Imaging the Creator, a longing for mastery and transformation lingers within the soul. Dazzling technologies strut before us as new idols pretending to meet those desires. However, we cannot expect technology to "do divine things for us." We remain restless and empty. Two ways stand out to overcome the anxiety and restless press of desire. The first is a kind of stoic or suicidal resignation. At age seventy, Deleuze called it quits. "Likewise, in Andrea Long Chu's writings, one can perceive a masochism, a suicidal longing to disappear under the imperious dictates of another's desire."[350]

The second strategy is to allow revelation to break through our self-enclosed project to fulfill ourselves. To accept our subordinate yet honored status as God's creatures. As such, our needs are known before we even ask him (Matt. 6:8). It is God who answers our infinite longings. Desire is not to be stamped out but integrated. And finally ordered by the One who created desire.

---

[349] Ibid., 41.
[350] Ibid., 41-42.

The rise of the "psychological man"

Carl R. Trueman believes the deep divisions in our society, the riots, the stretching of sexual boundaries, and so on, hold a particular motif in common. The key element that pulls these disparate developments together is the changed definition of the self.

> We think of ourselves in terms of our inner convictions, our feelings; we consequently interpret the purpose and meaning of our lives in line with this, seeing, for example, happiness in terms of an inner sense of psychological well-being. This is what sociologist Philip Rieff dubbed "psychological man..."[351]

In Chapter Eight, we discussed the dialogic nature of identity formation. Historically, one develops a sense of self through interaction with family, church, and society. Today, these forces are seen as obstacles to true personhood. Even biological reality must yield to one's inward reality. How did such a turnabout develop? Trueman proposes that the philosophical history of this highly subjective psychological self began with Jean-Jacques Rousseau in the Eighteenth Century.

Rousseau resented social conventions that quelched authentic living. He believed that education should be based upon natural instincts, not the corrupting, repressive influence of society. A child should be protected from such harmful influences as "... toy soldiers and church bells. Both

---

[351] "The Rise of "Psychological Man," *Public Discourse*, November 9, 2020. https://www.thepublicdiscourse.com/2020/11/72190/ See also, *The Rise and Triumph of the Modern Self: Cultural Amnesia, Expressive Individualism, and the Road to Sexual Revolution* (Wheaton, Ill.: Crossway, 2020).

are symbols of decadent society, through which the evils of war and established religion might corrupt the young."[352]

Considering that Rousseau abandoned his own five illegitimate children, one can only wonder at the hypocrisy of such a philosopher. At any rate, conviction that the authentic good lies within gradually led to an attack on the transcendent. Trueman writes:

> The 19th century is critical here. Hegel's phenomenology set the historical development of human consciousness at the center of his philosophical inquiries, thus potentially relativizing any specific historical expression of human nature. Marx famously turned him on his head, placing economic relations at the heart of history and thus making human nature itself a function of the changing means of production, thereby arguably intensifying its plasticity. Darwin's theory of evolution undermined notions of human exceptionalism by eliding the difference between human beings and other forms of life. And Nietzsche called the bluff of Kantian philosophy by declaring that neither claims to knowledge nor judgments of right and wrong could have any truly authoritative status in a world where God had been consciously removed from any active role in the picture of the universe with which Enlightenment philosophers operated. At this point, the psychological turn we find in Rousseau and the Romantics loses the confidence that there was such a thing as human nature that we all share. And with that move, all that implicitly remains of human purpose

---

[352] Colin Brown, *Philosophy and the Christian Faith: A Historical Sketch from the Middle Ages to the Present Day* (Downers Grove, Ill.: Inter-varsity Press, 1968) 82.

is the attaining of personal psychological happiness in whatever form happens to work.[353]

As the West's common understanding of human nature became increasingly changed by such thought-leaders, the impact of Freudian theory was growing as well. His theory of infantile sexuality put sexual drives at the center of human development.

> Freud made human flourishing in its ideal form identical with sexual satisfaction. It also—and most significantly—made sex a matter of identity and not primarily an activity. After Freud, sex is something you are, not merely something you do.[354]

Nevertheless, Freud had taught that civilization emerged as individual sexual desire succumbed to the demands of communal life. Repression of sexual instincts was necessary to build and sustain culture. But Marxists such as Marcuse and Wilhelm Reich "seized upon this idea of psychological repression as the key to solving one of the great lacunae in Marxist theory: how to enable the working class to develop a revolutionary self-consciousness."[355] In other words, when it was no longer obvious that the proletariat were economically oppressed, how were they to resist being dominated by the ruling class?

> The answer was the dismantling of traditional sexual codes. Reich and Marcuse saw such codes as effectively enforcing the normative nature of the nuclear family, something that the Marxist Left regarded as the training ground for social conformity and

---

[353] Trueman, "The Rise of 'Psychological Man."
[354] Ibid.
[355] Ibid.

obedience—a factory, if you like, for the production of mindless automata who will accept the bourgeois status quo with blind obedience. As children learn to fear, love, and obey the father, so they are prepared for the obedience demanded by political dictators such as Hitler and Mussolini.[356]

Watching the rise of Nazism, Reich had considered how the highly educated German people could so easily bow to totalitarian control. In 1936, he published his manifesto, *The Sexual Revolution: Toward a Self-Regulating Character Structure* in which he linked childhood sexuality with the political struggle. He decided that the unencumbered expression of natural needs and sexuality is the basis for political freedom. The first enemy to such freedom is the oppressive patriarchal family. And later, the church. The sexual codes advanced by these institutions are nothing but instruments of repression and control. They impede natural development, ultimately creating a submissive people. Reich called on the state to promote sex education and to intervene to protect children in their natural pursuit of (sexual) happiness.[357] Protect from whom? One is reminded of Monica Cline's training with planned parenthood—one that included an agenda to hide the curriculum from parents.

The dominant, repressive bourgeois class must be resisted. Trueman writes:

Revolution must therefore have at its heart the dismantling of the bourgeois sexual morality of lifelong monogamy, normative heterosexuality, and suppression of adolescent sexual activity. The psychological

---

[356] Ibid.

[357] *The Rise and Triumph of the Modern Self: Cultural Amnesia, Expressive Individualism, and the Road to Sexual Revolution* (Wheaton, Ill.: Crossway, 2020), 232-237.

self thus becomes central to the political struggle, as do sex and sexuality.[358]

So, the family with its emphasis on sexual fidelity is the problem? As a prophylactic to tyranny, this is exactly backwards. Solid, time-honored traditions passed down by the family build "thick selves"—the kind of people able to stand up to those who would abuse power. Nevertheless, the impact of such argument has been profound. Trueman does not see this slowing down, even as language itself is rapidly evolving to fit the narrative. The definition of oppression is a case in point. In the past, such a term entailed such self-evident events as being cheated, denied equal opportunity, or falsely imprisoned. Now, the term is more amorphous, merely a matter of words. Now, language police on college campuses suppress speech. "Oppression involves making people feel bad about themselves, less than fully human, while preventing them from being outwardly that which they are inwardly."[359]

The threat to religious freedom hovers ominously. Sex,

...ceases to be what human beings do and becomes what they are. From a Christian perspective, this is politically dramatic because it takes behavior that Christianity regards as illegitimate and makes it an identity society regards as legitimate and therefore requires all citizens to recognize for the common good. To object to homosexuality thus ceases to be merely to object to certain sexual practices or proclivities; it becomes the denial of the selfhood of another, an act of political violence.[360]

---

[358] Ibid.

[359] "The Impact of Psychological Man – And How to Respond." November 10, 2020. *Public Discourse*. https://www.thepublicdiscourse.com/2020/11/72190/

[360] Ibid.

Simple tolerance is not enough. Tolerance implies indifference which allows for moral disapproval. To allow such disapproval "grants legitimacy to precisely the kind of speech-acts that psychologized identities see as violence."[361] Further, one can speculate that identities grounded in fluctuating subjectivity certainly would be more likely to be hypersensitive to criticism and to demand affirmation. Inevitably, when identities are based on the shifting winds of inner experience, social upheaval and frustration are bound to expand. As an anxious king might kill the messenger of bad news, so might the growing cultural imperialism of the Left demand the head of those who would unmask their shaky agenda of self-fulfillment.

Trueman expects prosecution if not persecution. But ultimately, the church will thrive by being faithful to Christ and loyal to one another.

De-sexualizing the gods and the original sexual revolution

In uncovering many of the factors driving our cultural demise, David Kupelian reminds us that sex has always been a war zone and a "…dividing line between those attempting to obey God's laws and those rebelling against them (or denying they exist)."[362] He directs our attention to Dennis Prager's essay, "Judaism, Homosexuality, and Civilization." Prager argues that the Torah's demand that sex be confined to marriage not only made Western civilization possible but constituted an absolute revolt against the sexual chaos that had infused the entire ancient world.

---

[361] Ibid.

[362] *The Marketing of Evil: How Radicals, Elitists, and Pseudo-Experts Sell Us Corruption Disguised As Freedom* (Washington, DC: WND books, 2005, 2015) 194.

Ritual prostitution and sacred ceremonial sex had proliferated the nations surrounding Israel. Judaism, in stark contrast, required sex to be confined to marriage and, writes Prager, it changed the world.

> It is not overstated to say that the Torah's prohibition of nonmarital sex made the creation of Western civilization possible. Societies that did not place boundaries around sexuality were stymied in their development. The subsequent dominance of the Western world can largely be attributed to the sexual revolution initiated by Judaism, and later carried forward by Christianity.[363]

Perhaps it is time for a new sexual revolution.

Telling the truth about Alfred Kinsey

In a fairly short time, we have witnessed a cancerous growth of nihilistic and anti-rational sexual ideologies, a widespread drift from health and wholesome living (What an anachronistic phrase!), as well as from empirical science. Judeo-Christian attitudes generally held sway until the end of World War II. Then in 1948, Alfred Kinsey published his now discredited *Sexual Behavior of the American Male.* Unfortunately, the media happily endorsed this insect scientist as an expert and the destruction of our moral code began in earnest. Kinsey presented "evidence" that children are sexual from birth and behaviors we deemed perverted or immoral were actually normal. He claimed that infants and toddlers engaged in multiple orgasms. What the public did not know was that he employed pedophiles, rapists, and murderers in his studies. Pretending to do science, they molested thousands

---

[363] Ibid., 194.

of children producing fraudulent data that was swallowed by media, social scientists, and legislators.

Kinsey believed that any sex was legitimate, including, "pedophilia, bestiality, incest, adultery, prostitution, group sex, transvestitism, sadomasochism—and he worked to overthrow all laws prohibiting any of these perversions."[364] With large grants from the Rockefeller Foundation, Kinsey's influence was extensive. Soon his ideas permeated our society: the legal system reduced penalties for sex crimes, abortion was legitimized and legalized, the film industry pushed the limits of propriety and SIECUS, The Sexual Information and Education Council of the United States, was born. This group continues to infiltrate our schools with the fiction that children are sexual from birth. What's more, the pharmaceutical industry capitalized on the sexual revolution: the demand for birth control and the emergence of STDs brought new customers. The production of pornography skyrocketed. The divorce rate soared along with sex crimes, including child molestation. As a people, we would never be the same. Because of misleading and fraudulent data.[365] Judith Reisman has been attempting to expose the lies and bad science behind the Kinsey institute and sex education in our schools since the sixties.[366] Reisman, along with colleague Mary McAlister, continues to speak out in the U.S. and internationally.

Could personal issues power public ideologies?

Any consideration as to why people do what they do ought to carry the caveat that we cannot know another's heart. Finally,

---

[364] *Fighting the Kinsey Fraud: An Interview with Judith Reisman* by William Jasper. The New American, May, 1999.

[365] Interview with Dr. Judith Reisman. https://endsexualexploitation.org/articles/lunch-with-a-legend-kinsey-common-core/

[366] See *Sexual Sabotage: How One Mad Scientist Unleashed a Plague of Corruption and Contagion on America.* WND Books: 2010.

only God understands private motivations and behavior. We do wonder, however. What shapes a life or motivates a life philosophy? Could it be that those who would trouble society were as children, themselves troubled? We briefly note:

- Alfred Kinsey's parents were extremely legalistic Christians. His father was highly controlling and the young Kinsey grew up under strict rules. Prayer was the only activity allowed on Sunday. One might not be surprised that a young man might strain against such cords of control.

- Although Freud did not champion unrestrained sexuality, his antipathy to religion had helped seed the fruit of rebellion in the West. Paul Vitz found evidence in his childhood that offers insight to the genesis of this hostility. As a very small boy, his beloved Catholic nanny would take him to church. When he was about three, she was falsely accused of stealing and abruptly fired. Vitz suggests that such an early attachment loss may have stimulated a bitter form of reaction formation.[367]

- Friedrich Nietzsche's father was a pastor who died shortly before Friedrich's fifth birthday. The family then moved from their home and within six months, his little brother also died. Could these early traumatic events have shaped an atheistic, pessimistic philosophy?

- By the age of eleven, Wilhelm Reich was having sex with the chambermaid. Whether he considered it so, we would call this child abuse. In addition, he had a difficult time relating to his cold, authoritarian father but idolized his mother. At the age of twelve, he discovered her in bed with his tutor. Deeply conflicted, he

---

[367] *Sigmund Freud's Christian Unconscious,* (Grand Rapids: Eerdmans, 1993).

eventually told his father about the affair. The father's response was to beat her mercilessly. After months of such punishment, she committed suicide by drinking poison. Wilhelm blamed himself. One might understand how Reich may have come to hate what he considered to be a puritan, repressive culture.[368]

- Hugh Heffner's mother was a strict (and domineering?) Methodist who wanted him to become a missionary.

- Influential feminist, Simone de Bouvier (*The Second Sex,* 1949) was overcontrolled by her religious mother who demanded subservience to her strict morality and austerity. Finding herself far smarter than her classmates and able to discern hypocrisy among her teachers, she adopted a superior attitude to traditional morality and social conventions. At thirty years old, she lost her teaching position when her affair with a seventeen-year-old female student was discovered. Although they never married and had multiple paramours, she maintained a lifelong relationship with Jean Paul Sartre. Together, they advanced their godless agenda to find their own freedom and meaning.

- Kate Millett led an early assault on the patriarchy with her highly influential *Sexual Politics* (1970), a book described by *Time* magazine as the bible of the women's liberation movement. She grew up afraid of her father, an alcoholic who beat her. He ultimately abandoned the family, leaving her mother and sisters to fight off poverty.

Unloved or unprotected, would these thinkers not search for something—something different, better, profound? Nancy Pearsey reminds us that, "Clearly, the architects of the sexual revolution were driven by nothing less than a vision of

---

[368] https://www.thefamouspeople.com/profiles/wilhelm-reich-9371.php

redemption."[369] Were childhood wounds the source of such drives? Whatever the motivation behind these influencers, ideas do have consequences. Ironically, it appears that the most vulnerable to deceptive, destructive ideas are the next generation of children.

---

[369] Nancy R. Pearcey, *Love Thy Body: Answering Hard Questions about Life and Sexuality* (Grand Rapids: Baker Books, 2018), 134.

CHAPTER 12

Ideas Carry Consequences;
Division Spreads

For they sow the wind, they shall reap the whirlwind.
—Hosea 8:7

The kids, who looked to be in their early twenties, marched with crudely crafted banners, "Abolish ICE," "Feminists Against Borders." Random shouts of "F—the police!" "Down with white privilege!" and "Cops are baby killers" peppered the sunny Portland day. Mostly these appeared to come from white girls, who also seemed fond of brandishing their middle finger. At the information table, a young man handed out pamphlets demanding that the U.S. stay out of Venezuela. Other pamphlets included the Communist Manifesto and the Rainbow Solidarity in Defense of Cuba. Another young man explained that American imperialism may necessitate violence. "Preaching pacifism to the oppressed is not OK. So, if you want to come to PSU to give a speech, I'm going to be out there saying, no, you don't have a right to be using this space to send a genocidal message."

This student reminded me of my own experience as a young missionary in the Philippines where I met Bible school graduates who had embraced Liberation Theology. They were ready to fight the military dictatorship that had colluded with multinational companies such as Dole and Del Monte. These greedy companies grabbed vast stretches of farmland to produce export crops while impoverished laborers could pick pineapples all day without earning enough to buy a single can of that product. At the time, I wondered how Republicans could turn a blind eye to such exploitation.

Today, I wonder how American students can fail to grasp the horrifying legacy of Marxism. Progress through struggle—slaughtering millions labeled as oppressors. Justified by Hegel's theories of dialectical reasoning, Marx believed the Bourgeoisie class was an entrenched hierarchy built only by force. Therefore, a forceful revolution was necessary. This Portland protestor was espousing just such an ideology.

The villains today are not just greedy capitalists. According to David Horowitz, far-left radicals imagine "American society as a system of oppressive hierarchies based on race, gender, and sexual orientation… These hierarchies *must* be overthrown."[370] Inevitably, the sexes themselves are juxtaposed as contrasting classes. Can we not discern in this philosophy famed as light an assault on the Creator's primary template for human relationships?

Two deceptions hide in the shadows. The first centers around the concept of power. As we saw earlier, in God's economy, personal power is *power for* the other. God has positioned so-called power differentials to bless and to serve the other. The critical theory of progressive thought, on the other hand, seems to assume any such unequal distribution of authority or power is to be mistrusted. A related mischaracterization of God's vision for human differentiation denies that persons are designed to *come together*. Ironically, leftist ideology advertises unity but foments division. The signs of separation are everywhere.

---

[370] *Dark Agenda: The War to Destroy Christian America* (West Palm Beach: Human X books, 2018) 162.

Separated from the body

Although they claimed to be wise, they became fools...Therefore,
God gave them over in the sinful desires of their hearts to sexual
impurity for the degrading of their bodies. —Romans 1: 22-24

We have noted that in the repudiation of responsibility, problems must be due to someone or something else. When the self is the center, that center must be OK, not wrong or weak or broken. The desires and perceptions of the self must be defended. Prior to the Fall, such self-validation was unnecessary; the possibility for failure and evil remained in the Tree. To ingest its fruit was unnatural as the humans were not designed to deal with evil. As the stomach vomits bad fish, so the guilty soul spits out culpability. "The woman you gave me..." The classic culprits have always been the neighbor, another country, or political party. It would appear that for some in gender studies, it is the body itself that would cause such indignation. The body is wrong—it limits me, my truth. The "good" is defined individually without reference to tradition, other people or even reality. Psychiatrist Glynn Harrison sites theologian N.T. Wright as calling ancient Gnosticism the "controlling myth" of our age. The ancient Gnostics believed

> the source of the self is found by looking within. They share a revolt against the external, against the body, against nature itself. Christians would say they both tap into a fissure that runs through the human heart—a revolt against God and the reality that he has created.[371]

In contrast to the harmony depicted in the Garden of Eden, the discord spread by rebellion emerges sooner or later

---

[371] Harrison, op. cit., 17

as an argument with reality itself. For some, this quarrel would begin early with an assault on the body—the body of a child, in particular, those body parts that represent the future of the human race. Careful observers of infancy know that the self emerging from the mother/infant dyad is an embodied self. Children intuit whether they are safe or loved by the way they are spoken to and held. They experience wet, cold, hunger, and pleasure long before they have words. It is through the body that infants initiate communication and receive the ministrations of others. To cause a child to doubt his own body by validating gender confusion can create incalculable destruction. To disaffirm a child's physical reality in order to affirm his feelings invites the question: "If I cannot trust the reality of my own body—the ground of everything I have known so far—how can I ever know what is true or false?" Yet, this is the direction of liberal politicians who continue to sign legislation that forces public acceptance of transgender mythology.[372]

Is it not so that whenever a movement denies the wisdom or the values embedded in the natural world or expressed in revelation, one's goals become extremely subjective? National columnist Gene Lyons highlights the absurdity to which Women's Studies can sink to in a search for some arbitrarily defined value of equality. According to Lyons, Prof. Karla A. Erickson, a sociologist at Grinnell College, who teaches a class called "Gender and Society," has stated that breast-feeding makes her feel like a cow. She protests that on the one hand, nursing her infant unfairly imposes restraints on her own "spatial mobility and time," while on the other hand, this feminine ability also gives her an unfair advantage over her husband in winning the baby's affection and attachment.

---

[372] "Governor Newsom Signs Bill to Fund Sterilizing Trans-Treatments for Minors and Adults" Sept 28, 2020. https://www.californiafamily.org/2020/governor-newsom-signs-bill-to-gund-sterilizing-trans-treatments-for-minors-and-adults/

This practice "must be renounced in the interest of gender equity. Baby gets a boo-boo; baby runs to mommy. And that would never do."[373]

Lyons quotes Erickson's rationale for opposing breastfeeding:

> It's one thing our bodies do that reinforces the social differences between men and women ... Sometimes we have to do a runaround our bodies to ensure equity. Sometimes we have to do some social engineering to help dislodge our social aspirations from the dictates of our glands and gonads.[374]

Professor Adrienne Pine, in her class "Sex, Gender and Culture" at American University is likewise embarrassed by her biology. The whole debate about the breast as being more natural than the bottle

> leads down a slippery slope of biological determinism... To be honest, if there were an easy way I could feed my child without calling attention to my biological condition as a mother, which inevitably assumes primacy over my preferred public status as anthropologist, writer, professor, and solidarity worker, I would do so.[375]

Professor Pine, as a single mother, prefers that her achieved status as a professional takes primacy over her "biological condition" as a mother. As Ms. Pine elevates her role as professor over her mothering functions, she inevitably

---

[373] Gene Lyons, "Be on the lookout for breast-feeding, the latest classroom controversy." Times-Standard, Humboldt Times, August 22, 2013.

[374] Ibid.

[375] Adrienne Pine. "Expose`ing My Breasts on the Internet," **Counterpunch**, Sept. 05, 2012.

denigrates motherhood and the family; in her article, she states that she must pay $75/day for day care for her infant and even more when the baby is sick.[376] One might well wonder, does she love the infant or resent her? Acknowledged or not, motherhood lies "at the very core of the experience of being female... As a biological reality, motherhood is supremely indifferent to ideology, to historical or technological 'progress,' to culturally imposed norms and values."[377]

Having achieved significant parity in public life, some progressives now demand that gender differences be eliminated altogether. The recent demand by Wesley women illustrates the victory of this ideology on campus. No more are they to be referred to as women, but as students. The power of this philosophy has even infiltrated into the field of medical education. According to the *Journal of the American Medical Association*, medical schools now refer to "parents" who give birth while in residency. One reads halfway through the article before the word "mother" appears and then only as a problem for lactation and the need to pump while in the middle of a long surgery.[378] Apparently, in the battle against transphobia, policy changes are not enough. Speech must also be controlled. Incredibly, a University of California medical school professor was recently forced to apologize for referring to pregnant "mothers."[379]

---

[376] Ibid.

[377] Susan Maushart, *The Mask of Motherhood: How Becoming a Mother Changes Everything and Why We Pretend It Doesn't.* (New York: The New Press, 1999), 241-242.

[378] Bridget M. Kuehn, "Fixing the parent trap for resident physicians," March 4, 2020. JAMA Network. https://jamanetwork.com/journals/jama/article-abstract/2762693?guestAccessKey=1a76b95f-3e71-4d5c-b5d2-b19c6990dfed-&utm_source=silverchair&utm_medium=email&utm_campaign=article_alert-jama&utm_content=olf&utm_term=030420;

[379] Med Schools Are Now Denying Biological Sex - by Katie Herzog - Common Sense with Bari Weiss (substack.com)

While woke students might deny sexual difference, younger girls cannot seem to do so. While their older sisters repudiate male privilege, it would appear that many girls covet it, renouncing their femininity. Troubled by their body, they seemed to have absorbed some subtext that masculinity is the prize. Abigail Shrier's book, *Irreversible Damage: The Transgender Craze Seducing our Daughters,* posts a disturbing image on the front cover: a little girl stands with a round hole in her middle. Awash in androgynous and transgender dogma, are we surprised that young girls are confused? Mistrusting tradition, their parents, and even their own body, these children ask: "Who am I?" "Where is my place?" Shrier puts it bluntly: Unopposed progressive ideology mutilates children. This phenomenon

> ...has nothing to do with real gender dysphoria and everything to do with our cultural frailty. Teenage girls are taking courses of testosterone and disfiguring their bodies. Parents are undermined; experts are over-relied upon; dissenters in science and medicine are intimidated; free speech truckles under renewed attack.[380]

According to lesbian provocateur, Camille Paglia, the PC culture in the universities and its unthinking embrace of androgyny and transgenderism both emasculates men and puts us on the brink of cultural suicide.

> Gender doesn't really exist. Everything is all about expanding women's rights and also terminating men. And defining men out of existence. Masculinity is by definition toxic. I have always been fascinated with the concept of androgyny and studied it at Yale but the

---

[380] Shrier, 3.

more I explored it in history, the movement toward androgyny occurs in late phases of culture as a culture is starting to unravel. You see it throughout history. In Greek culture, the statues of young men that used to be robust now are like wet noodles, soft feminine-like young men.[381]

Why is gender necessary? Why might the attempt to dissolve sex differences carry sinister overtones? Family physician and psychologist Leonard Sax lays out many psychological and medical facts in his book, *Why Gender Matters*. Sax writes:

> One hundred years from now, scholars may look back at the disintegration of early 21ˢᵗ century culture and conclude that a fundamental cause for the unraveling of our social fabric was the neglect of gender in the raising of our children—not only in our schools, but also the disbanding of gender separated activities across generations, and in the near elimination of single gender communal activities: women with girls, men with boys. I wonder what those future historians will say about how long it took us to recognize our mistake, to recognize that *gender matters*.[382]

Separated from mom

Standing in line at Walmart, I was only vaguely aware of the song on the store's speaker system. Then the DJ began an interview with the singer. Her answer to his questions about her future projects caught my ear. Speaking about her little

---

[381] https://www.youtube.com/watch?v=I8BRdwgPChQ
[382] *Why Gender Matters: What Parents and Teachers Need To Know About the Emerging Science of Sex Differences* (New York: Doubleday, 2005) p. 251. The second edition, 2017, expands the data and deepens the arguments.

boy, she noted, "I struggle with mom guilt. Men more easily go off to work. When I walk out the front door, I leave my heart." I thought to myself, "What an elegant summary of the issues!" Of course, maternal angst accompanying women's migration from home to work has stimulated much discussion in recent decades. How to assuage her discomfort? Mary Eberstadt, on the other hand, is not as concerned about a mother's feelings. Rather, she brings our attention to an even more troubling observation: that little ones suffer when mom is away. This fact was highlighted by her ten-year-old daughter as she returned from volunteering at a local daycare center. The girl's happiness at caring for toddlers that day was ruined by the unrelenting shrieks of a little boy with an earache who could not stop crying, *mommy! mommy!*

Eberstadt cites numerous data that daycare children are more susceptible to getting sick and more likely to grow up unhappy, angry, and aggressive.

> Contemporary feral behaviors among children and teenagers—from suicide rates to the increase in elementary school violence—have increased in tandem with the vanishing of many adults from their lives. There is simply too much suggestive evidence to deny the connection.[383]

Eberstadt reminds us what many would deny. That is the apparent correlation between what the Surgeon General has declared as a public crisis in mental health for children and adolescents and the meteoric rise in single-parent families. In addition, the rate of working mothers with children under the age of six rose from 46.8 percent in 1982 to 64.6 percent in

---

[383] *Home Alone America: The Hidden Toll of Day Care, Behavioral Drugs, And Other Parent Substitutes.* (New York: Sentinel, 2004), 27.

2000. In short, we have been raising a generation of children who are sadder, lonelier, and angrier.

Cycles of separation

As progressive agitators spread the rumor that men are wont to oppress women, men retreat. Feeling abandoned or unwanted, women become suspicious and angry, falling back on their careers as men fall by the wayside. As sex roles are repudiated, neither sex takes cues from their elders. Mothering and fathering roles slip into conflict or confusion. If they have children at all, actual parenting suffers.[384] Young moms turn to Yahoo articles that caution them about not being sexist or transphobic.[385] Intimidated by the watchful eye of woke culture, they abandon common sense along with the assumptions their grandparents grew up with. They offer little truth to give their kids, no anchor to test reality. Could it be that they themselves have been cheated from such an anchor?

An astute chronicler of the fallout from the sexual revolution, Eberstadt wonders at the high animosity found on so many campuses today.[386] Considering the generally affluent status of college students, where does all the angst and anger come from? Eberstadt posits an answer: Angry cries of victimization are due to the fact that the offspring of the hippie

---

[384] The importance of gender roles in parenting is the particular focus of the research studies featured in the book edited by W. Bradford Wilcox and Kathleen Kovner Kline. Although phrased in scientific and politically neutral terms, the thrust of these studies supports what has been evident for millennia, viz., that males and females parent differently and in essential ways. *Gender and Parenthood: Biological and Social Scientific Perspectives* (New York: Columbia University Press, 2013) 13.

[385] How to Answer "Is That a Boy or a Girl?" and 5 Other Gender Questions Tara Santora, September 4, 2020 https://www.yahoo.com/lifestyle/answer-boy-girl-5-other-154837077.html

[386] "The zealous faith of secularism: how the sexual revolution became a dogma." (*First Things*, January, 20018).

generation actually have indeed been cheated. Following a religion of unrestrained freedom, many boomers did their own thing. They had children but neglected them. In short, many students today have been robbed of "social capital"— the identity, security, and spiritual direction which traditionally is linked to a stable family life. Having lost these things, "the dispossessed former children of the West are furious… The antagonism is not just political, it's primordial."[387]

One wonders as well if there does not lurk some subterranean motive for revenge. Could the tendency to repudiate the binary contain a subtle rejection of mom and dad? Could the eagerness to repudiate the patriarchy have something to do with fathers who didn't love or protect them or simply were not there? On the other hand, could the pornographic exploitation of women as it exposes and cheapens the reproductive equipment, have something to do with a repudiation of motherhood?

In the Genesis story, the serpent invites humans to defy the absolute limit to human capacities: *The prohibition not to eat of the tree is of no consequence, only designed to restrict your freedom.* Does not the denial of sexual differentiation follow a similar spirit to repudiate boundaries to human possibility? Further, the repudiation of gender requires the rejection of gender roles. The denial of gender roles invites denial of responsibility—a denial of obligation toward the other and inevitably toward children. In addition, to pretend the sexes are the same does not excite to love or romance. Worse, it swoops the legs out from under a society, trumpets the death of what Gilder called the sexual constitution and, in time, the death of the family itself.

---

[387] https://www.lifesitenews.com/news/the-2020-election-chaos-can-be-linked-to-the-sexual-revolution

The poisoning of pediatrics

The reach of the sexual revolution has, unfortunately, embedded itself in the very institutions designed to give guidance and protection to the next generation. Alexander Webster writes in *Touchtone* that the battle for the souls of our children began in the sixties as unbelief infiltrated our schools. Then the battle for the bodies of our children began in 1980 when the American Academy of Pediatrics (AAP) embraced a theory of sexual autonomy in which adolescent children could obtain contraception without parental consent. The battle for the very identities of our children began more recently when "...willfully confused and perverse ideologues adamantly insisted on pseudoscience grounded in the mercurial notion of 'gender,' a historically linguistic term pertinent to inflected languages but woefully misapplied to divinely engineered human biology."[388]

Webster describes the moral slide of the AAP as one that began to appear thirty years ago when 56 percent of the membership supported abortion on demand for adolescents. By 2013, the policy statement on "sexual minority teenagers" had already become

> Chock-full of political buzzwords such as "homophobia, heterosexism, gender identity, gender expression, and transgender," as well as confident proclamations (sexual minority youth should not be considered abnormal) and recommendations.[389]

---

[388] Alexander F. C. Webster, "Do you know your child's doctor? The politicization of pediatrics in America" *Touchstone*, January/February, 2020.p. 34. See also, Leonard Sax, M.D., Ph.D., Politicizing Pediatrics: How the AAP's Transgender Guidelines Undermine Trust in Medical Authority - Public Discourse (thepublicdiscourse.com)

[389] Ibid.

The recommendations include an essentially default affirmation of transgender adolescents and referrals for the process of transmission and advocating that adolescents receive full access to contraceptive procedures without parents' knowledge. Webster does celebrate the fact that a new alternative American College of Pediatricians (ACPEDS) was established in 2002. Although small in number, these pediatricians defend traditional concepts of marriage, human sexuality, and parental authority. They embrace the essential role parents play in their children's lives and the benefits of sexual abstinence until marriage. Accordingly, ACPEDS is vilified as a hate group and its positions are denounced as "anti-science." The Southern Poverty Law Center and the Human Rights Campaign are the loudest detractors.

Webster refers us to the 1990 United Nations "Convention on the Rights of the Child." At that time, there was already a growing global consensus:

Adolescent children are autonomous and self-determining, self-realizing, "autonomous" individuals who possess "human rights" to freedom of expression, thought, conscience, religion, association, assembly, and education—even in opposition to their parents' or guardians' desires—and are fully capable of making their own *moral* decisions.[390]

Webster quotes philosopher Mark J. Cherry, who points to a universal philosophy of radical secularism. The intention is to drive a wedge between parents and their children. Under the guise of "best interest" of the child,

Advocates of the liberal state seek to limit the bonds of family loyalty, to reduce the influence of parental

---

[390] Ibid., 36.

authority vis-à-vis children, and to paint the traditional family in an unflattering light with wide-ranging implications for the bioethics of pediatric decision-making.[391]

Citing Jesus' warning in Matthew 18 about those who would cause little ones to stumble, Webster celebrates the Protestant and Roman Catholic pro-family organizations and urges those in his religious tradition of Orthodox Christianity to become more involved.

Education as indoctrination

I recently chatted with a fourth-grade public school teacher. Her curriculum included material that encouraged each child to consider themselves special and unique. They were asked to reflect on questions such as, who is the real you? What do you really like? What do you want to become? Not bad questions in themselves, if you consider such topics to be the purview of a public school. But there was no opening, no hint that a child might consider any future role in the family—nothing about mothering or fathering.

Such an omission is by design. In fact, the sexuality education sponsored by SIECUS, the teachers' unions, Planned Parenthood, and the ACLU specifically instructs teachers to avoid words that imply the sexes belong together. Terms such as "boyfriend/girlfriend" or "husband/wife" are to be eschewed in favor of the generic "partner." This program to brainwash our children was ostensibly designed to protect gay or trans children from feeling excluded or being bullied. According to Family Watch International, however, "CSE is designed to change the social and gender norms of society,

---

[391] Cited in Webster, p.37. See Cherry's book, *Sex, Family, and the Culture Wars*, 2016.

promotes high-risk sexual behaviors and encourages even the youngest of children to experiment sexually."[392]

Various forms of CSE are saturating public schools across the country. California, of course, leads the way. The Board of Education, as evidenced in the California Healthy Youth Act, aggressively mandates changes in the way teachers present sex education.[393] In 2019, I described in *The Christian Post* some of the imperious phraseology woven into this curriculum:

> With barely concealed menace for traditional attitudes or contrary opinion, progressive ideologies are enforced. Educators "must" affirm that a person may be attracted to the same or different genders. "Your instruction teaches that any of the different sexual orientations is normal." Not only must this instruction include examples of same-gender relationships, but must also explore the harms of negative gender stereotypes. "Your instruction has activities addressing and debunking negative gender role stereotypes." "You refrain from: suggesting that girls care about love and emotions... Talking only of young mothers and not young fathers, and so on." [394]

Kindergarten is not too soon to begin indoctrination:

> Teachers are to explain to children that their sex is merely assigned at birth and may not match their "true" gender identity. Teachers in no uncertain terms must

---

[392] "The War on Children" www.stopCSE.org

[393] Activists at the California Teachers Union secretly mock parents who might complain. Leaked Audio Reveals How California Teachers Recruit Kids Into LGBTQ Clubs (theepochtimes.com), Nov. 21, 2021.

[394] Kuiper, "Sex: God's design vs. comprehensive sexuality education," August 29, 2019 https://www.christianpost.com/voice/sex-gods-design-vs-comprehensive-sexuality-education.html

affirm and normalize such conditions. "Your instruction explains that a transgendered girl is a girl and a transgendered boy is a boy… and that there are gender identities other than male or female." Books and videos that embrace non-gender binary as well as homosexual orientations are to be actively promoted. "[395]

CSE requires Middle schoolers not only to be exposed to oral and anal sex, but teaches them how to do it. High schoolers are invited to explore their possible gender identities or sexual orientations. They are also encouraged to know their rights to receive birth control or abortion services at any age—without parental knowledge.[396] "Taken as a whole, the thrust of CSE is to sexualize children, deemphasize abstinence and ultimately delegitimize the traditional family."[397]

Parents and church leaders can fight back and a growing body of literature helps to negotiate the complexities.[398] New parent groups, gratefully, have sprung up across the country to oppose the sexualization of children.[399]

---

[395] https://sex-ed-facts.com/elementary-school/

[396] https://sex-ed-facts.com/high-school/

[397] Kuiper, "Sex: God's design…" A more thorough analysis can be found in the article by the International Organizations Research Group, August 2018, Briefing Paper Number 16 "Seven Reasons to Reject "Comprehensive Sexuality Education" https://c-fam.org/wp-content/uploads/CSE-Briefing-Paper-8.26.18.pdf?fbclid=IwAR0WhSZCKUCZ75MKN-dSTUhkyqKLoW-ZTTwmh6e_cOTzxCgvyNm02bapCQdg ; see also, "How Schools Groom Kids for Sexual Predators" https://www.washingtontimes.com/news/2020/jul/15/how-public-schools-groom-kids-for-sexual-predators/?inf_contact_key=c-003c8e837f4ef9b2ae6532bf0c8881a842e902fbefb79ab9abae13bfcb46658

[398] For example, see Preston Sprinkle, "The Center for Faith, Sexuality, and Gender," CFSG Pastoral Papers_14 (centerforfaith.com)

[399] For example, Protect Child Health Coalition; https://www.informedparentsofwashington.com/, https://www.facebook.com/groups/InformedParents California/, https://www.massresistance.org/ A free book offers parents specific guidance in these issues. Back-To-School-For-Parents_Edition1.pdf (familypolicyalliance.com); see also 5 Tips When You Discover Your Kid Is Viewing Porn - NCOSE (endsexualexploitation.org).

Unwin learned that it took three generations before a society finally collapsed under the weight of sexual license. However, he could not have known of the dizzying rate of change the Twenty-first Century has brought us. Rather than a slow slide, it would seem we are being shoved off a cliff. This push—camouflaged as an indignant need to affirm one's true self—centers around sex. The assault on traditional attitudes towards sex is both ingenious and nothing new. Frankly, it is old policy, a reintroduction of lies and temptations with the surefire result of disruption and division.

Sex and the serpent

Do pediatricians and educators really want to put a wedge between parent and child? To invite children to doubt both the data of their own body and their parents' authority? We do not allow eight-year-olds to determine their bed time but are told we must affirm their feelings about their genitals! Beyond the historical analyses discussed in the last chapters, we wonder, "Is something else going on?" Could we be witnessing an iteration of an ancient strategy? Where natural order is inverted and the purpose of sexuality subverted.

In filling the whole earth with God's goodness (1:26 – 28), the sexes were to function in union with each other. This plan was to be protected. As a boundary to human choices, the tree of knowledge protected Adam and Eve from the fatal mistake of substituting self for God. In submitting to this limit, they would be protected from pursuing false identities. Furthermore, obedience to this limit would point them to their true nature, which as Bonhoeffer claimed, was freedom for God. This freedom was to be actualized in union with each other.

The plan barely gets going before disaster strikes. We note that the serpent appears immediately after we read how united the humans were (Genesis 2:24 – 25). The Adversary seems to grasp the obvious: this element of oneness is essential to the great mandate to populate the earth. The serpent has his own agenda: that the humans neither unite nor proliferate.

One need not agree with all the conclusions of this book to agree that the Bible is clear: As Christians, we face an unseen battle with an enemy, a liar (John 8:44) whose intention is to destroy us (1 Peter 5:8). This diabolical energy, identified as Satan, a fallen angel, appears at once to disrupt God's intentions for Adam and Eve. But why the hatred? And why are so many problems related to sexuality? Describing *the rage of the prince of darkness,* Mosgofian and Ohlschlager offer a glimpse into his motivation:

> At the crux of the matter lies Satan's fierce hatred towards humans because they are able to procreate. Satan lacks the power of God to create as he wills, and lacks the privilege of man to procreate after his own kind. Since Satan cannot touch God, he seeks to rob God's created beings of life.[400]

Whether from envy, fear, or rage, the goal of the devil is to oppose human flourishing. Paul reminds us not to be unaware of the devil's schemes (2 Corinthians 2:11). We discern an intention to divide and deceive.

The serpent's first move disrupts their sexual unity. According to the Köstenbergers (*God's Design for Man and Woman: A Biblical-Theological Survey*), the fall of humanity "… was engineered by a complete reversal of the divine design."[401] Bypassing Adam, Satan undermines his authority, disrupts the flow. Eve is tempted to act on her own.

---

[400] Peter Mosgofian and George Ohlschlager, *Sexual Misconduct in Counseling and Ministry* (Word, Inc., 1995), 294.
[401] Wheaton, Ill.: Crossway, 2014, 41.

Instead of God's authority being mediated from Adam to the rest of creation, the biblical fall narrative recounts how the Serpent (Satan) approached Eve, who took the initiative, with Adam following her lead, in breaking God's commandment.[402]

In concert with this divisive strategy, the serpent attacks the protective limit. "Did God really say…?" In doing so, he cleverly awakens values essential to her very nature as imaging God's character, namely, the principles of freedom and fairness. "It's not fair that you should be forbidden to partake of that which pleases you." Next, he impugns the nature of God. "For God knows that when you eat of it your eyes will be opened and you will be like God, knowing good and evil" (3:5). As if God is threatened that they would know too much. *(As if your parents are ignorant of your true self.)* Indignation now partners with desire. Eve succumbs to the beguiling fruit and Adam silently follows.[403] Against the promise of ever-expanding life, the seeds of death are sewn.

The Canaanites soon emerge as the poster people for rebellion and sexual license. The strategy to lie about the goodness of God was highly effective with the polytheists in the ancient near East. Clay Jones unpacks the religious and cultural backdrop behind the conquest of the Canaanites. Comparing their moral failure to our own, Jones warns that judgment follows sexual chaos. As idolatrous polytheists, they denied the one true God and one true reality – a set-up, if you will, to believing and accepting anything. Thus, the Canaanites were free of any natural or true frame of reference, allowing them to practice adultery, child sacrifice, homosexuality and bestiality. Temple sex involved eroticism and sensuality, naked priests, transvestites and pederasts in the worship of the

---

[402] Ibid.
[403] Ibid., 45.

goddess Inanna/Istar. Following their sexually out-of-control gods, incest was common. Bestiality and underage sex were common features of Baal worship. Perhaps the most hideous image of Satan himself can be seen in the face of Molech, as wailing children were placed in his fiery arms.[404]

Having breached the original boundary to keep us from evil and to guarantee our freedom, we chafe at our fallen condition. Agitated and homeless, we search for that lost freedom and that lost love. We search in all the wrong places and come up empty and alone. As a youth, St. Augustine came to understand the truth of the human condition when he wrote these now famous words, "You have made us for yourself, O Lord, and our hearts are restless till they find rest in you." Having discovered that rebellion and sexual debauchery left him broken, he was able to turn to that "living water," the source of both freedom and love.

---

[404] "We Don't Hate Sin So We Don't Understand What Happened to the Canaanites: An Addendum to 'Divine Genocide' Arguments." *Philosophy Christi,* Vol. 11, No. 1, 2009.

CHAPTER 13

Engaging Culture with Promise and Hope

*If you knew the gift of God and who it is that asks
you for a drink, you would have asked him and he would
have given you living water.* —John 4:10

A friend tells the story of an acquaintance of hers, a white missionary lady serving in a Native American territory. One night, the woman's husband, a Native American himself, was leading a Bible study in their home. The couple had been making positive inroads with the Gospel in the small, close-knit community. However, one young man despised mixed marriages and was particularly hostile to the faith, even though he often came around the house. On this particular evening, he boldly walked into the living room as the husband spoke. Flopping himself on the floor, he lit a cigarette. He then proceeded to blow smoke at her husband, who simply continued to read from the Scriptures. The wife fumed. Unable to sit any longer, she got up and retreated to her bedroom. Pouring out her irritation to God, she finally asked him what she should do. The answer came back loud and clear: "Give him an ashtray." She did so, and this simple act of kindness deeply touched the young man, who now teaches his own Bible study.

Jesus tells us that the Father understands our needs. After praying, this missionary understood that the man's deeper need was for acceptance. Or, maybe, recognition that he was angry. And, perhaps, that he needed an ashtray.

So, how do we engage with those whose views of sexuality seem to threaten us or our society? Or with those who would do far more than blow smoke in our face? If we are to follow Christ's injunction to love, then perhaps a place to start is by understanding them. What makes them tick? Chapter Eleven described two kinds of motivation driving those who would undo traditional sexual mores. The first is private—an individual's struggle to meet personal needs or manage dysphoric feelings. The second emerges as a political and dangerous drive to remake society itself. But, we wonder, do these private and public programs to defy sexual boundaries have anything in common? Are the desires of the ideologue and the sexual seeker similar? We might find that what they need is not so different from the longings that haunt everyone born this side of Eden.

Understanding human needs

On close inspection, several common desires can be discerned in those who would defy traditions, laws and even nature itself. The simple wish for freedom and the desire for meaning or purpose are certainly universal wishes. Then, of course, we all need love and community.

The Genesis story described the original "gifts of being," Including the ingredients needed to thrive and live forever. Defying the single boundary that would protect their nature and destiny, the humans resorted to their own strategies to meet their needs. In doing so, they brought death, sabotaging the most basic need of all—to survive. For creatures designed to live, the cessation of being is unthinkable. So, born in sin and rebellion, man not only must try to meet his own needs, but manage the dread of death. As Becker showed, there are many ways to soften and deny this final reality. These "immortality projects" include for some, the pursuit of success or

money. For others, it is the temptation of status or power.[405]
The arena of sexuality emerges as a particularly curious field
of such operations.

The sexual agenda and the promise of happiness

It is impossible to overestimate the significance of sexuality.
Eros promises satisfaction along multiple levels, including
sensual excitement, love, and community. And, not to forget,
the pathway to survival of the species itself.

One's sexuality is hard to ignore. Every sensation, every
awareness is mediated through the body. Its very shape is
charged with meaning. What might a woman's wide hips
suggest? Or her breasts, located in the foreground, ever a
reminder that this female carries something of significance.
Something soft, representing nurture; something powerful,
able to sustain life. We find in a man's chest not mammary
glands but pectoral muscles. Does not this fact carry implications? Why do men on average possess 40 percent greater
upper body strength? Why are they taller, have deep voices?
Or consider the penis. Why does it harden? What is its aim
and what is its product? In short, does not each gendered body
affirm and energize a purpose and meaning beyond itself—a
dual telos of communion and procreation?

Let us also consider theological design. Sexuality is an
intrinsic order, a primary relational template involving differentiation and complementarity. And the only mechanism to
fulfill the mandate to be fruitful and fill the earth. In contrast,
autonomous or anonymous sexuality denies such purposes,
fragments and divides. The self is the center—the operational
impetus and the measure of all things.

Inasmuch as any hopeful endeavor is driven by significant need, its failure will be felt all the more deeply. When

---

[405] *The Denial of Death.*

sexual pursuits fail, the consequences are often heartbreaking. Rejected lovers and divorce victims often fall into depression. Too many transgendered people sink into despair after their reconstructed body fails to fulfill their dream of wholeness.[406] We have seen that a defiant sexuality, as it repudiates God's laws, wise traditions or taboos, is a terminal sexuality, without fruit, without progeny. As with other *causa sui* pursuits, sooner or later, an individualistic sexual agenda brings heartache.

Shame

It was never God's intention that Adam and Eve know unhappiness. Yet, immediately after disobeying, they feel shame. Realizing they are naked, they cover themselves. Then, hearing the "sound of God walking in the garden in the cool of the day" (Genesis 3:6), they hide. When confronted, they make excuses and blame. Shame is uncomfortable. As is guilt, but shame is deeper. Sexual shame is deeper yet, representing a spiritual, ontological mistake. When confronted with his sin with Bathsheba, David understood this and cried to God, "Against you, and you only have I sinned." More than a misstep to be acknowledged or repaired, shame is being exposed, being *seen* as lacking. More than a sin to be confessed and forgiven, but a sense that one's very self is exposed as wrong. One solution is to hide or to cover the eyes of the looker.[407] This is so with our sexuality. Perhaps, especially with our sexuality.

Wanting to be just like God, the first humans arrogated to themselves that which did not belong to them. This was a

---

[406] As Andrew Walker points out, the thing transgendered people are looking for is "a way to make their mind's perception, their heart's desires, and their body's construction "match"—to feel wholeness, rather than dysphoria." *God and the Transgender Debate: What Does the Bible Actually Say About Gender Identity?* (The Good Book Company, 2017), 87. See also https://www.dailysignal.com/2017/08/23/sex-change-myth-trying-change-ones-sex-will-always-fail/

[407] Or, as in the play, *Equus*, to blind the eyes of horses representing religious judgment.

deep failure, touching the very nexus of what it means to be a self—that orientation toward God and the other. They lost something essential and now cover themselves at the point of their sexuality, with its promise and obligation toward the other. As if aware they have transgressed an absolute boundary of being. Not that they had made a simple mistake, but in failing to resist the temptation to be "like God," they had confounded their very nature. Karl Barth writes,

> And the awful genius of sin is nowhere more plainly revealed than in the fact that it shames man at the center of his humanity, so that he is necessarily ashamed of his humanity, his masculinity and femininity, before God and man, and every attempt to escape this shame, every self-justification, or concretely every denial and suppression of sexuality can only confirm and increase the shame.[408]

Naked innocence is no longer possible. Nakedness now means exposure, as being wrong. To think themselves to be just like God was a shameful thing. They know this in their genitals, the most vulnerable parts. These are the locus of differentiation, the organs of promise and the gifts by which they were to love each other and enact their vocation to be fruitful. Covering is now appropriate, a recognition that something vital is lost. Bonhoeffer explains:

> In shame man acknowledges his limit... Man's shame is his reluctant acknowledgment of revelation, of the limit, of the other person, of God. Therefore, the preservation of shame in a fallen world is the only—although most contradictory—possibility of

---

[408] Barth, 292.

acknowledging the original nakedness in the blessed-ness of this nakedness.[409]

Understanding the social and psychological weight of the genitals, traditional societies retain the ability to call out a certain degree of shame. When communities promote modesty, they recognize there is something necessary in the covering of sexual parts. That there is a responsibility, a mystery, a gravitas around sexuality—to be kept hidden, held as sacrosanct for a special purpose. Simple dress codes recognize this reality and protect from shame. When boys must tuck their shirts in and girls observe rules regarding the length of their skirts, modesty is enforced. And so is mystery. Mystery and modesty authenticate the significance of sex and the value each sex brings to the other.

A shameless society?

As modesty has faded from public discourse, shamelessness has grown. One might expect, however, that as a sexually profligate society, shame would be a common symptom. If indeed, sexual sins touch the human soul more deeply ("The sexually immoral person sins against his own body," 1st Cor. 6:18), where is the shame? Perhaps it has been erased by a devious media. I recall as a boy watching Divorce Court and being shocked at the antagonists' willingness to discuss private details on national television. Then followed decades of the likes of Jerry Springer, as he happily exploited the sexual failures of naïve guests. The appetite for such programs remains strong. They can be found every afternoon, right after school.

But has shame really faded in the Twenty-first Century? Or is it merely buried, or projected outward? In the act of covering and hiding, Adam and Eve blame and rationalize.

---

[409] Bonhoeffer, *Creation and Fall*, 79.

Not much has changed. Monica Lewinsky, who has endured more shame than we can imagine, has recently re-emerged in the public eye. She offers some insight.

> We have created, to borrow a term from historian Nicolaus Mills, a "culture of humiliation" that not only encourages and revels in Schadenfreude but also rewards those who humiliate others, from the ranks of the paparazzi to the gossip bloggers, the late-night comedians, and the Web "entrepreneurs" who profit from clandestine videos.[410]

Anonymous web surfers zero in on someone who has made a mistake or social *faux pas* and excoriate them. Perhaps it is no coincidence that it is the young, as products of a secularized education, knowing little of sin or redemption, who are the ones most likely to savage each other. As if guilt and shame, unidentified, stirs within. Energy agitating for an object.

In a secular world, such feelings are restless, without target, nor method of absolution. Without acknowledgment of sin, there can be no process of reparation. Without punishment or a system of sacrifice, there is no codified scapegoat. Nor is there, without God, an object of worship. Yet, the needs for God and for redemption not only linger, they permeate social discourse. Becker described the phenomenon of heroism, the public adulation of outstanding figures as transference objects, replacements for God. As these heroes win games and awards, we identify with their success. They help us feel we have overcome impotence and failure. We make them larger than life and, in their worship, believe we have cheated death. Yet, such worship does little to assuage our own guilt or shame.

So, we sacrifice them. YouTube commentator, Sammy Lazarus describes the meteoric rise of Britney Spears followed

---

[410] "Shame and survival," *Vanity Fair*, June, 2014.

by mental breakdowns as an example of how fickle and vicious the public can be with its stars.

> That's what we do. We raise a humble human to the status of God and smash them down again just to prove they are mortal. In our secular society, we fill the godless gap with celebrity. And we take pleasure in cheering on the underdog until they're not the underdog anymore. Then we destroy them.[411]

Lacking knowledge of a loving creator, the need to worship is transfigured to idolizing actors or athletes. Lacking the concept of sin and unaware of the promise of atonement, the need to feel whole requires scapegoats. When we discover our heroes have clay feet, we switch from adulation to scorn.

Why have sexual boundaries? (In celebration of prudery)

Armed with the latest woke issue, finger-pointing has become a national pastime. Sexual shame as it points to deeper issues of relational failure is denied, modified, and displaced onto surfacy stuff. Superficial right and wrongs act as manageable rules, more easily digested and applied to others. A generic, amorphous guilt floats about, inviting everyone to feel bad about unconscious racism or presumptuous assumptions of heteronormativity.

The Bible is more specific about sin and more serious about sex; we are guilty before God, not our Facebook friends. Both testaments are consistent in promoting sexual self-control. As discussed previously, a cavalier sex causes pain. As Walsh reminds us:

---

[411] https://www.youtube.com/watch?v=eQq841rg-dg May, 2020.

The incidence of sexually transmitted disease has soared … That attractive person you see might be not only a potential sex partner but also a future plaintiff in a lawsuit. The more sex, the more heartbreak; the less "repression," the less romance.[412]

Conservative traditions protect us as well as embrace the mystery of the *imago Dei*. God is a relational God; his intention was to animate his nature on the earth and to do so, he fashioned his representatives in the shape of sexual duality. Such a modality requires self-limitation, the opportunity and obligation to pour love into the counterpart. Maturity and self-control are prerequisites. Therefore, it behooves a society to promote rules. For example, children should not have sex.

To follow God's design of sexuality, boundaries are necessary—a *moral* force, if you will. With a belief in right and wrong, good and bad, judgment follows. The man who molested his niece needs to be punished. Everything is not okay and we know this. Sin brings judgment because sin hurts people. Rules are necessary and we judge those who break them. Yet, not designed to judge, humans rarely seem to do it well.

The head of John the Baptist and the problem with moral judgment

Perhaps you have read the novel, *The Scarlet Letter,* in which a woman is shunned by her Pilgrim community after her child is born out of wedlock. This book seems to be popular in public schools as it highlights the hypocrisy and judgmentalism of a religious community that shames a young woman by forcing her to wear a large red letter "A" ("Adulterer") on the front of

---

[412] Michael Walsh, *The Devil's Pleasure Palace: The Cult of Critical Theory and the Subversion of the West* (New York: Encounter Books, 2015), 149.

her dress. We can imagine the indignation as a tenth grader reads this book. *How could a community justify such public humiliation?* We wonder as well, how many never-married mothers or members of the LGBTQ community carry a deep hurt or offense toward a religious community that judged or shunned them.

On the other hand, judgment, whether from within or without, is unavoidable. When confronted by the prophet Nathan, David repented. Not so Herod when confronted by John. Neither he, nor his sister-in-law/wife turned from their sexual sin. Herodias, instead, seethed at the messenger and strategized how to silence him. Then one night, bound by lust and a party spirit, Herod allows himself to be captivated by her daughter's seductive dancing and makes a stupid promise to the girl. Her mother is ready (*How dare he judge me!*). Weakened by sin and pride, Herod submits to her demand for John's head. Could Bill O'Reilly be correct in his observation that secular progressives share a single motivation in their hostility to conservative values: "to be free of judgment?"[413]

Exposure and concealment

In the beginning, God appears to express two initial responses to sin. Bonhoeffer discusses the dialectic between exposure and concealment. The humans are ashamed and hide. God allows this. He does not shame them. He does speak to them. They must know what they have done. But he also clothes them. But not with neutral smelling leaves from fig trees. These lie about their condition and fail to protect their bodies. Animal skins offer a more suitable leathery protection. Animal skins also tell the truth with their lingering smell of death.

Jesus also concealed and exposed. To those whose sins affected the public, he exposed publicly. He called out the

---

[413] *The Culture Warrior* (New York: Broadway Books, 2006).

religious leaders who, because of their position of authority, were responsible for harming those under their charge. On the other hand, "love covers a multitude of sins" (1 Peter 4:8). Jesus spoke privately with the woman at the well and repudiated the public shaming of the woman caught in adultery.

The church: "the light of the world"?

How do we address a culture in decline? What do we say to a society awash in mystifying sexual messages? Perhaps one answer has to do with individual gifting, the fact that Christ's calling to us to be salt and light is a corporate mandate and that each of us represents only one part of the body of Christ. And we engage with our neighbor in different ways. A pastor friend suggested the analogy of a highway heading toward a cliff. Those with the gift of teaching, prophecy, or preaching are the ones on the highway. With megaphones and signs, they warn anyone who will listen. "Stop! Do not drive yourself and your children over the cliff!"[414] Then, there are those with other gifts, such as mercy, help, or encouragement. These are those waiting at the bottom, caring for and restoring the broken.

Engaging culture from the pulpit

Concerned that the clergy avoids controversial issues, Stephen Nichols, the president of Reformation Bible College, cites a poll indicating that 22 percent of evangelicals believe in gender fluidity. One in five Christians think that "gender is a matter of choice"? He worries that such gender confusion threatens an entire generation. Rather than hearing the Word

---

[414] Individuals can support a variety of ministries, e.g., see the video series https://rescuingourchildren.net/

of God, "… many American evangelicals are instead listening to the changing voice of culture."[415]

Christians thinking like everyone else. Do we blame our preachers? Michael Brown appears to do so. As I read his chapter, "Jezebel and the Silencing of the Prophets," I wondered if comparing timid preachers today with the false prophets of Elijah's time wasn't a bit unfair. Brown charges that just as the wicked Jezebel silenced the prophets in First Kings, a similar spirit of intimidation has silenced Christian preachers today. Brown argues that the gospel is not always positive, that God can be angry and that hard prophetic messages do not only belong to the Old Testament.[416]

Pastor Jon Tyson would agree. Believing it a form of self-ishness not to tackle the hardest issues, this New York City preacher challenges pastors to "run toward the controversy." Reminding us that Jesus regularly offended people, Tyson also explains that such preaching exhibits grace and love. The bottom line? "If I don't help people form a theology of these issues, the culture will gladly give them that."[417] Certainly, there is truth here. On the other hand, one might wonder just how much influence a weekly half-hour sermon can have when most Christians consume countless hours staring at the TV or their smartphone.

---

[415] Michael Faust, "22% of U.S. evangelicals believe in 'gender-fluidity,' report finds." *Christian Headlines*, September 11, 2020. https://www.christianheadlines.com/contributors/michael-foust/22-percent-of-evangelicals-believe-in-gender-fluidity-report-finds.html?inf_contact_key=8e781770a94e1d05ddd0ced-7b04cd78e1b0a3f0fd3ee5d9b43fb34c6613498d7

[416] *Jezebel's War With America: A Plot to Destroy Our Country and What We Can Do to Turn The Tide.* (Lake Mary, Florida: Frontline, 2019), 138.

[417] "Run toward the controversy: Why NYC pastor Jon Tyson's goal is to 'winsomely offend everybody.'" *CT Pastors Special Issue*, Fall, 2020.

Engaging culture from the pew

Believers don't need a pulpit to stand behind in order to stand for truth. For some, engagement may simply involve supporting organizations such as The National Center on Sexual Exploitation, Family Watch International, Million Moms, or Focus on the Family.[418] Others might be called to jump into politics. Anyone can write letters to oppose CSE or monitor school board decisions. All of us are called. Paul encourages older women to mentor younger ones and older men to train young men. Can we not enlist the retirees in our churches to implement such a wise strategy?

While marching at the Capitol, distributing petitions, and writing letters as energetic culture warriors, it is easy to forget that our battle is not against people, but spiritual forces (Ephesians 6). It may also slip our mind that prayer is the most powerful force. While praying, we must let love be our guide as we defend the defenseless, work for truth in politics and science, and promote life wherever we can. Why? Because those who defy natural and spiritual law, sooner or later, find themselves in a dead end, wounded in soul and body.

The church as a hospital

My client, a Sunday school teacher and church elder, hung his head as we sat in silence. In the previous session, he had confessed that he knew he should love his wife but that he neither liked her, nor was he sexually aroused by her. I appreciated his openness. In this session, however, he was reluctant to admit that he had slipped into old homosexual liaisons over the weekend.

As Christians, we are often accused of being hypocrites. Was my guy a hypocrite as he taught the Bible the following Sunday? Or what about the woman from a very conservative

---

[418] See also, *Biblical principles for political engaging* https://frc.org/engage.

church who invited me to sleep with her after a session? Each of these Christians regretted what they had done or said. I could offer them grace for I, too, have stumbled in my walk with the Lord.

Have you ever shuffled into a church service, watched the smiling worshippers while you yourself felt depressed or like you didn't fit in? Did not measure up? Contradictions. On the one hand, we each hold some grasp of the proper and righteous behavior, attitude or emotion. Yet, too often, we know the good and have not done it. Indeed, how then do we answer the charge of hypocrisy?

The answer, in short, is that the charge fits. Some struggle with sexual failure. Others may come to realize they carry too much jealousy, or fear, or anger. Happily, God does not define us by our failure or our feelings. Justified by faith, sin is not the final word. We understand that, as representatives of the divine likeness, we fall short of the loving reciprocity found in the Trinity. God does not abandon us when we fall into disorder. Instead, as Anderson puts it, "God creates the space and time in which disorder can learn of the wisdom of that divine Word."[419]

This is grace that gives people time to grow. As believers in Christ, we belong to the "already and the not yet." We understand that the kingdom of God did indeed break into this present age with the incarnation of Christ but will not yet be fully realized until he returns. Christians then live in the "eschatological overlap" between the present, evil age and the perfect age to come.[420]

In Romans 7, Paul acknowledges the contradiction of knowing what the perfect law of God requires and one's sinful proclivities. The answer can only be the work of Jesus Christ who delivers us from condemnation (Romans 8). Does this

---

[419] *On Being Human*, 129.

[420] For a full explication of this doctrine, see George E. Ladd, *A Theology of the New Testament* (Grand Rapids: William B. Eerdmans Publishing, 1974).

mean our behavior does not matter? "What shall we say, then? Shall we go on sinning that grace may increase?" (Romans 6:1). Of course, behavior matters. Sin is real. However, because we have been saved by the blood of Christ, that behavior is not determinative of who we are and who we are becoming. Anderson recounts the story of Martin Luther who had often been tormented by doubts and conflicts. Then one day, he went to his table and wrote in chalk the words, *baptizatus sum*, meaning, "I have been baptized!"

> And then he promptly went about his work with the assurance that this was the final word concerning the state of his soul. The body of Christ dares to baptize that which is not yet whole and gives the bread and the wine to those who are not yet what they will be. This is what it means to say that we are justified by faith. Where this takes place, there is a cure of souls.[421]

Andrew T. Walker declares that the church ought to be the safest place for people to be open and talk about their struggles. It has been said that some 85 percent of the LGBT community have come from Christian backgrounds. How have they experienced the church? In discussing people with gender dysphoria, Walker offers several markers of a New Testament church. Citing James 2, he calls the local church to be a "compassionate community," one that does not make superficial distinctions as if "… the Son of Man came to seek and save good people, not the lost."[422] The church should also be a "listening community." Are we "quick to hear and slow to speak" (James 1:19)? Of course, we have our convictions but let us not forget that we are not a country club for those who have "made it;" much more like a hospital for the wounded.

---

[421] Anderson, 204.
[422] Walker, 124.

Engaging persons in pain

How are we to deal with the individual who may be close to the cliff or who has already fallen? What do we say to the fifteen-year-old who believes she is really a boy? Or the doctor who's been arrested for molesting his patients? One answer is that we meet them. Jesus did not only address large crowds. He connected in kindness with individuals. Many of these were not "good people." In fact, the "righteous" religious leaders were quite offended that he "ate and drank with sinners" (Luke 5:30).

But what if our conversational partners do not agree that there is any moral issue in their behavior? Do not believe in sin. What if they are comfortable—whether it be cohabiting, looking at porn, or pursuing same-sex attractions? We have already reviewed Jesus' encounter with the woman at the well. He saw past her sexual infidelities to her real need for "living water." Before introducing "the Lord's prayer," Jesus declared that "the Father knows your needs before you even ask him" (Matthew 6:8). Can we believe that? Those who would challenge sexual traditions demand freedom from any imposition on the possibilities they envision for their lives. Do we believe God is the one who gives freedom? Many demand equality—a world that is fair to all. And they wish to be recognized for who they are, not forced into artificial molds but to be accepted as unique and valuable beings in their own right. We wonder, as we consider the following parable, do we not find a God who actually understands such people. Who really does comprehend the deepest needs that motivate the human soul? And not only what we need, but our helplessness to meet that need.

The pursuing father

"Patriarchy" is a dirty word today. But is it understood? New Testament professor Ken Bailey invites us to look deeply into the heart of God to answer this question. As a scholar steeped in Middle Eastern culture, Bailey suggests that the better title for the parable of the prodigal son is the "the parable of the pursuing father." Having lived in Lebanon, Jerusalem and Cyprus, Bailey offers several insights into the story. Referencing Muslim, Jewish and Eastern Christian sources, he advances some thought-provoking observations.[423]

The parable is part of a trilogy beginning in Luke 15 with the complaint about Jesus that "this fellow welcomes sinners and eats with them." Bailey notes that according to the Babylonian Talmud, rabbis did not eat with common people. In response to their criticism, Jesus tells the story of a shepherd who goes out to find a single lost sheep, a woman who searches for a lost coin, and a father who pursues two lost sons, better known as the Parable of the Prodigal Son. The last story is full of surprise and contradictions. Bailey offers the following insights:

- The boy requests that his father, while still alive, give him his inheritance. This is unheard of. This is tantamount to wishing the old man were dead. Any Middle Eastern patriarch would have thrown him out at once. Equally incredulous, this father grants the request.
- The young man does not "repent" as has been traditionally understood. As with the lost sheep and coin, repentance in these parables equals "acceptance at being found." Bailey points to Arabic versions of the story that more accurately capture the original

---

[423] "The pursuing father: what we need to know about this often misunderstood Middle Eastern parable." *Christianity Today,* October 5, 1998.

meaning. Rather than feeling remorse, the phrase translated "he came to his senses" refers to a devious, manipulative thought process. In other words, he got smart and concocted a confession that would suggest heartfelt repentance. In fact, Bailey notes, the phrase "I have sinned against heaven and before you" is a quotation borrowed from Pharaoh who was trying to manipulate Moses to stop the plagues. The prodigal was "thinking of himself (I am dying of hunger) not of his father's broken heart."

- At the time of Jesus, any young man who lost his inheritance to Gentiles would be severely punished. If he dared return home he would face the *qetsatsah* ceremony. "The villagers would bring a large earthenware jar, fill it with burned nuts and burnt corn, and break it in front of the guilty individual. While doing this, the community would shout, "So-and-so is cut off from his people.' From that point on, the village would have nothing to do with the wayward lad."
- Knowing his son will fail, the father "waits day after day, staring down the crowded village street to the road in the distance along which his son disappeared in arrogance and high hopes." Aware of the shaming and shunning that awaits the boy, the father knows that if he can intercept him, he will head off the *qetsatsah* ceremony.
- The father spots him a long way off. Again, breaking the mold of Middle Eastern patriarchy, the father pulls up his long robes to run to greet his son. "Traditional Middle Easterners, wearing long robes, do not run in public. To do so is deeply humiliating."
- Before the son is able to give his speech, the father has already kissed and hugged him as a mother would; he covers him with a fine robe, puts a ring on his finger, sandals on his feet and calls for a banquet. It is not

to celebrate that he was lost and has decided to come home but that he was lost and is found.

Bailey writes:

So, who found him? The father did! Where did he find him? At the edge of the village! Thus, in the father's perception, the Prodigal was still lost and dead at the edge of the village. Even as a shepherd was obliged to go forth and pay a high price to find his sheep, and the good woman sought diligently to find her coin, even so the father went down and out in a costly demonstration of unexpected love to find and resurrect his son.[424]

But what of the older son? He is resentful and refuses to come to the banquet, "an unspeakable public insult to the father." Once again, we find amazing grace as the father, risking public humiliation, goes out to find his other son, who is lost in a different way.

In this famous parable, we discover a father who "gets" humanity. He understands the younger son's need for freedom, to find his own way. And later, his need to be protected from failure, shame, and rejection. He also recognizes the elder brother's need to be recognized for who *he* is, as well as his concern for equality and fairness. Most of all, he understands their need for forgiveness.

Who among us has not been lost in some way—caught in the dualism between good and evil, flesh and spirit? Or perhaps we find ourselves looking down on single moms or a college student who declares he has always been a girl. We may have forgotten what it feels like to live every day in dissonance, to carry contradiction deep within. Perhaps we

---

[424] Ibid.

have forgotten as well the freedom of acceptance we possess as believers. That we live, as Paul did, free from judgment (1 Cor. 4:3-4; Rom. 8:1). As we fight for our society and the future of our children, let us remember the individual, the one hungering for wholeness. Who is that *person* behind the drag queen's garish outfit? Why is this feminist professor of gender studies so angry? What is their story? Let us find them and listen. And, perhaps, when they are ready, let us tell them our story. How we found ourselves too weak and too conflicted to "find ourselves." How we felt hopeless, but were given hope. How we were broken but heard a message of wholeness. And that we were lost, but let ourselves be found.

Index

A

Abolition of Man, The, xiii
abortion, x, 13, 14, 75, 204, 236, 252, 256
abstinence, 197, 253, 256
adultery, 56, 67, 69, 77, 98, 192, 236, 271
affirmative care, 85
American College of Pediatricians, 253
Anderson, Ray S., 25, 26, 44, 123, 125
androgynous, 201, 247
antinomianism, 213
asexual, 78, 214
attachment, 32, 76, 94, 107, 108, 113, 120, 131, 155, 199, 205, 237, 244

B

Bailey, Kenneth E., 65, 66, 69, 71, 277, 278, 279
Barth, Karl, 37, 38, 46, 121, 137, 142, 143, 144, 145, 149, 265
Bathsheba, 64, 264
Becker, Ernest, 53, 55, 57, 59, 61, 262, 267
bestiality, 56, 57, 88, 236
Bloom, Allan, 57, 78, 202, 203, 204, 205
Bly, Robert, 132, 133
Bonhoeffer, Dietrich, 19, 22, 40, 41, 47, 265, 266, 270
Bork, Robert, 205, 206, 207, 208, 213, 214
boundaries, 24, 25, 29, 31, 32, 35, 36, 55, 63, 108, 155, 158, 159, 176, 195, 197, 204, 222, 223, 229, 235, 251, 262, 268, 269
breast binders, 85
Brown, Michael, 272

C

California Healthy Youth Act, 255
Carnes, Patrick, 81, 82
Cherry, Mark, xiii, 253, 254
child pornography, 79
child sacrifice, 56
Chodorow, Nancy, 117, 118
Communist Manifesto, 241
complementarity, 123, 125, 138, 139, 161, 164, 171, 181, 263

Comprehensive Sexuality Education, ix, 255, 256
critical theory, 218, 242

D

de Bouvier, Simone, 238
de Castillejo, Irene, 110, 112
Deleuze, Giles, 226, 227, 228
Derrida, Jacques, 219, 220, 226
doctrine of objective value, 216
drama queens, 62

E

Eberstadt, Mary, 173, 249, 250
Eldredge, John, 133
Eldredge, Staci, 112, 170
Eliot, T. S., 214
Elliott, Elizabeth, 161
Elohim, 23
equality, xiv, 6, 8, 17, 32, 58, 86, 111, 118, 121, 128, 142, 143, 161, 166, 167,
        196, 204, 205, 206, 208, 244, 276, 279
Erikson, Erik, 14, 169, 172, 198
eros, 55, 225, 263
Esolen, Anthony, 4

F

familism, 190
fetishist, 62
Focus on the Family, 273
Frankfurt School, 218, 224
Franks, 226
Franks, Angela, 226, 227, 228
freedom, x, xiv, xv, 1, 12, 25, 26, 27, 29, 30, 31, 32, 36, 41, 42, 43, 44, 45, 48,
        52, 55, 59, 63, 97, 130, 135, 137, 140, 145, 155, 156, 158, 168, 183, 185,
        186, 187, 188, 190, 193, 197, 201, 203, 204, 206, 207, 210, 213, 214,
        218, 221, 222, 223, 224, 225, 232, 233, 234, 238, 251, 253, 262, 276,
        279, 280
Freud, Sigmund, 53, 89, 100, 225, 231, 237
Friedan, Betty, 14, 15

G

Garden of Eden, 22, 243
Gay Pride, 58
Gay-Straight Alliance, 214

gender, xii, 6, 8, 12, 14, 17, 21, 62, 84, 85, 86, 87, 88, 93, 94, 112, 113, 117, 118, 119, 121, 125, 140, 159, 161, 164, 165, 166, 167, 168, 171, 182, 201, 202, 209, 211, 214, 215, 218, 220, 221, 225, 226, 227, 242, 243, 244, 245, 246, 247, 248, 250, 251, 252, 254, 255, 256, 271, 272, 275, 280

gender dysphoria, 17, 84, 86, 225, 247, 275

gifts of being, 24, 262

Gilder, George, xvi, 113, 193, 194, 195, 196, 197, 198, 199, 200, 201, 202, 251

Gilmore, David, 163

Gnosticism, 243

Goldberg, Steven, 129, 207

Grossman, Miriam, 13, 80

Grudem, Wayne, 127, 142

H

Haight-Ashbury, 2

Harrison, Glynn, 97, 243

headship, 125, 127, 128, 129, 130, 146, 147

Hite Report, 207

Hoff Sommers, Christina, 9, 117, 118

homosexuality, 56, 94, 233, 234

Horner, Althea, 104, 113

humiliation of women, 196

I

identity, x, 5, 7, 24, 58, 74, 86, 87, 93, 98, 113, 114, 125, 127, 145, 155, 156, 158, 164, 171, 173, 177, 194, 195, 197, 199, 209, 211, 214, 224, 227, 229, 231, 233, 251, 252, 255

imago Dei, 25, 269

incest, 56, 57, 90, 236

inclusive language, 222

intimacy, 2, 11, 47, 48, 54, 58, 61, 77, 80, 97, 98, 125, 135, 147

J

Jesus, xvi, 23, 33, 37, 38, 64, 65, 66, 67, 68, 69, 70, 71, 72, 95, 98, 123, 124, 128, 134, 135, 139, 140, 146, 149, 155, 168, 254, 261, 270, 271, 272, 274, 276, 277, 278

Journal of Human Sexuality, 95, 96

K

Kierkegaard, Soren, 53

King David, 64

King, Nicole, 14, 16

Kinsey, Alfred, 90, 235, 236, 237
Kohlberg, Lawrence, 211, 212
Kreeft, Peter, 34, 52, 168, 210
Kuby, Gabriele, x
Kupelian, David, 234

L

Legutko, Ryszard, 221, 222, 223
Lewis, C.S., xiii, xiv, 19, 34, 63, 215, 216, 217, 218
LGBTQ, 58, 255, 270
Liberation Theology, 241
Lois Lane syndrome, 180
lust, 30, 49, 64, 159, 197, 228, 270

M

Mahler, Margaret, 103
manhood, 45, 94, 109, 116, 127, 129, 163, 169, 171, 195
Manichaeism, 191
Manning, Brennan, 24
Marcuse, Herbert, 224, 225, 231
marriage, xiii, 3, 7, 15, 40, 58, 77, 80, 97, 113, 127, 128, 129, 137, 141, 148, 149, 158, 159, 177, 183, 186, 188, 189, 191, 193, 198, 199, 221, 223, 226, 234, 235, 253
McGuire, Ashley, 16
Mead, Margaret, 116, 128, 193, 198, 207
MILF, 60
modern liberalism, 205, 206, 213
modesty, 5, 197, 204, 266
moral judgment, 269
motherhood, 7, 98, 137, 160, 171, 173, 246, 251
mother/infant dyad, 100, 244

N

natural law, 154, 216, 217, 223
Nietzsche, Friedrich, 230, 237

O

Oedipus complex, 53
Ortlund, Raymond C., 32, 129

P

Paglia, Camille, 247

paraphilias, 88, 89, 91, 92
partnership model, 125
Pascal, 60
Passno, Diane, 11
patriarchy, 7, 129, 138, 177, 204, 207, 218, 221, 238, 251, 277, 278
Pauling, Joshua, 8, 18, 116
pedophilia, 57, 78, 236
perversions, 56, 57, 59, 236
Peterson, Jordan B., 176, 180, 218, 219, 221
Pharisees, 67, 69
Piper, John, 32, 127, 129, 130, 139, 161
Planned Parenthood, ix, x, 254
Pope Benedict XVI, 228
pornography, xi, 3, 10, 11, 21, 57, 79, 80, 81, 82, 83, 98, 196, 236
pre-nuptial chastity, 187
prodigal son, 277
promiscuity, 80, 186
prostitution, 56, 80, 141, 235, 236
puberty, 62, 74, 84, 85
pursuing father, the, 277

R

radical feminism, xiv, 12, 155, 206, 208, 213
Rank, Otto, 53, 55, 59
rape, 76, 221
rapid-onset gender dysphoria (ROGD), 17
reciprocity, xv, 123, 125, 167, 274
Reich, Wilhelm, 231, 232, 237, 238
Reisman, Judith, 236
relativism, 192, 202, 217
repression, 54, 60, 219, 225, 231, 232, 269
Richter, Sandra L., 24
Rousseau, Jean-Jacques, 229, 230

S

salvation, 34, 123, 144, 207
same-sex attraction, 93, 94
Sax, Leonard, 8, 118, 248
second wave feminism, 18
secularization, 7
self-righteous, 5, 68, 72
sensuality, xv, 49, 54, 56, 57, 89, 204
sex addiction, 81

sexism, 6, 118, 222
sex reassignment surgery, 17, 85
sex roles, xii, 5, 17, 117, 118, 120, 160, 167, 171, 207, 250
sexualize children, 256
sexual orientation, 21, 93, 95, 96, 242
sexual rhythm, 194, 195
sexual suicide, 193
sex week, 54
shame, 3, 40, 42, 46, 49, 67, 74, 81, 82, 89, 90, 91, 93, 94, 119, 204, 227, 264, 265, 266, 267, 268, 270, 279
Shrier, Abigail, 17, 247
SIECUS (Sexual Information and Education Council of the United States), 236, 254
Solzhenitsyn, Aleksandr, 219
stay-at-home mothers, 16
STDs, ix, 13, 16, 17, 18, 19, 236
Stern, Daniel, 106
Stonewall riots, 58
submission, 135, 137, 169
suicide, 85, 238, 247, 249
Summers, Larry, 6
super theory, 221, 222, 223, 224, 227
Sweden, 84, 85, 86

T

taboo, 12, 55, 56, 57, 60, 80, 177, 203, 216, 264
tao, 63, 216, 217
Thielicke, Helmut, ix, 122
tolerance, 19, 91, 180, 182, 213, 234
traditionalists, 65, 72, 154
traditional roles, 71
traditional societies, 56, 162
transcendence, 55, 56, 58, 60, 62
transgender, 3, 17, 58, 84, 86, 87, 214, 215, 244, 247, 252, 253
transgenderism, 84, 98, 247
trans woman, 225
tree of the knowledge of good and evil, 26
Trueman, Carl R., 156, 157, 229, 230, 232, 233, 234
trust, 5, 12, 30, 37, 46, 47, 77, 136, 137, 170, 178, 218, 244

U

Ullman, Chana, 177
Unwin, J.D., 185, 186, 187, 188, 198

V

Vietnam War, 1

W

Winnicott, Donald, 100, 101, 102, 105
woman at the well, 65, 72, 271, 276
women in combat, 208
women's liberation, xii, 193, 195, 238
women's studies, 207, 244

Y

Yahweh, 23, 24, 29

Z

Zimmerman, Carle, 189, 190, 191, 192, 193, 198
zoistic dead cultures, 186

www.ingramcontent.com/pod-product-compliance
Lightning Source LLC
Chambersburg PA
CBHW021707120626
46545CB00004B/1449